Service Provider Strategy

Proven Secrets of xSPs

Anne M. Burris

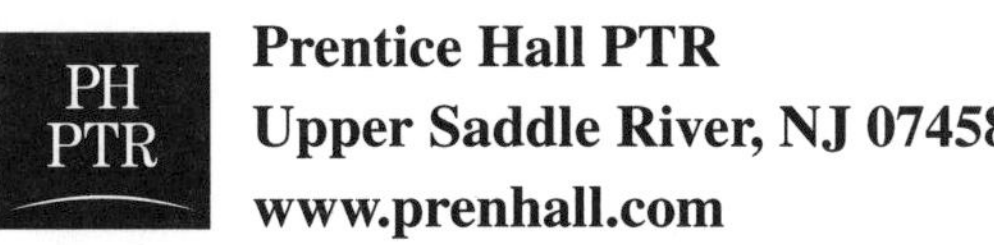

Prentice Hall PTR
Upper Saddle River, NJ 07458
www.prenhall.com

Library of Congress Cataloging-in-Publication Data Available

Burris, Anne M.
Service provider strategy : proven secrets of xSPs / Anne M. Burris.
p. cm.
Includes bibliographical references and index.
ISBN 0-13-042008-5
1. Application service providers. 2. Internet. 3. Business enterprises--Computer networks. I. Title.

HF5548.32 .B867 2001
384.3'3--dc21

2001041416

Editorial/Production Supervision: *Jan H. Schwartz*
Acquisitions Editor: *Jill Harry*
Marketing Manager: *Dan DePasquale*
Manufacturing Manager: *Alexis R. Heydt*
Buyer: *Maura Zaldivar*
Art Director: *Gail Cocker-Bogusz*
Interior Series Designer: *Meg VanArsdale*
Cover Design Director: *Jerry Votta*
Cover Design: *Nina Scuderi*
Editorial Assistant: *Justin Somma*
Composition: *Aurelia Scharnhorst*

Prentice-Hall, Inc.
Upper Saddle River, NJ 07458

Prentice Hall books are widely used by corporations and government agencies for training, marketing, and resale.

The publisher offers discounts on this book when ordered in bulk quantities. For more information, contact Corporate Sales Department, Phone: 800-382-3419; fax: 201-236-7141; email: corpsales@prenhall.com or write Corporate Sales Department, Prentice Hall PTR, One Lake Street, Upper Saddle River, NJ 07458.

Printed in the United States of America

10 9 8 7 6 5 4 3 2 1

ISBN 0-13-042008-5

Pearson Education LTD.
Pearson Education Australia PTY, Limited
Pearson Education Singapore, Pte. Ltd.
Pearson Education North Asia Ltd.
Pearson Education Canada, Ltd.
Pearson Educatión de Mexico, S.A. de C.V.
Pearson Education-Japan
Pearson Education Malaysia, Pte. Ltd.
Pearson Education, Upper Saddle River, New Jersey

This book is dedicated to:
Mom, Chris, and DEZ

Contents

Your Account

amazon.com.

Amazon.com
1850 Mercer Rd.
Lexington, KY 40511

Billing Address:
RIchard J. Schiller
15 Magnolia Street
Westbury, NY 11590
United States

RIchard J. Schiller
15 Magnolia Street
Westbury, NY 11590
United States

Shipping Address:
RIchard J. Schiller
15 Magnolia Street
Westbury, NY 11590
United States

WillowGrov

bytb12393/-3-/8539/std-us/1511609/516-338-4304

Your order of May 30, 2002 (Order ID 104-0103906-4503937)

Qty.	Item
	IN THIS SHIPMENT
1	**How to Go to College Almost for Free** Benjamin R. Kaplan paperback (1-2-4) 0060937653
1	**Service Provider Strategy: Proven Secrets for xSPs** Anne M. Burris paperback (1-2-4) 0130420085
1	**Foundations of Service Level Management** Rick Sturm paperback (1-2-4) 0672317435

This shipment completes your order.

17/bytb12393/-3-/box/WillowGrov/8539/std-us/1511609/0530-18:26/0530-19:39

Preface

What is an xSP? Why would an xSP need a strategy primer?

Service provider nomenclature seems to change almost hourly: ASP, CSP, MSP, ISP, and so forth. What is fashionable one day is passé the next. A service provider—application, content, management, Internet, and so on—is sometimes forced to re-engineer its image to stay aligned with market trends as a way to assure ongoing revenue streams. Enter the "xSP." An xSP is any service provider, coming from any industry, no matter the specialty that offers goods or services over the Internet for a fee.

This book is written primarily for individuals considering a start in the service provider industry, service providers already in the business, individuals or corporations selling to or working with the service provider segment, and any others interested in a different perspective on what it takes to be successful in this business. Those new to the service provider industry will gain valuable information about the market, key players, and helpful tools to get started. This book is a good review for service providers and will give ideas on how to streamline operations. For those interacting with xSPs, this book gives more detail about the business, its needs, and a perspective about the people in the business. To voyeurs, or those just interested in getting more information about this segment, the book will give a good basic overview of market trends, and generally what it takes to be an xSP.

The book is divided in three parts. Part 1 gives an overview of the market, its operational challenges, and how service providers position themselves. Part 2 is about specific, unique, examples of companies coming into the market. Unique, because these case studies discuss how contributing companies are entering the market, focusing on the challenges each faced, and solved. Part 3 is a more in-depth discussion of the industry's seven operational challenges: organization/operations, partnering/alliances, sales/marketing, service provisioning, customer care, billing, and infrastructure. In-depth is a relative term. Each operational challenge is a complex subject and could be the subject of an entire book. This book, which gives the reader a high-level understanding of the topic, can be used as the starting point for more research. For quick guidance, a checklist is part of every chapter. Appendices round out the book, providing more specific tools to help service providers along the road to success.

No one can be an expert at everything, and the writer is no exception. She would like to thank those reviewers and contributors who helped make this book possible, and those close to her heart, for their patience while it was being written.

The only limitations are those of imagination. That's the good news and the bad news. Hopefully, readers will gain new insight into how to work more efficiently and successfully, while broadening their vistas to creatively face challenges.

PART 1

Introduction to the Seven Operational Challenges

CHAPTER 1

Level Setting

The service provider concept is not a new one. It's based on the service bureau model, a successful scheme that has been around for a long time. While service providers offer a similar service, their differences are encapsulated in the technology used and how business is executed. A service provider is a company, in any industry, that offers services, or resources, over the Internet, via appliances, to help solve the problems of, or give information to, people or enterprises. Here appliances do not mean necessarily traditional household appliances like refrigerators, washing machines, or ovens—but it could! Appliances are any item, including household appliances, which can receive and/or send information or services from/to service providers.[1] In today's world appliances are normally devices like computers, mobile phones, personal digital assistants (PDAs), and so forth. The services are normally paid for on a pay-per-use, monthly fee, or transaction basis.

Service providers are made up of four main components that they either own or partner for:

- A communications backbone
- Hardware/software/operational infrastructure
- Content or applications to be offered to end-users
- Services that can encompass system management, system integration, or business process consulting

If the majority of these items are procured via partnerships, the provider may be called a "virtual" service provider. There are so many service providers in the market today that they differentiate themselves by core competency to keep brand awareness. There are many different labels, like application service providers (ASP), content service providers (CSP), management service providers (MSP), hosting service providers (HSP), business service providers (BSP), Internet service providers (ISP), and so forth. Now something called an "xSP" is entering the market. The idea behind the xSP concept is that service providers share a common *taxonomy*, or makeup, which is differentiated at the edge, or by provider core competency. The taxonomy includes the challenges discussed in this book: organization/operations, partnering/alliances, sales/marketing, service provisioning, customer care, billing, and infrastructure.

How service providers work through these operational challenges is the difference between their success and failure. As mentioned earlier, the concepts are not new, nor are they unique to the service provider industry. Successfully negotiating these challenges will result in the service provider being able to maintain a loyal customer base, increase its market share, maintain profitable revenue streams, and decrease its operational costs.

Traditional service bureau outsourcing services rely on the ability of the outsourcer to consolidate the customer's people, processes, and technology gaining efficiencies and economies of scale. Outsourcers build shared infrastructures to recognize additional efficiencies. The success of outsourcing firms is a result of their ability to aggressively reduce client costs while maintaining, or enhancing, the performance of their client's systems. Outsourcing firms typically map contracts to specific customer requirements and, over time, cost structures inherent in custom platforms and contracts result in higher operational and contract costs.

Moving to a service provider model for the first time, particularly when transitioning from other established models, can be risky. For the provider, offering Internet services has value over the traditional outsourcing model because sales cycles are shorter, sales costs are lower, and they are able to reach a larger customer base. The sales cycles are shorter because offerings are standardized and the services can be faster, more efficiently, and less expensively offered to potential business customers, as well as to the consumer market.

Every company, no matter the industry, has to provide a product to an identified customer segment(s) at a price and quality the market will support. The differentiator comes in how the company executes its business. The focus of this book is to help readers understand more about the business, its challenges, and give some tools for success. As a result, the service provider has a better chance of ending up in the media for all the right reasons, instead of as a side story telling readers who got ownership of the corporate mascot used in advertising campaigns.

When considering any business, it is best to first understand the industry and why it is important in the global marketplace. This chapter discusses the market, general global trends, and why services provided over the Internet will continue to be important.

1.1 History

In the late 1960s, the U.S. Department of Defense (DOD) provided funding to the Advanced Research Projects Agency (ARPA). It was this agency, in conjunction with research funded by ARPA grants, that eventually developed the "internetwork" between local area networks (LANs) and wide area networks (WANs) which became known as the Internet. In the late 1970s, the National Science Foundation (NSF) funded a project to build CSNET—the computer science network. As a result, many computer scientists were using the Internet by the mid-1980s. Connecting all these intellects meant that even more Internet development research, proposals, and projects came forward. ARPA created the Internet Activities Board (IAB) as a venue to coordinate all these happenings. In 1985, the NSF was funded to create NSFnet as a way to link researchers at 100 universities by linking the five NSF supercomputer centers. Toward the end of 1991, the NSFnet backbone was reaching its capacity and it was clear that the U.S. government would not pay for the Internet indefinitely. About this time IBM, MERIT, and MCI formed Advanced Network and Services Inc. (ANS), a nonprofit company. In 1992, ANS created ANSnet forming the base for the current Internet backbone.

Information technology began evolving from the simple running of private propriety software, through driving the desktop environment via LAN/PC deployments, into real-time environments, running open network software, and supporting real-time transactions/interactions. The transformation from voice to data, the resultant changes in running/managing information technology networks, and the exponential growth of data networks, are the trends that made the Internet a ubiquitous component of present day business environments.

The service provider model is a catalyst for changing the way vendors think about delivering goods. It began as a way to more directly address specific business and consumer needs by offering components, like backbone, network management, and Internet access. This basic trend expanded to include service delivery, customer care, billing, and mission critical application services.

Other factors also contributed to the growth of the Internet model. When software vendors began looking at the small and midsize business markets as a target for additional opportunities, they realized that these smaller companies could not afford the new technologies, or the staff to manage/support them. The service provider model offered an ideal way to satisfy the needs of this market segment. Internet-based technologies began to enter all aspects of the corporate intranet and extranet and provided a new business model based, not on time or location, but on connectivity. Technology became available to address availability, security, quality of service, Web-based instrumentation, scalability, management, and other issues needed to support high-volume, mission-critical operations.

1.2 Why Work with a Service Provider?

The advent of the Internet has greatly changed the business and consumer marketplace. It fills gaps in a number of areas:

- Efficiencies in economies of scale and business processes
- Operational cost savings
- Locating skilled resources
- Faster time to market for products and services
- Higher reliability
- Enhanced customer retention

Not every company, not even some of the largest in the world, have the people, people skills, or the resources to manage and support many of the new applications required. Using a service provider can offer immediate access to the needed technologies and trained personnel, reducing hiring and training costs.

Companies are looking for ways to lower implementation risk and maintain economies of scale, while being able to use new applications and technologies that may further their competitive edge. Many corporations may not be able to generate the volumes to assure economies of scale and are concerned about the risk of implementing "bleeding edge" technologies. Service providers take away that concern by offering services on a per-use basis. This further reduces capital expenses resulting in a more favorable financial picture. Another benefit of the model is faster implementation time because the service is already up and running at the service provider. Faster implementation time means the user sees service benefits sooner, possibly leading to faster returns on investment.

Corporate customers are looking for the most effective interconnection to public networks with enhanced performance. Service providers' core competency is to offer just such interconnections. In addition, most service providers offer service level agreements ensuring the customer a fast and reliable mechanism to offer new, higher quality products and services.

Businesses are constantly on the lookout for ways to better understand customer behavior, increase customer-switching costs, and increase customer interaction. New customer relationship management systems, campaign management systems, and quality-of-service applications are available, but can be very expensive and risky to implement. Enter again the service provider that can offer these sorts of services faster and at lower risk.

Businesses of all sizes are looking for ways to minimize investment in never-ending hardware and software upgrade cycles. The right service provider shoulders the burden of making sure technology is up to date, patches are installed, versions updated, and so forth. Service level guarantees guard against business loss from unplanned infrastructure downtime, lessening the complexity of infrastructure management for the client.

The Internet has brought global markets within the reach of all businesses, no matter their size. To take advantage of these new markets, companies are looking for infrastructure that will help them offer their goods or services internationally in an efficient manner, and within expense guidelines. Service providers can help businesses launch international trade, not only through provider services, but also via their communities of interest, offering customers new ways to expand their global reach.

Customers expect service providers to work with them as a partner in their business, shouldering some accountability for success. They expect a simple, understandable value proposition and pricing model, and for the service provider to align with their corporate values and vision. Service providers will notice that service buyers are changing from the traditional IT department managers in favor of business and financial managers. It is the needs of these buyers that should be incorporated into service provider value propositions.

1.3 Why Use the Internet in Business?

1.3.1 New Revenue Streams

Businesses in mature industries use the Internet as a way to add new revenue streams or enhance old ones. The communications industry is a good example where bandwidth devaluation is causing carriers to find new ways of generating revenue. With the huge growth in the data services market, voice carriers are looking for ways to add IP products to their portfolios. Competition is further forcing differentiation in what—and how—end-users purchase and interrelate with communications services vendors.

1.3.2 Access to New Markets

The Internet is a way to access new markets via new channels and find new customers. It offers new venues for brand promotion and gives companies new ways of doing business. An example could be a manufacturing firm that uses the Internet to find new buyers, or sales channels, in new regions by leveraging brand to create international communities of interest. Figure 1-1 shows another way to offer new product mixes and to access new markets.

1.3.3 Increase Market Share

Bundled service provider services may be a way for companies to increase their market share by increasing the identified customer base. An example of this could be a U.S.-based small/medium business using the wider reach of its service provider to access all North and South American businesses having similar needs. Internet-based service bundles may make the product mix more interesting to a broader number of potential clients. For example, bundled offerings that include Internet functionality could give retailers access to buyers or markets heretofore inaccessible because of geographic or technological infrastructure barriers.

1.3.4 New/Better Ways to Interact with Existing Customers

New Internet enabled customer care systems can be a better way to maintain close associations with customers and to make goods and services available 24 hours a day, seven days a week. These systems also gather large amounts of data on customer buying habits. This intelligence can be used to provide better product definition and sharper marketing/sales campaigns.

1.3.5 More Efficient Supply Chains

Those with a view into the entire value chain can better maintain customer control. Manufacturers are becoming service providers as a way to enhance their supply chains, and lower their costs of goods sold.

Whatever the reason, or however a company uses the Internet as a part of doing business, it must be accompanied by a deep commitment to change and flexibility. The rules are different than those of traditional industry and change very quickly.

Figure 1-1 Companies are using the Internet as a way to offer new product mixes and to access new markets.
Printed courtesy of Kenneth Myers.

1.4 Trends

1.4.1 Quality of Service

Quality of service (QoS) will continue to be the differentiator between service providers. This one issue creates great stresses upon the core components involved in providing services. For example, private peering (P2P) will become more important as high bandwidth services become ubiquitous. The motivation for P2P arrangements is to improve network reliability by cutting down the number of router hops, or number of times a packet is forwarded to the next router, lowering the incidence of packet loss. Being able to control routing enables each peering partner to offer QoS guarantees to business customers. These QoS guarantees are difficult to offer when traffic goes through a public network access point (NAP). Private peering establishes a clear, high-bandwidth line between two ISPs, enabling traffic traveling over that connection to be monitored and controlled more carefully. As a result, traditional ISPs will feel the pressure of providing ongoing, highly available connectivity to high bandwidth users, both technically and operationally. This result may mean new business models for ISPs around pricing, bandwidth resourcing, and bandwidth allocation. QoS concerns are visible throughout all aspects of service delivery and customer fulfillment, including, but not limited to, service set up, changes, billing, and service deactivation.

1.4.2 Convergence

End-to-end services will create barriers to entry for potential competitors. These include multiple local access options (cable, xDSL, fixed wireless), integrated access with managed customer premise equipment (CPE), and end-to-end service level agreements (SLAs), including the local loop. All of these trends require the convergence and integration of data, voice, wireless, and any heretofore unknown future trends. The convergence needs to happen seamlessly and can mean fundamental changes in how service providers are doing business, not just aggregating new sets of applications. How providers will activate, deliver, and bill for these new converged services is still a question that needs to be examined.

1.4.3 Consolidation

Service providers are in a land grab to get big fast while maintaining flexibility. As consolidation continues, the market should see some megacarriers emerge that will dominate the market. These companies will probably focus their core competency on offering the best global, end-to-end services (best new services), and/or supporting these services through technology leadership (hot new technologies). They are driven by a need to move into the higher value services markets quickly and they will have the capital to acquire companies with the technology or services already developed. Market downturns, coupled with a lack of venture capital funding, mean consolidation will continue and will most likely increase.

An example is Internet data center (IDC) services. If it takes approximately two years for an IDC to recognize its full potential and investments to be recouped, a market downturn could make IDCs good candidates for consolidation.

Mergers are allowing providers access to larger markets and scarce resources, better economies of scale, the ability to mount more focused and effective marketing campaigns, and more advertising and commerce revenues. Top players seek to obtain scale through acquiring data center facilities, service expertise, operational processes, and customer base. Consolidation is a way to get to market faster and less expensively with high margin new services. It also means a lot of back-end integration to ensure seamless service provisioning to the end-user.

1.4.4 Market Acceptance of Internet Services

Whether business-to-business or business-to-consumer, the biggest change has come in the general acceptance of Internet services. On the demand side this is evidenced by a greater corporate Web presence and increased levels of outsourcing among mature corporations. Consumer acceptance is seen in the volumes of Web-based purchases over the holiday season. On the supply side, it is evidenced by the global build out of high technology data center facilities able to support mission critical services. New and more creative pricing policies and services show understanding of market needs and acceptance of risk to gain and enlarge market share.

Markets for provider services are large. Just how large is the debate among market analysts. What is certain is the upward trend in the number of Web access devices, purchases over the Internet, and increases in the dollar amount of these purchases. These trends are affected by local economic cycles, but over time they continue to increase. In fact, economic, regulatory, and cultural issues are among the main factors affecting global Internet use. These issues account for the majority of regional disparities in commercial transaction volume and Internet commerce development. In any case, Internet services are not going away and vendors continue to instrument their products for Internet use.

1.4.5 Where's the Money

There will be a continued shift away from services charged on a flat fee, like simple access, toward services that can be value priced. Providers are trying to create high switching costs by creating entire user business environments. Once customers are integrated into these environments, it is uncomfortable to change providers. In the banking world this is the equivalent of electronic bill payment. Once all the paperwork is in place for electronic bill payment, it is time consuming and uncomfortable to change banks. The provider walks a fine line of customer perception in regard to pricing for such services. The customer must perceive a fair price for fair value, but the provider must offer the service profitably. New entrants to the service provider world will be subject to brave new business models, such as market expectations for low price, or free, software or services. Providers need to be creative to make money in such environments by understanding well their operational and capital expense positions.

1.5 New Services

As services undergo margin squeeze, providers look for ways to differentiate services they offer and wring more from their current infrastructure. The Internet is becoming a utility used as a base for other value-add services. Hosting is a good example of a maturing service trend used as a base for other value-add services. There is a perceived glut of IDC space and providers are starting to feel downward pressure on prices for simple hosting and collocation services. This forces providers to expand service offerings to maintain their market differentiation. Service expansion can take the form of higher SLAs, more/different management services, security services, and so forth.

New service functionality and how the provider communicates the functionality value to focus markets are limited only to the provider's imagination. Some of the most compelling of these services fall into the broad areas of:

- Field-force automation (FFA): technology that helps field workers do their jobs more efficiently by getting information to them where they work, allowing them to communicate with their dispatchers or home offices.
- Education: services that run the gamut from consumer to corporate market and include all aspects of learning and training as well as distance learning, student lending, banking, apartment search, auto search, and so forth.
- User automation: dynamic services that support corporate or consumer users in daily work or personal life such as business travel support or getting faster, more accurate responses to requests for proposals (RFPs). They are smart services; their dependent components are self-adjusting to changes in the service environment. An example is the business traveler with reservations for air, hotel, and car services. If the traveler's flight is delayed, or canceled, smart services will adjust the reservations and meetings automatically, taking the burden off the individual.
- Storage and disaster recovery services: data volume increases make storage more of a factor. Disaster recovery and business continuity services will always be of prime importance as mission critical operations become automated.

These service segments will include aspects of business process, services, vertical focus, and technology. They need infrastructure, as discussed in Chapter 15, "Infrastructure," that will support traditional and new access devices, such as wireless. Here is a partial list of specific applications and services:

- Messaging
- ICE (Integrated Collaborative Environment)
- TCA (Team Collaborative Application) solution sets
- E-commerce
- CRM
- Supply chain
- Procurement
- Web design/hosting
- Business process management
- MRO
- Marketing
- Trading community management

Whatever the service there is a shift toward global reach and wireless access, meaning the appropriate infrastructure needs to be in place. As services become more complex, buying patterns slow unless their value to corporate and consumer customers is clearly articulated. Providers continually need to keep the bigger picture in mind as a way of continuing to meet, and exceed, customer needs. They need to drive the market, rather than react to it.

1.6 Challenges

To be successful, providers must constantly think of ways to communicate their unique value to end-users. As seen in Figure 1-2, service providers may decide to offer their core competency direct to end-customers as a retailer, branded wholesaler, or offer their services via a retail channel. Customer rapport becomes more difficult the more removed the provider is from the end-customer.

Other challenges include:

- New competitors
- Commoditization of services
- Voice/data and other future types of convergence, meaning integrating disparate networks
- Maintaining profitability
- Increasing market share
- Adding value for all end-users
- Financing
- Decreasing the time it takes customers to reach the full revenue potential
- Insulating the business from economic bad times
- Serving markets in real time, while paying for the infrastructure needed to do it
- Staffing and expertise
- Integrating infrastructure

These are age-old problems. The difference is the speed of the Internet market.

Addressing these challenges successfully can be based on luck, skill, or by having sponsors with very deep pockets. In any case, having a skilled staff that understands the business is going to be key; otherwise, it is just a question of how long the money lasts. In this highly fragmented industry, service providers are looking for ways to control their environment, enabling a

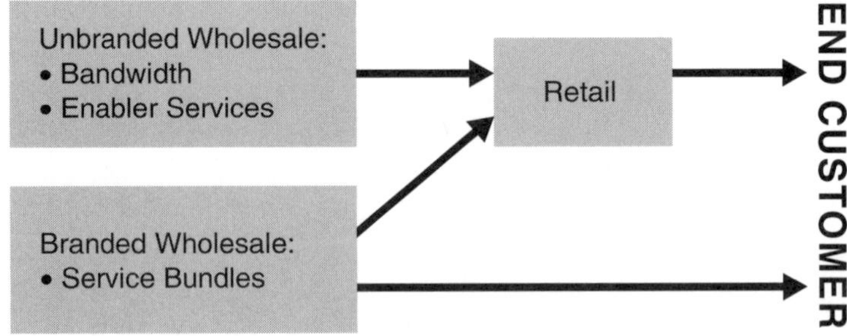

Figure 1-2 Service provider business models.

move from pain toward gain. This book is oriented to those who want to make their own luck and understand how planning and creative partnering can be used to leverage core competencies and build solid business practices.

1.7 Endnote

1. Most people would not consider a refrigerator to be an Internet appliance, but recent advances include prototypes of this sort of appliance sending and receiving information relating to warranties, break/fix information, product replacement, the family information center, and so forth.

CHAPTER 2

Basic Operational Challenges

All companies have at least four goals:

- Keep their current customer base
- Increase market share
- Develop high margin products and services
- Decrease operational expenses

Achieving these goals is based on skilled operation and organizational discipline. That said, being in the right place at the right time also has a positive effect. Success, obviously, can make the difference between a profitable company and a shuttered one. The operational challenges (see Figure 2-1) in trying to achieve these goals may be greater in some industries than others and service providers are no exception. Their operational challenges fall into seven basic categories:

- Partnering and alliances
- Organization/operations
- Sales and marketing
- Service delivery and provisioning
- Customer care
- Billing
- Infrastructure

Typically these operations fall into "customer-facing" and "back-office" functions as seen in Figure 2-1. This chapter gives a high level overview of each challenge as a basis for the case studies in Part 2. Part 3 discusses each challenge in detail with checklists that service providers can use for guidance.

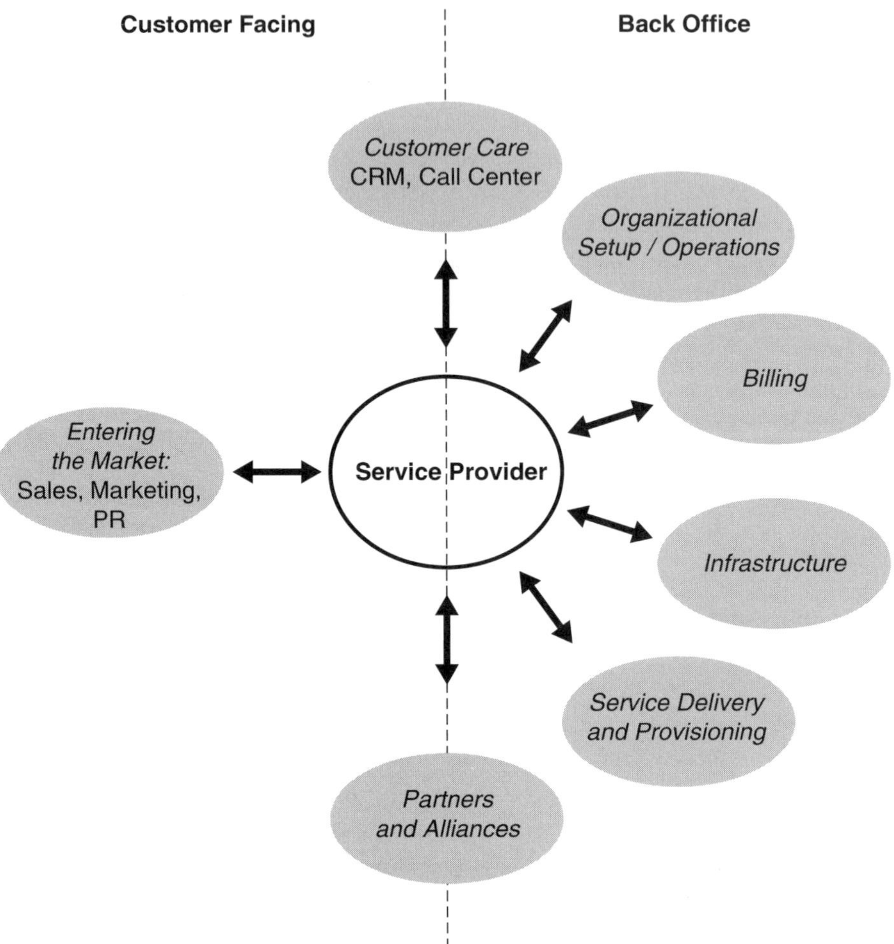

Figure 2-1 The basic operational challenges.

All organizations have key measurable objectives that they use to define business success. Here are some examples:

- Increasing market share by *x* percent
- Closing x number of sales by (date)
- Increasing revenue/customer by *x* percent
- Utilizing *x* percent of IDC (internet data center) floor space by (date)
- Profit targets of x percent by (date)
- Measuring customer satisfaction
- Churn (customer turn-over) rate during the quarter not to exceed *x* percent

To reach these goals, the provider must be committed to fundamental change. An Internet-focused company must have the commitment of top management that actively pursues, controls, and maintains the corporate strategy and vision. People must be given the proper tools to be successful and rewarded when goals are met. Likewise, personnel should be remunerated to discourage them from building empires that take focus away from the common strategy. The service provider must be constantly challenged to be a market maker, defining the best of breed in the market. Once the core competency is defined, the provider needs to perform due diligence and choose the best partners and alliances to fill the gaps identified in the service offering and delivery. This is not a mature industry and there are no rules, so service providers need to be flexible and nimble in order to survive. If the provider is a corporate spin-off, the parent company must allow this flexibility. Most importantly, the provider must be customer centric and customer focused.

2.1 Partnering and Alliances

Strategic partnering and alliances are essential for service providers to remain competitive in today's cutthroat environment. Partnering takes many forms and may be instigated to share things like information, resources, funding, equity, and so forth. No matter the form of the partnership, it should support the business objectives of the service provider and fill an identified gap in the business strategy. Normally, when creating a solution, a service provider tries to find a partner when filling identified gaps is too expensive, and/or too slow to do in-house. Partner strategy can be simplified into six steps shown in Figure 2-2.

Phase One entails identifying gaps in the service provider's organization and strategy that can be filled by partners. Then the service provider needs to prepare a partner profile and investigate potential candidates that fill its needs. After potential candidates are identified, the service provider needs to review the choices for business risk, looking to see if the candidate is financially viable, has management expertise, and so forth. Then the negotiation process begins.

Negotiation strategy and process is not the focus of this book, but here are some questions to ask:

- What are the main outcomes desired from the negotiation?
- What is the service provider's position? The other company's position?
- What are the service provider's walk-away points for each issue?
- Does the service provider understand the other company's organization?

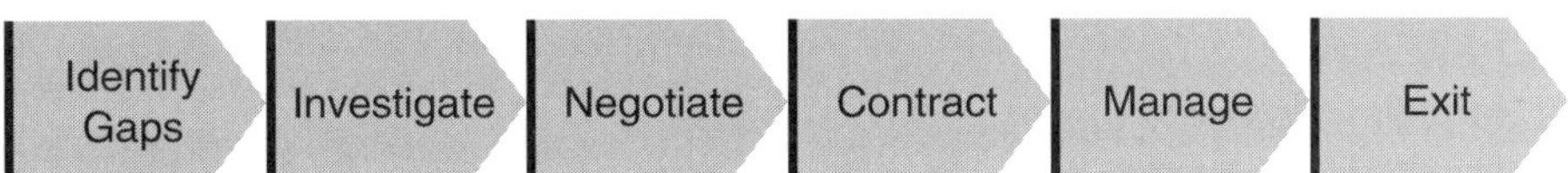

Figure 2-2 Partner strategy execution.

After contract signing the partnership goes into management mode for ongoing care and feeding. The last phase represents partnership exit, if/when partners determine the association is no longer viable.

Many of the same factors that break up marriages destroy partnerships: poor foresight, poor planning, and lack of quality management after the partnership is announced. Partners must share fundamental values and business philosophies and must agree to contribute required resources upfront to make the partnership work. The most effective partnerships are between people who bring different skill sets to the table and respect each other's expertise.

In most cultures, written agreements are important and force partners to think through partnership details. Partner conflict is prevalent and service providers should do their best to focus a partner as much as possible, mapping them against the overall product or strategy. Partner focus must be communicated as a function of overall partner management.

Partnerships may be used for sales and marketing, or more core development and intellectual capital creation. Sales and marketing partnerships may include things like joint business development/sales calls, funnel sharing, joint seminars and conferences, new sales initiatives, marketing collateral, demo centers, and so forth. Core development partnerships where a joint product is involved usually mean a more fundamental investment in time and materials on both sides. Partnering with vendors can offer significant sales opportunities for the vendors and new markets for the service providers. Some vendors offer sell-to/sell-with programs to service providers, with offerings along the lines of locating venture capital, services development, sales/marketing, and so forth.

Partnering and alliances are important in any business, but especially so for service providers. They may permeate all aspects of the service provider business and cannot be taken for granted. Partnering takes many forms and is a way to quickly gain entrance to markets, increase product/service functionality, and decrease operational expenses. The corporate relationships may be strategically agreed at high levels between companies, but must promote good working relationships at the field level in order for the partnership to be executed successfully. Alliances, like marriages, have lifecycles and the service provider must understand its goals in each of the phases, keeping focused as the relationship progresses. Sometimes, formal relationships are not built until initial success is achieved. Sometimes formal relationships are needed right away, especially when investments and joint development is involved. Exit strategies must be considered early on in the relationship so that parting is more equitable—one never knows when a future relationship will again be desirable.

2.2 Organization

The key to the xSP model is the consolidation of service delivery capabilities, allowing the service provider to leverage economies of scale and reusable service components. For the model to work, the services must be delivered from the xSP or xSP-partner-managed facilities tha support many clients, using common platform configurations. Keeping common platform configurations lowers the cost of operations and makes service delivery, management, and support more efficient with fewer errors. There may be many component service providers needed to offer an entire end-to-end service, but one of them must take the lead, accepting responsibility for service availability and quality. The service provider taking that responsibility will own the customer relationship and maintain brand equity by establishing direct contact with that end-customer.

2.2.1 Organizational Structures

This book discusses two high-level logical organizational structures that depict how service providers can be organized for both ramp-up and ongoing operations. These organizations loosely map to service delivery operations, as seen in the traditional telecommunications models: the Telecommunications Management Network (TMN) model, the Telecommunications Operations Map (TOM), and the Provisioning, Assurance, and Usage (PAU) model.

The TMN model (see Figure 2-3) shows how the business is logically managed, TOM (see Figure 2-4) maps processes into different operational functions, and PAU (see Figure 2-5) maps these processes into the provisioning, assurance, and usage functions of the business. The most important thing to remember when organizing a service provider is that there must be a customer-centric focus to organization and processes.

2.2.2 Staffing

Organizational staffing depends on guidelines set up around cost containment and productivity balanced against the provider's service's roadmap. Finding the right employees is a bit of an art form. Try to make an ideal employee profile that incorporates the desired skills and personality traits. What books would he/she read, what hobbies would the successful candidate have, what trade shows would they frequent? Does a recruitment booth make more sense at a wine festival or a technical conference? Company reputation has a lot to do with recruiting and retaining the best employees. Do research to understand what others inside and outside the service provider think it's like to work there. If consultants are used for recruitment, the provider should not abdicate candi-

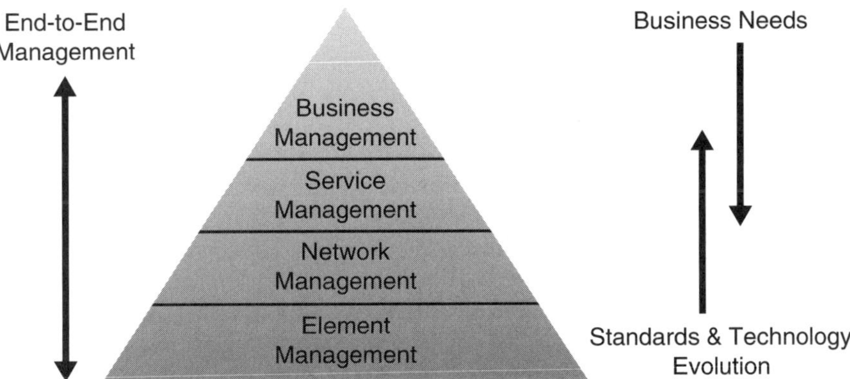

Figure 2-3 The Telecommunications Management Network.
© TM Forum's Telecom Operations Map.

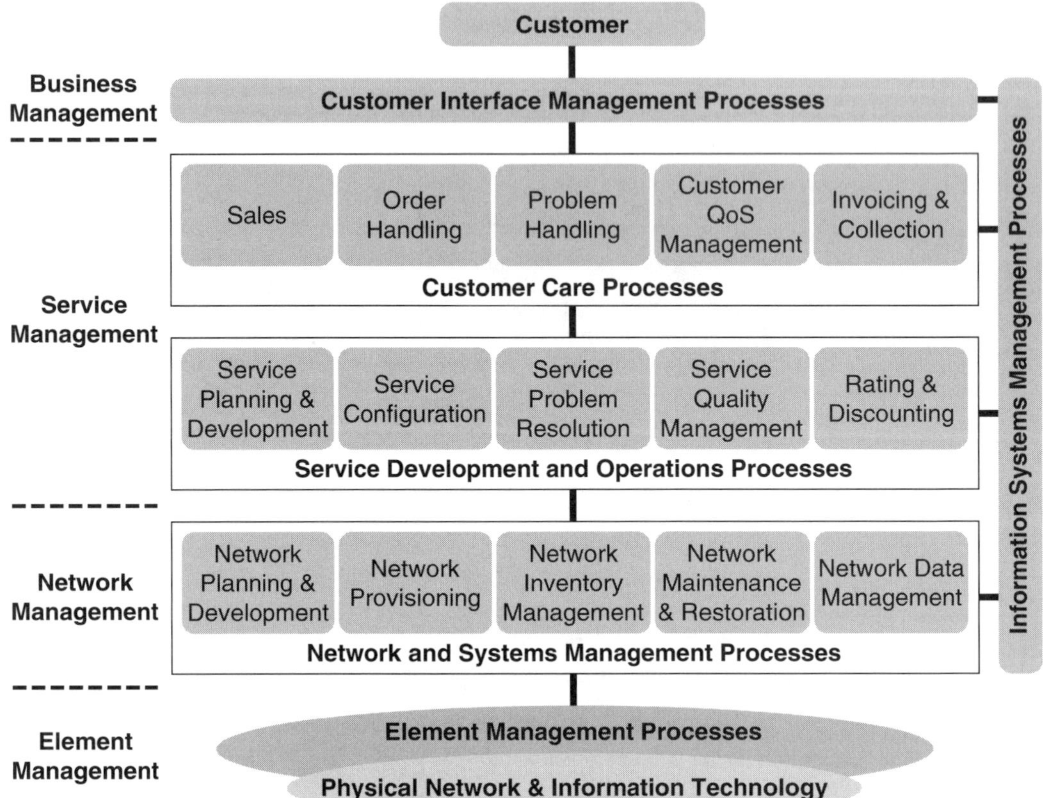

Figure 2-4 The Telecommunications Operations Map.
© TM Forum's Telecom Operations Map.

date specification and hiring. The consultant can leave at the end of the day; these employees will be working for the provider for quite some time, in the best of worlds, and are a big investment in time and money. Involve a selection committee when it comes to hiring for key posts.

2.2.3 Decision Making

In general, when entering the market, service providers should focus on key processes and create some decision boundaries, versus rules, to empower key managers without limiting their authority and creativity. These boundaries should include guidelines on corporate mission/vision/goals, business priorities, financial profit/loss, timing, and exit. Key to this philosophy is communication. Communication shouldn't be exclusively top/down, but should incorporate bilateral methods. All levels of the organization need to know what is most important to the owners/stockholders, understand market dynamics, corporate strategy, key company issues, and so forth. There must be venues for every employee to add useful input or criticism without feeling his/her job is in jeopardy.

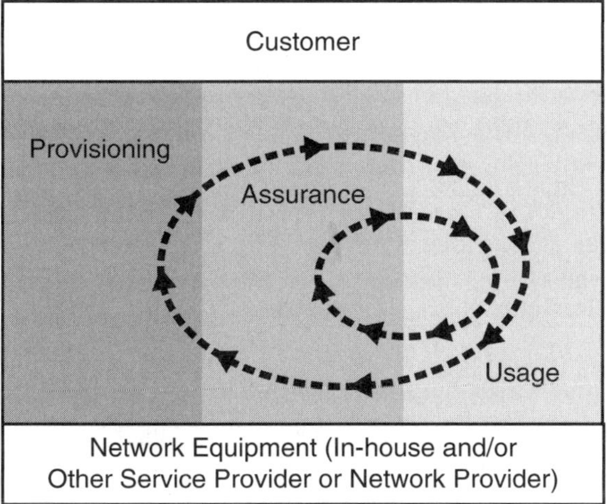

Figure 2-5 The Provisioning, Assurance, and Usage Model.
Published courtesy of Hewlett-Packard Company.

2.2.4 Growth Strategies

Primary growth strategies fall into the following three general categories:

- Organic
  - Recruiting and retention
  - Differentiation
- Partners and alliances
- Mergers and acquisitions

Organic growth seems to be preferred in more stable market environments where providers have time and local labor resources. Partnering and alliances will occur in normal business as the provider identifies gaps in service functionalities and channels to market. Mergers and acquisitions are more common for those Internet players and market situations where a key capability is needed fast or in the case of rapid geographic expansion.

2.2.5 Investments

As part of the general service provider organization, decisions need to be made about how much revenue will be reinvested in research and development (R&D), marketing, education/training, recruitment/retention, infrastructure technology, sales, and so forth. A lot depends on the core competency of the provider, their position in the market, and business goals. Analysts seem to show a mean average of 5.5 percent of revenue reinvested for R&D purposes, 5 percent for educational purposes, and 6.5 percent for marketing purposes.

2.2.6 Project Value Methodology

Service providers should be preoccupied with deciding which projects or services to implement sooner rather than later, so it makes sense to say a few words about project valuation trends. Besides the typical internal rate of return (IRR), economic value added (EVA), and net present value (NPV), and so forth calculations, providers are emphasizing more and more the value of a loyal customer base and the effect a new system or service will have on their most profitable customer segments. This should be the focus of the provider's project office.

The first step is to determine the value of the customer base affected by each project. Then the provider needs to look and consider which projects under consideration will provide the greatest return in protecting or enhancing customer value in the shortest amount of time. To determine the most profitable customer segments, the provider needs to measure the revenue generated per customer, the probability of retaining each customer, the cost of retention, and the cost of acquiring customers. Taken together, this information will show the effect of the customer segment on the company's bottom line. The project office should then look at its project list and determine which projects will have the most positive direct effect on the identified customer segment(s). The relative costs of these projects can then be analyzed, together with other information, against the financial considerations of the customer segments to make an informed go/no go decision. The result is that the provider will first implement those initiatives that have the greatest effect to the company's bottom line.

2.2.7 Organization

There is no secret formula to set up an organizational structure for a service provider; rather it is dependent upon process design and people effectiveness, as well as profit targets and desired overall customer support levels. Chapter 10, "Organization," will give suggestions for organizational roles and titles, personnel organizational models, and estimates for resource numbers, as well as a list of processes needed to operate effectively. When the service provider decides on its services roadmap, it can also decide on its core competence—what it wants to be famous for and when it will be, or needs to be, profitable. After this, the service provider can better decide how it will staff, partner, and outsource. When outsourcing a portion of its operations, a service provider must perform rigorous due diligence and manage these associations carefully for quality performance. Staffing plans normally are developed in conjunction with the detailed sales, marketing, and operational plans.

2.3 Entering the Market

It is helpful to think of everything the service provider does for a client in terms of a solution. Before entering the market, it is important to correctly understand customer needs and have a clear roadmap to profitability. Labeling the company, its service offering, or affiliations, is necessary for brand awareness in the market. Service providers should be aware that market identity with the label may have adverse affects. An example of this is the dot.com label after the market crashed and so many went bankrupt. Providers using this label could feel direct results on their industry visibility, reputation, earnings, and shareholder value.

2.3.1 Determining Customer Needs

It's difficult for a service provider to define a solution for a customer segment that is "needs-oblivious." There are four essential elements to determining if potential customer segments understand a perceived need:

- They can articulate their issues.
- They can offer evidence, financial or otherwise, that a problem exists.
- They can articulate the impact, financial or otherwise, a solution would have if the problem is fixed.
- They can list the functions a potential solution needs to address.

After customer needs are assessed, the service provider needs to think strategically about what services to offer and what functionality to bundle. These bundles will change as a function of the services lifecycle, product mix, competition, and changing target customer markets. Some services might be bundled as a way to enter a market and be priced to "buy" the market as a loss leader for a certain amount of time.

Sales and marketing is a critical area for any service provider, especially in such a highly competitive market. Service providers use many sales forces that fall under the broad headings of direct and indirect. Traditionally, sales forces were organized by industry matrix solution set. As Figure 2-6 illustrates, providers have been evolving through several stages of sales organization, from:

- Product lead
- Geography based
- Service line

toward solution based and vertical expertise organizations.

This progression shows an evolution toward understanding customer needs and a progression toward consultative selling. Selling service provider services to potential customers is more complex than traditional product sales because it normally directly affects many divisions across the organization. This can mean a larger deal size and more decision makers involved in each sale. It also means that sales calls will be at the executive level in the prospective company. By moving from left to right in the continuum in Figure 2-6, sales people better understand, and are better able to articulate, how their Internet services will affect the core customer business. That

Figure 2-6 Sales force organization evolution.

said, many providers are still trying to understand how to perfect the consultative selling model, many leaning toward a team selling approach pairing a sales person with a consultant and a technical lead. Typically, the leads are then reviewed for viability by a management team.

Direct sales teams are the most expensive and normally focus on key service provider customers. Indirect teams are less easy to control, but less expensive. These sales teams are homed in on the customer groups as defined by the focus of the channel. This helps mitigate the risk of having most of the provider revenue being based on only certain customers.

2.3.2 Pricing

Pricing models are limited only to the imagination of the service provider and acceptance by the market. Contracts include such models as:

- One time set up fee and ongoing set periodic fees thereafter
- Per transaction, fixed rate
- Per transaction, rate based on volume of transaction
- Risk/reward monthly rate based on business success. Normally ceilings and floors are associated with this.
- Cross selling, pricing discounts based on selling to provider/customer client bases

Service providers want to offer pricing benefits to those customers willing to sign multiyear contracts. Some will offer special rates to customers that have a service or product that can be cross sold to other provider customers. This is one way of bundling more value added services into the provider's services mix.

2.3.3 Marketing Communication

Marketing communication should be simple and understandable to the target audience–it should untangle the Web. The service provider should build brand recognition through communications channels and defend the brand as much as possible. Partners and customers may pay dearly to be associated with a trusted brand. Build a loyal following that will communicate, by word of mouth, the advantages of the brand to new customers.

Providers want to be market makers, defining the market. There are disadvantages to this strategy, for example having to educate the marketplace about advantages of the new service and working through legal questions arising out of new models. Advantages of being first to market normally far outweigh the disadvantages and include things like price definition, brand recognition, market share, and so forth.

The service provider's go-to-market strategy includes information about:

- Customer need, market drivers, and customer segmentation
- Customer needs awareness levels
- The service offering description
- Service pricing, placement, and promotion

Strategy is executed via a series of plans, including plans for:

- Sales
- Marketing/Marketing Communications
- Resourcing
- Partnering
- Operations, and so forth

Service execution components include:

- An owner
- A small number (maximum of three) measurable objectives
- Marketing, sales, staffing, partnering, and so forth.
- Plans to achieve those objectives
- Testing the plan
- Gathering the resources to execute the plan
- Executing the plan(s)
- Formulating a plan when the market and competition reacts to the services
- Ongoing execution review
- Developing an exit strategy

2.4 Service Delivery and Provisioning

Efficient service delivery is one of the differentiators in the service provider business and providers need to understand the service costs, timing, and delivery process. Service delivery is the service provider infrastructure and processes needed to deliver a service to either an individual or enterprise. It includes all aspects of the customer lifecycle including:

- Purchase: from order entry through testing
- Activation
- Maintenance
- Up-sell
- Exit

Service delivery (see Figure 2-7) and provisioning need to be in synch, efficiently linking many parts of the organization. Typically, the processes to deliver and provision new services, or changes to existing service, are set up so it is impossible to control the entire process. There are usually point-to-point, tightly linked processes involving resources and technology between departments that are difficult to optimize.

Typically, these processes are a mixture of systems and human elements with no one coordination point. A change in one aspect will have a domino effect on the others. For example, automating order entry means the links to other aspects of the provisioning process need updating to reflect the automation.

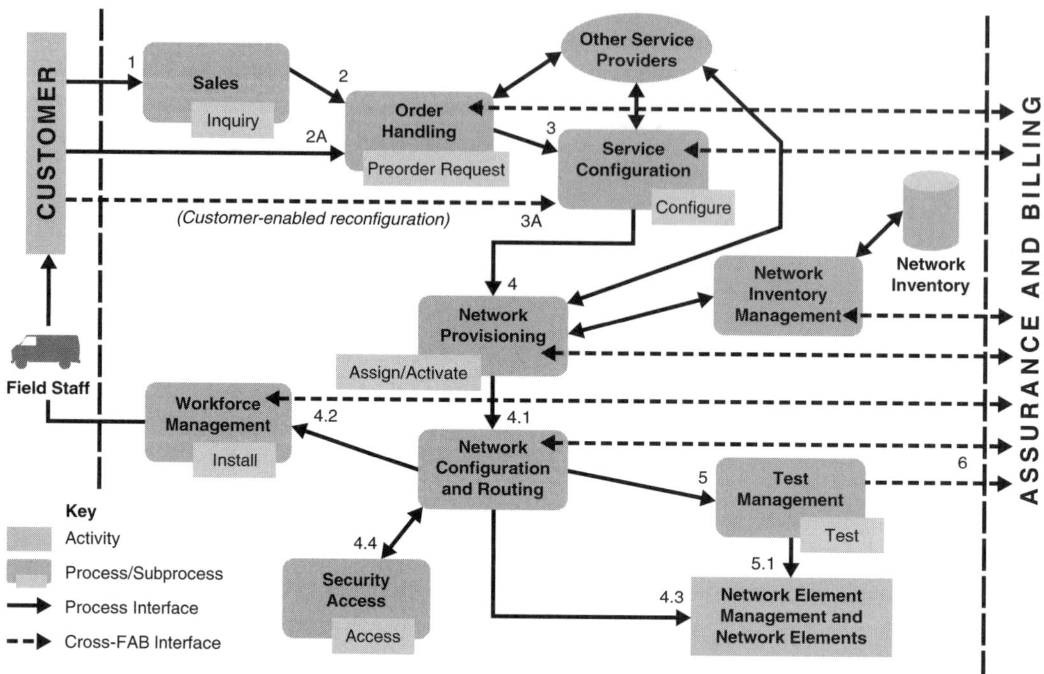

Figure 2-7 Generic service delivery processes.
© TM Forum's Telecom Operations Map.

Service delivery for a new service consists of four high-level provisioning areas–sales/negotiation, order capture/handling, service configuration, and provisioning/activation. The more preconfiguration, the more steps can be bypassed.

The following are generic processes for service delivery of new services and link into Figure 2-7.

- Step 1—selling. The customer inquires, negotiates, and decides to buy a service. If the service can be self-provisioned the customer can go directly to Step 4.
- Step 2—order request. An order request is created and the sales staff checks that it is feasible to supply this service to the customer. This normally includes some sort of product catalog and network inventory.
- Step 3—service request. If the service is feasible, a request for the service can be generated.
- Step 4—provisioning request. Configuration parameters are set up, work force assigned to install the CPE, network elements are configured, access checks are performed.
- Step 5—activating the service.
- Step 6—test request. The service is tested to see if it is working and can be released to the customer.
- Step 7—service delivery complete. Control passes to the service assurance and billing processes.

One of the biggest single operational investments made, in dollars and manpower, is a flexible automated provisioning system. Provisioning is the step in the service delivery process when configuration parameters are set up, the work force installs the customer premise equipment, network elements are configured, access is checked, and so forth.

2.5 Customer Care

When customer churn is high something is inherently wrong with service and no provider can afford to lose profitable customers. Customer relations are the most important element of a successful business and a differentiator in the market. To be successful, providers should create a single view of the customer that is available throughout as a way to streamline sales and customer support functions. Only by having a single view of sales, delivery, billing, and customer care can service providers run their business efficiently. The provider should be organized in a way that customers can handle all their business through whichever entry channel they choose.

Call center business applications are inherently operational (local) and can be independently justified. Information they use, acquire, and share needs to be analyzed and processed (global, systemic) for use in developing new processes and services.

Operational No solution stands alone; each exists in an operational context. Successful customer care solutions are systemic, rather than point-to-point. These systems must integrate:

- Computer/telephone user interfaces (CTI)
- Call flow
- Work flow
- Call handling scripts
- Sales and marketing strategies and tactics
- Business objectives

Analytic The operational information must be stored, normally in a data warehouse, and analyzed, or processed, for those needing a combined view of the customer's situational environment. To do this, system designers need to know what departments or individuals will benefit from, or be affected by, the information flow. More specifically, they need to understand how the following interact:

- Applications
- Databases
- Processes
- People
- Functions

Information must be processed in a way that will work best for the provider through specific analysis and profiling techniques.

Impact All of this means understanding the impact of information on the organization. How will access to more in-depth, consolidated customer information affect different areas of the organization? The correct answer will have a dramatic effect on the company's bottom line. More complete customer information available to more areas of the company should mean a closer customer relationship, better products, lower customer churn, and higher revenues.

When discussing customer service, service providers normally think in terms of:

- Controlling costs
- Improved customer service representative (CSR) efficiency
- Better customer service and interaction
- Improved image
- Integration

Each customer contact is an opportunity to reduce risk of churn and increase revenue. Each touch point must be able to capture the customer contact event with enough information to improve the next contact and to anticipate future needs.

Customer care is also an opportunity to extend interaction beyond normal business hours meaning more opportunities for revenue generation and customer satisfaction. Self-care options with electronic interfaces give customers control over their environments and lower frustration factors. These options also lead to lower costs because customers can help themselves and, hopefully, solve their own problems. The provider can choose to support and facilitate chat rooms using these interfaces as a way to build brand loyalty. It is also an excellent way for the provider to get closer to the customer and get first-hand customer feedback.

Any customer care system must have measurable objectives and monitoring systems. These are the keys to managing market perception of the service provider. Customer relationship management systems are more than just call centers. They are the glue that link information between different operational areas of the service provider to give one view of the customer. Operational management systems link day-to-day information while analytical management systems show trends and help management understand overall business performance. Customer relationship management (CRM) systems will be a critical enabler for high value services and will eventually expand to touch all points of the organization.

2.6 Billing

Billing for IP services is significantly different from billing for circuit-switched telephony. Mediation is harder; bytes, bandwidth, and QoS provide a more appropriate basis for pricing than minutes. Billing systems need to take a high volume of usage information from many sources and rate them, real-time, while applying universal discounting and settling charges, some of which are roaming, with diverse business partners. Customers expect self-provisioning and care with instantaneous results to their service. To keep up with these trends, billing systems need to be scalable, flexible, and robust with abilities to easily update tariff plans and rating logic. There also needs to be an ability to set up APIs and protocols that will work with

"Webified" and "non-Webified" applications since industry standards are not defined in this highly fragmented area. Service providers are looking to billing as a source of new revenue by enabling charging for advertising, cross sell/up-sell, and as a new wholesale service that can be offered to service providers who decide to outsource these functions.

2.7 Infrastructure and Availability

Over the years, the landline telephone and the cellular network have developed thousands of interconnection points to exchange traffic among network operators. Users, confident of connectivity and quality standards, have come to expect consistent pricing and quality in both environments. Similarly, cellular and landline network operators are accustomed to the costs and revenues associated with internetworking through an established traffic tracking and revenues settlements system. Since the Internet is an entirely new kind of global network, it has presented unique challenges from an infrastructure and availability standpoint.

Client/server software is not optimized for xSP delivery over the network. Challenges when offering non-Web-enabled applications include software delivery, maintenance, revision control, and backward compatibility. Even if the software is already Web-enabled there could be operational problems that need to be overcome before it is service ready. Testing and benchmarking in a nonoperational environment is key before going live.

Modular architecture can ease deployments, upgrades, and system enhancements. Capacity planning and forecasting for new services is very difficult and providers need to have alternative forms of capacity until customer usage statistics are available.

Service provider infrastructure needs to be scalable, flexible, dependable, supportable, secure, and manageable. These characteristics are needed throughout the delivery chain from service origination through to the final customer. Usually they are measured by SLAs. Service levels are often governed by the links between members of the delivery chain and are dependent on the chain's weakest point. Service providers just entering the market will probably offer the most basic SLA possible and will include only those elements over which the provider has direct control. More complex SLAs, while highly desirable from a customer point of view, can only be offered by those providers in tune with, and experienced in, operating a complex delivery infrastructure. Whatever architecture is used must support the service provider's business.

2.8 Summary

In reviewing the operational challenges it is important that the service provider understands its current state: What is good today, what is unacceptable, and why. Then the provider must understand the future state: What does a successful future look like, in a quantifiable way, and why. The gaps identified between today and the successful future are the basis for a sound execution plan to move away from pain, toward gain.

Part 2 shows how service providers around the world identify, face, and work through the operational challenges described in this chapter.

PART 2

Case Studies

CHAPTER 3

Case Studies: An Introduction

Part 2 takes into account real-life examples of how service providers face and meet the seven operational challenges identified in Part 1. These case studies are taken from examples in each of four super regions in the world:

- Asia Pacific: Acer CyberCenter Services, Inc.
- Europe: KPNQwest
- Latin America: Triara
- North America: PartnerCommunity, Inc.

The case study content in the following chapters was obtained during interviews and it is important to understand that, even though direct quotes are seldom used, the information represents the direct points of view of those interviewed. Each chapter begins with a high-level overview of the market to give the reader some contextual frame of reference for the case study.

There are common issues apparent across the world within the seven operational challenges:

- How best to interact and work with corporate stakeholders
- How best to communicate to the market
- How to find and retain the best people
- How to get services to market quickly
- How to maintain close ties with customers
- How to test and monitor infrastructure
- How to partner most effectively

The case studies will show how these companies have faced these, and other, issues.

From a contextual standpoint, there are some global trends to keep in mind that affect the service provider business. Multinational providers that ignore national differences when rolling out services are heading for failure. They should factor in the various stages of readiness in different countries before launching a new service. The Internet is global in scope, but local in impact. Due diligence is needed to understand which countries should be targeted first with each service. The propensity to use a service is based upon three factors:

- Economic and business environment
- Cultural factors
- Regulatory issues

For example, whereas Internet use is global, Internet commerce may be more popular in the United States; Europe may lead in wireless Internet services trends. Internet use should increase as more businesses come online, new functionalities become available, and children using Web-enabled educational tools come into the work force. Media continues to play an important role in promoting Internet use.

Services, in general, appear to focus on four major customer segments:

- Small/medium businesses
- Large enterprises
- Vertical industries
- Consumers

The definitions of each vary by region, country, and service provider within the country. Some countries in Asia Pacific are kick starting Internet use among small and medium businesses by offering government-subsidized programs that begin automating supply chains.

Today when a company decides to use an Internet service from a service provider, the initial implementations, either for internal or external use, still tend to be the first such projects undertaken in the enterprise. This means the sales cycle may be longer, and more people within the prospective customer organization may need to be educated. While this situation may lead to larger value orders for the provider, the initial support costs for this customer profile will invariably mitigate some, if not all, of the extra revenue.

Not every service provider will own an IDC, but all Internet services are based on one somewhere. This means that if the service provider decides not to build its own, it must partner with one, or several, providers that do own IDCs. It also means that the partner should understand the hosting business and its ability to offer the services, and service levels, required now, and in the future.

Finally, throughout the world customers look to service providers as a business partner, not just someone who offers Internet services. They look to the provider as a source of infrastructure services, and also to help with new ideas for gaining new customers, service fulfillment, coselling, advertising, and so forth. This puts the provider in a unique position that must not be taken for granted or abused.

CHAPTER 4

North America – PartnerCommunity, Inc.

The North American market represents one of the largest and most homogenous in the world. For the purposes of this book, North America encompasses Canada and the United States of America with all its holdings. This region is one of the most open and uniform from a regulatory standpoint and makes one of the better breeding grounds for new Internet technologies. It is also one of the more competitive markets in the world.

4.1 The North American Market

4.1.1 Customer Needs

Many North American businesses already have some interface to the Internet, even if it's only an informational Web page. What is changing now is that corporations are looking at more cross company unified Internet implementations. This means reviewing Web-enabling applications already installed for efficacy and updating applications to Web-instrumented versions, and reviewing production, support, sales, and marketing operations. To keep ahead of the competition, North American businesses want to use new technologies to understand, and make the best use of, customer data and enable the real-time sharing of operational information.

From the demand side, businesses are looking for ways to use the Internet to expand customer interaction and market reach. Businesses want to work with service providers to open more sales and marketing channels. From the supply side, businesses are looking for service providers and system integrators to use the Internet as a way to make supply chains work more efficiently. By using applications available on a per-use basis, companies are also able to lower capital expense outflows.

4.1.1.1 Service Provider Operations

The majority of service provider operations began with a more traditional approach. Geographically based organizations had responsibility for account management, service delivery, and so forth. As service offerings changed and became more complex and pan-regional, providers began implementing more national processes to assure quality levels. As services change from single applications toward a solution set focus like CRM, or technology focus like wireless or broadband, or a more business model focus like a vertical industry, providers are changing their go-to-market approaches. As the services become more complex, providers are forced to focus more on integration skills across applications. Older market entrants are retooling to maintain brand distinction, as the service provider market becomes more mature.

Pure service providers are hitting up against dot-coms, independent software vendors (ISVs), consulting companies, and so forth, which may already have a large installed base with companies interested in the newer complex services. Competition to get a foothold in the limited number of large enterprise clients is high. North America has severe IT resource constraints that make the situation worse. Service providers are looking for customers that can create longer ongoing business, versus the fast implementations of the first wave. Since the resources of ideal customers are financially limited, there is severe pricing pressure and many customers are requesting results-based pricing.

Providers are partnering overseas to gain expertise and develop skills in new service areas, like wireless, that are not common yet in North America.

4.2 Case Study – PartnerCommunity, Inc.

4.2.1 Company Overview

In June 2000, Dr. John Yin, formerly chief technology officer and corporate strategist at Daleen Technologies, Inc., founded PartnerCommunity, Inc.[1] Daleen is a publicly traded software company that develops billing and customer care solutions for service providers. The PartnerCommunity concept was developed in late 1999, and was cultivated as an internal Daleen project during the first half of 2000. In June 2000, Daleen incorporated the unit as a separate company, and Yin was named president and CEO. Daleen, which made the initial cash investment, continues to be the majority owner. PartnerCommunity is headquartered in Boca Raton, Florida.

PartnerCommunity has 22 employees, and its main business is delivering Internet-based *partner chain management*™ services for communications, content, application, and infrastructure service providers. Using its software solutions, PartnerCommunity enables members to find and form new partner relationships, integrate systems and business processes, and automate and manage the operation of key business functions between companies. Members are able to manage service offerings, create and manage contracts and service level agreements, process trouble tickets, automate ordering, and manage settlement functions in collaboration with partners. This makes it possible for PartnerCommunity members to bring new service offerings to market, and expand distribution channels, with greater speed, ease, and flexibility. As a result, members are able to accelerate time-to-revenue, ensure customer satisfaction, and secure current and future success.

According to Dr. Yin, the company went into business because, "the irreversible trend of digitalization, [means] services will become the dominant form in which value is delivered to [the] user. In fact, communication, content, computing, and applications are all becoming services." For reasons discussed in detail later in the chapter, the delivery model for services has shifted dramatically away from single, vertically integrated providers to collaborative teams of service providers that go to market in the form of a virtual ecosystem or partner chain.

Service providers that are building and operating partner chains have undertaken sometimes-massive projects to integrate their business processes and enterprise software systems with those of trading partners. Historic methods of integration, primarily EDI and custom software development, are being abandoned as too brittle or expensive for the fast-paced operating environment of the 21st century.

State-of-the-art business process and application integration requires the use of extensible Markup Language (XML) and business-to-business (B2B) integration servers. But, as illustrated in Figures 4-1 and 4-2, even the state-of-the-art has a significant shortcoming—it is enormously complex and very expensive to build a point-to-point integrated network among multiple trading partners. Each trading partner must implement, and maintain, software that handles protocol and data translation, messaging, and workflow management for each and every one of its trading partners.

PartnerCommunity streamlines the point-to-point process and application integration approach with a hub-and-spoke architecture (see Figure 4-3). With this architecture, a service provider integrates once—and only once—with PartnerCommunity's hub. PartnerCommunity is one of the only companies to address partner chain management problems with a value proposition:

- Enabling service providers to leverage the core competencies of others in a collaborative value chain. This enhances the service provider's ability to offer its customers the right solution at the right time.
- Enabling service providers to build flexible value chains through a scalable hub and spoke, Internet-based architecture. This enhances the service provider's ability to manage changes in its business model, customer base, and value chain or operating environment. For example, an existing trading partner might develop a relationship with one of the service provider's key competitors, be acquired, or even go bankrupt.
- Reducing significantly the cost and time required for integrating, automating, and managing intercompany business processes between service providers.
- Increasing customer satisfaction and retention by enabling service providers to offer complete, seamless solutions to their customers and to minimize any inter-service providers delays, inconsistencies, and disputes.
- Leading to higher revenue and margin for service providers.

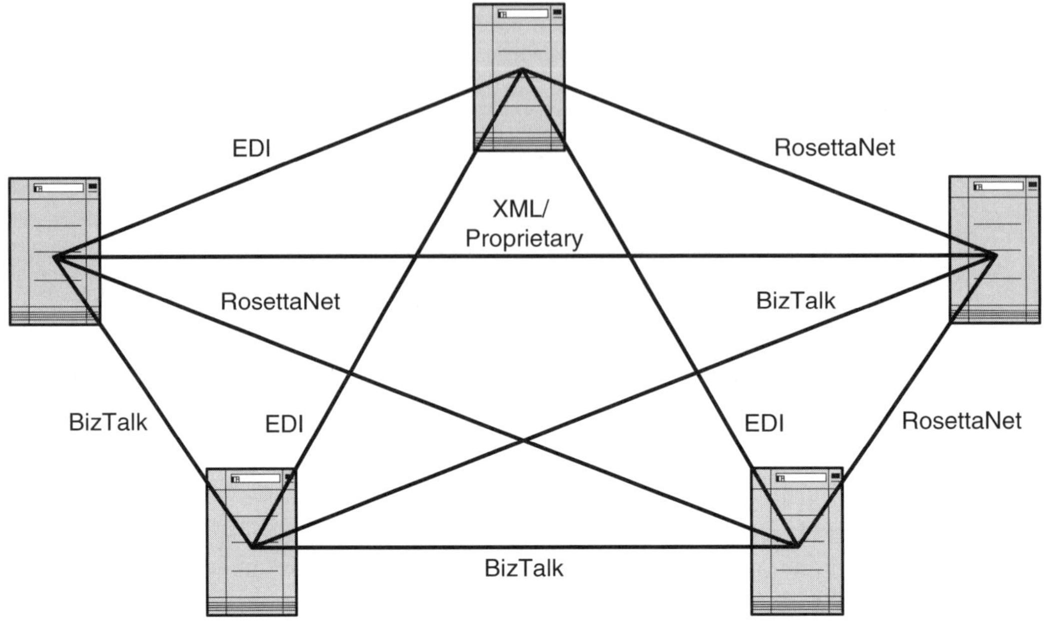

Figure 4-1 Enterprise integration.

PartnerCommunity services are charged on a subscription and transaction fee basis. Customers who become members of PartnerCommunity pay a flat subscription fee to sign up. In addition, PartnerCommunity charges transaction fees based on the total transaction dollar value between trading partners. PartnerCommunity also licenses its products to service providers who want to form their own private communities.

Reference customers include TeleComputing, CyLex Systems, Inc., and Cedar Group. Through product preintegration with Daleen software, all Daleen customers can automatically integrate with the community hub. PartnerCommunity is pursuing a similar preintegration strategy with other operational and business support software vendors.

Partner chain management for service providers has very different requirements from supply- and demand-chain management for enterprises. Collaborating service providers need to deliver integrated services to their customers 24 hours a day, 7 days a week, with a single bill and a single point of customer contact. While there are hundreds of B2B exchanges and platform vendors in the market today, its focus on service providers and on real-time integrated partner

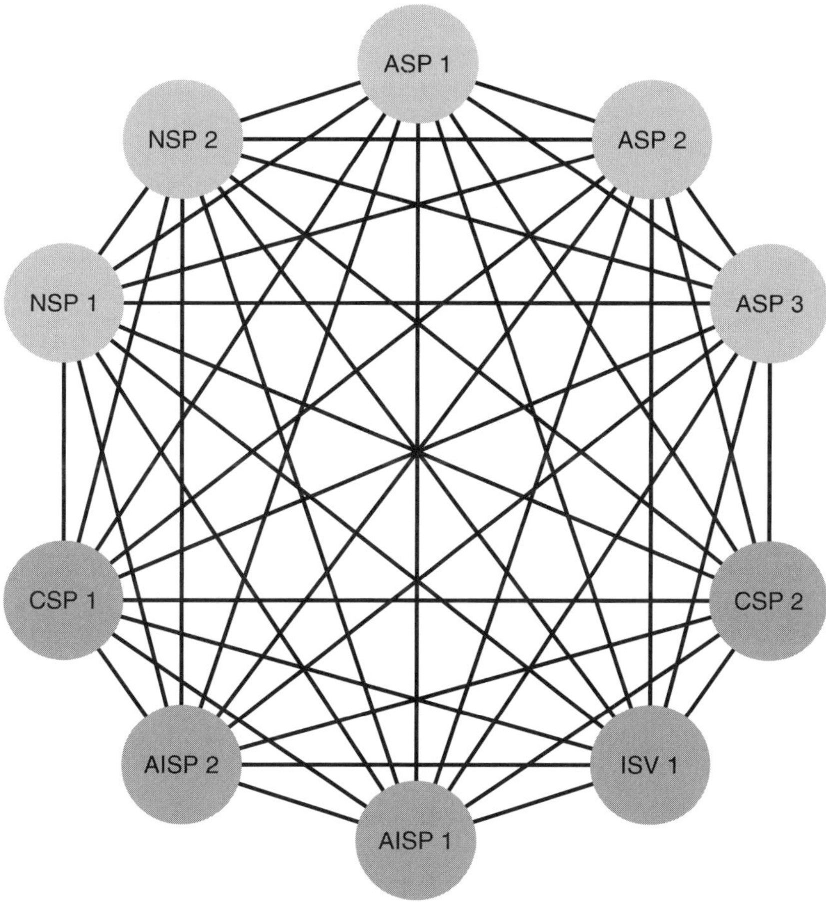

Figure 4-2 An integration nightmare.

chain management services is what fundamentally moves PartnerCommunity apart from past and present would-be competitors.

4.2.2 Local Landscape Overview

Even though its solutions are critical to service providers throughout the world, PartnerCommunity chose to focus first on business in North America. This was logical because it's a big market, it's close to home, and PartnerCommunity knows it better than any other.

The North American market is extremely competitive. It is the place where everyone wants to try out new ideas, new concepts, and new services. "North America is also a great environment for startups from a technology standpoint," says Yin, "because it is ahead of most regions of the world in most new technologies, with the exception of, perhaps, wireless technologies."

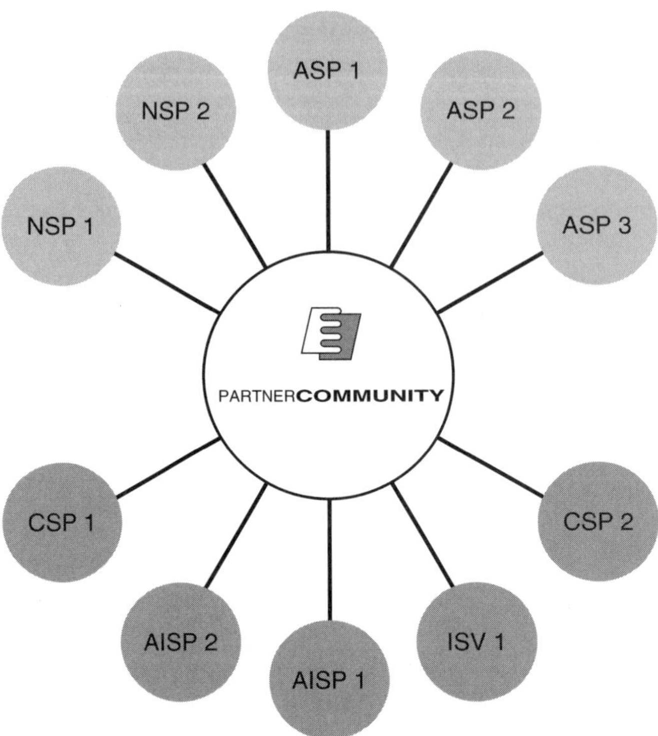

Figure 4-3 Back-end integration with PartnerCommunity.

The regulatory environment in North America is more open and uniform than that of other countries, so it creates the perfect place to test and create products and services. For example, Europe has different regulations in each country, and service providers need to adapt their operations to work within multiple, individual frameworks. North American requirements, on the other hand, are relatively consistent between the United States and Canada, meaning that service functionality offered can be introduced more quickly to a larger number of potential customers.

4.2.2.1 Competition

There are no other companies in the market, yet, which enable xSPs to build their value chains, or ecosystems, in such a flexible way. This gives PartnerCommunity a first mover advantage in the market. According to Yin, "PartnerCommunity does not consider aggregators to be direct competitors because they tend to aggregate a particular set of applications to satisfy a particular set of end customers. ASP enabler services, on the other hand, are mostly focused around enabling applications to work in an Internet, service-based environment."

PartnerCommunity doesn't pretend to understand the needs of a service provider's end-customers, or what services the provider should offer. PartnerCommunity focuses on giving service providers the ability to build and operate an ecosystem, together with the front and back office environment needed to successfully support the services that the providers want to offer their customer bases.

4.2.2.2 Partnering Infrastructure

Enabling collaboration among service providers is PartnerCommunity's core business, and as such, its leaders understand why and how service providers operate.

First, service providers must focus on a core competency. The ever-accelerating pace of change in each industry, and technology in general coupled with fierce competition, makes it almost impossible to keep up with everything that goes on. Nevertheless, customers of these service providers still demand complete solutions that incorporate new functionality and technologies. For example, customers want to get all of their communication services (broadband, wireless, local, and long distance) from the same provider on a single bill and have a single point of customer support. It is extremely difficult for one service provider to build the infrastructure and to provide all these services directly.

Second, the rapid commoditization of a particular service can ruin the service provider's business. The shelf life for value-added services is relatively short before service providers start to feel margin squeeze from competitors. They need to continuously expand functionality to increase revenue per customer, margins, and general market share, while minimizing customer churn.

Third, wholesale and retail service providers need channels for their services. Their immediate customers may differ; for example, a wholesale content provider customer might be a small to medium ASP or retail channel. Eventually, all service providers use either a direct or indirect channel to reach their end-user markets—be it consumer or enterprise. ASP services, for example, may be most appropriate for small- and medium-size businesses, but a direct sales approach to such customers is inefficient and, therefore, too expensive. It makes sense in this case to create a partnership between a telecommunications service provider and the ASP. One has customers but needs value-added services, while the other has value-added services but needs customers.

PartnerCommunity's services are targeted toward service providers that want and need to quickly offer new services to market. Typically, when a service provider wants to offer a new service, it needs to:

- Define the service requirements and functionality gaps between its capability and the requirements.
- Go through an RFP process to find the partners needed to fill gaps in order to provide the entire service functionality.
- Establish business relationships, including contracts and service level agreements, and integrate with selected partners to create an offering with the desired functionality.
- Set up service delivery processes.
- Manage the value chain, offering, service quality, support, and customer satisfaction.
- Bill for the services.
- Divide revenue among service partners.

In the past, communications companies would try to do all this inhouse or through acquisitions. This approach is expensive, risky, and takes a long time. There is no guarantee that the requirement for the new service is either pervasive or long lasting, or that the margin for a service will be sustainable. This approach often requires a service provider to step out of its core competency.

There is a fundamental shift in how service providers decide which applications and software products to offer. As services become more complex, service providers need to have a strategy for partnering with other service providers as a way to mitigate risk, lower operational expenses, and speed time to market. Providers need the capability to partner with other service providers who have previously implemented similar services; but how can this be done? If the provider partners with others, how does it ensure a flexible value chain? If it is not satisfied with its partner, how does it change partners after the service is already offered in production without jeopardizing quality? What happens if the partner goes out of business? To answer these questions, service providers need to focus on five major areas when offering multiple partner services:

- Partnering: How do you find the right partner based on the current understanding of customers' requirements? How flexible is the value chain? Can partners be substituted/ added, both technically and legally, without creating a ripple effect to others in the service fulfillment value chain? Can customer data be moved from one provider to another?
- Service description: How are customers' needs translated into services offered by the partnering service providers, and how are the services described, delivered and supported consistently to the customers? This may not be trivial if the service providers are from different industries.
- Contract and ongoing management: What kind of support, or services, is needed to negotiate the contract and service level agreements? How will the contract and service level agreements be managed on an ongoing basis, real-time?
- Service delivery: How will orders and provisioning requests be routed real-time to service partners in such a way that there is a seamlessly integrated workflow to support partners and end-customers? How will trouble tickets be routed real-time and seamlessly between multiple partners in the fulfillment chain?
- Billing, settlement, and customer care: How is the customer usage information shared so that the customer can be billed correctly and on time? How are billing settlements handled? How is revenue split between partners determined on a real-time basis? How are service level agreement violation settlements done accurately between partners? Who owns the customer and customer data?

Service providers probably will not create the entire service, preferring to focus on core competencies, while partnering for the added functionality needed. This model will continue well into the future. Meanwhile, end-users continue to demand more complex complete solutions. There is a gap between what the customer wants and what the service provider that owns the customer can realistically deliver. The provider can't very well tell its customers to go to another service provider directly to fill in the gap, because it may lose those customers to the other service provider. End-users don't have the patience, or resources, to coordinate multiple service providers, work through multiple contracts, or track trouble tickets through multiple providers in case of service problems.

PartnerCommunity offers an enabling environment where service providers can aggregate and bundle partner offerings seamlessly, offering the full solution to the customer. Traditional partnering processes are not efficient, scalable, or flexible enough. PartnerCommunity was founded as a way to solve these integration problems and relieve management issues. It acts as a facilitator, supporting service providers with the partnering infrastructure needed to get to market quickly. The specific areas of facilitation includes:

- Partner directory
- Contracts
- SLAs
- Service order and provisioning between service partners
- Billing settlement between service partners
- Trouble ticket management

This is why PartnerCommunity positions itself as a service provider enabler, versus a wholesaler or aggregator. It allows service providers to substitute a particular partner, and add or subtract partners, in the value chains without major disruptions to business.

The network based hub-spoke architecture allows service providers to use whatever protocols they want and mediates these protocols, allowing service providers to talk between themselves. This means service providers can set up, or change, partner relationships without worrying about integrating or changing data protocols or formats. A case in point is a service provider that wants to offer the same service on both coasts of the United States. This service provider needs to work with one partner on the East Coast and another on the West Coast to offer the same service. In this case the two service partners may require two different provisioning protocols or data formats, a burden for the service provider because it would have to deal with two different integrations. PartnerCommunity mediates between the partners, allowing them to keep their internal protocols and data formats. In other words, instead of point-to-point integration, PartnerCommunity acts as a hub between the service providers. The service providers do one integration when they join the community, and afterward they are able to communicate with all other community members on the hub on an almost real-time basis. This significantly reduces the risk, cost, and time required to offer new services.

4.2.2.3 Outsourcing

There are three challenges in the outsourcing process:

- How will the service provider decide on its core business focus?
- How will the service provider get its people, especially line managers, to think strategically, so they don't build empires?

- How will the service provider find companies offering the desired services that also meet other business and cultural fit criteria, such as similar interests, investment/growth cycles, and attention to detail?

PartnerCommunity outsources its data center, data center operations, human resources (HR), and facilities management functions. Its philosophy is that a company should know what its core competency is and keep it inhouse. Anything that doesn't increase tangible value to customers and shareholders should be designated as noncore and should be outsourced.

PartnerCommunity's core competency is providing partner management services to service providers. To provide these services, it focuses on:

- Maintaining its domain expertise in service provider operational and business support systems (OSS, BSS).
- Building the right software solutions to solve real-world partner management problems that service providers have.
- Delivering the highest quality in both its service offerings and customer support.

PartnerCommunity's domain expertise is based on its association with Daleen's customer care and billing solution development and Daleen's service provider customer base.

Service providers must have the discipline to decide on their core competencies, set up boundaries around them, and not include inappropriate items under the core competency umbrella. Providers must understand that they can't do everything equally well. After the service provider decides on its core competency(ies), it should make a list of things to outsource, ranking them from greatest to smallest cost savings. Outsourcing some things will result in better financial returns than other things, and the provider should review transaction costs, comparing the cost of doing things internally versus externally, while completing the ranking exercise. Costs should include not only monetary consideration, but also management attention, impact on cycle times, and opportunity costs.

If a function is kept inside, would it be necessary to develop a "real" core competency? Not always. For example, if PartnerCommunity decided to have an inhouse HR manager, no real core competency development is needed, but sooner or later it will probably outsource the function because the company is small. This is also an example of a function that could be outsourced, but is not at the top of the outsourcing list because it results in a very small financial benefit. Building and running a data center, on the other hand, is very expensive, requiring specialized expertise. PartnerCommunity will choose to outsource data center services first because it is not their chosen core competence, the service is expensive, and it would take too much time and money to develop this functionality and expertise inhouse. At a later time it may choose to outsource a less costly function like HR management.

Once the decision is made regarding what to outsource, the service provider must find the best company offering the desired services. Service providers create a short list via RFPs and word of mouth. After this, it is up to exhaustive due diligence to determine which company offers the best quality and functionality at the best price.

The service provider must make decisions on how the outsourcing company will be managed on an ongoing basis. At PartnerCommunity, one person is responsible for each relationship. The person in charge is usually the individual whose authority covers the functionality that was outsourced.

4.2.2.4 Getting Buy-In

There is always some reason a line manager can give as to why certain functionality should not be outsourced. The CEO needs to understand the industry, its challenges, and its technologies, to keep a neutral perspective and not get swayed by people with opposing agendas. According to Yin, "Many companies and line managers I interviewed tell me why they can't outsource. These very bright and motivated people believe they can do things better than everyone else and do not trust their partners. Interdependency will be a key characteristic of the new ecosystem-based economy. For example, Wal-Mart relies on its partners' just-in-time delivery to minimize inventory and reduce cost. It is up to the CEO to articulate the corporate vision and strategy in such a way that everyone understands why outsourcing is important. He or she must build consensus among the management team about what is a core competence and what isn't, and have the discipline to stick with that decision. Without this consensus, outsourcing decisions cannot be made consistently and reliably.

"The Company CEO needs to understand the business," says Yin. "If the CEO doesn't understand a specific function, he or she doesn't have a frame of reference on which to base outsourcing decisions." Given the fast pace of change in both industry and technology, the CEO must have the interest and capacity to learn quickly and on an ongoing basis. The best way to acquire information about happenings in the industry is through reading, including publications like this book, networking with people in the business, and going to conferences.

Finding outsourcing companies offering the desired services with the right business and cultural fit is a challenge. Outsourcing providers often think that all their customers are alike—one solution will fit all companies using their services. Reality shows that each customer's business is different. The service provider seeking the outsourced services needs to understand, and make a decision based on a trade off between outsourcing companies that are:

- Market leaders—fast growing, high market share, high capitalization, financially stable, but not the same focus/functionality offering desired.
- Niche players—companies that may have more fit around functionalities offered, but not be as financially strong.

There will be a symbiotic relationship between the outsourcing provider and the service provider wanting to use their services. The companies need to work together, developing a win-win situation so that the outsourcing provider gets enough money for services to continue development and growth, and the service provider gets the desired service functionality at the desired quality and price point. There is risk involved in outsourcing that can, in part, be mitigated through contract exit clauses. These should include plans to migrate data to a new outsourcing provider if the present provider's service does not meet quality standards, it goes out of business, or its prices become noncompetitive. Using common sense and scenario planning can go a long way to prepare both parties for situations that might need to be addressed in the future.

4.2.2.5 Partnering Advice

When identifying partners, the service provider first needs to understand the gaps in its value chain. These gaps should be determined by first understanding end-customer needs. Then the service provider can identify gaps between the offering, what the service provider core competencies are, and what else is needed to provide the full solution. For example, a DSL provider focusing on the small/medium business market may find its customers want more than plain DSL, they also want Internet Web hosting, email, and calendaring functions. It should be obvious to the DSL provider that its core competency is providing DSL service, and it would be a risky proposition (expensive, time consuming, and so on) to develop these other services inhouse. Without this added functionality, the DSL provider may start losing customers and margin. If the DSL provider is only serving a small community, it is probably an easy decision to find a local partner that can offer this added functionality at a reasonable price. It becomes a challenge if there is no obvious provider. Then the DSL company needs to do a lot of due diligence and negotiation to find the right one.

If the service provider understands its industry well, and the players in it, the job of creating a short list of alliance partners will be a relatively simple one. There are many reasons why finding the best alliance is a challenge. Maybe the service provider is new to a vertical industry, maybe there are many niche players in the market with new technology heretofore unknown, or maybe several potential partners appear to have similar offerings. In these cases service providers need to do a lot of due diligence to find suitable partners. There are services available, like PartnerCommunity's partner matching service, that can help in these situations.

In general, partners should share a common vision and understand the win-win proposition for each. If the partners don't understand what each side gets out of the relationship, the alliance probably won't last very long because there is no incentive to continue working together.

When identifying partners to use as sales channels, the service provider needs to identify its target customer segment(s) and what solutions this segment needs. Once the target segment(s) is understood, the decision is taken on whether a direct or indirect sales approach is warranted. This decision is based on several factors, not the least of which is cost of sales and propensity to purchase via one channel over another. Financial modeling should help determine if acquisition costs are lower/higher than the potential revenues from the focus market(s). Many service providers don't take the time to go through this simple exercise and end up spending far more on customer acquisition than they will receive in revenue. For example, while many small/medium businesses can benefit from the ASP model, ASPs have not been very successful in the small/medium business market because they approach the market with an expensive direct sales approach, which cannot be cost-justified with low recurring revenue. It makes much more sense in these situations to partner as a way of leveraging these costs and the market entry price. By leveraging customer lists between partners, the providers are able to offer an enriched service bundle to a larger customer base—both partners win.

Most service providers aren't patient enough for the partnership to bear fruit. It can take a long time for partnerships in more traditional industries to create acceptable returns for the parties involved, but the Internet world forces things to move at a faster pace. Patience is needed for results even in Internet time, but service providers may not have that luxury. Significant outlays for public relations and joint development add to other cash flow constraints and put pressure on getting revenues in as quickly as possible from all venues. Service providers should be on the lookout for ways to accelerate returns on partner relationships. This is why partner chain management is becoming so important. Unless you can accelerate the partnership life cycle, even the most promising partnerships may not get enough time to ripen. Successful partnerships usually require that both parties put in required investments and resources at the start, not only after results are received. If one side wants to put in resources only after results occur, this might be a warning sign that there is no upfront commitment nor a perceived value in the relationship from both sides.

Managing conflict needs to be explored at the beginning of the relationship. Conflict resolution and escalation processes need to be in place before contract signing and should be included as special clauses in the contract. Expectations need to be understood and managed. For this, communication between parties is key. Communication shouldn't stop at the partner level, but should also continue to the level of end-user customer as a way to prevent conflict. Finger pointing among service providers in front of their customers is an easy way to ruin a partnership.

Once conflict occurs, the provider needs to use all of its management skills to rearticulate the reasons for the partnership and why the parties established it in the first place. Both parties need to be willing to work out their differences. Good partner relations are based on good personal relationships between people in the partner companies and between service providers and their customers. Communications should be ongoing, not just when things are going badly.

Partnerships do, unfortunately, sometimes fail. Exit provisions should be covered in the contract, but there are other issues. Service providers should preplan for all eventualities and review process and technical integration points. If these points are hard-wired, changing partners will be more challenging, as the barriers to change are higher. It will take time to reintegrate new software and processes. The contract should stipulate time frames and responsibilities if reintegration occurs. It shouldn't take six months and a lot of money to migrate if the partnership doesn't work out. There needs to be some inherent flexibility so changes can occur without too much upheaval. For example, processes should be established for migration of data and information from old to new service providers, in case change is warranted. The contract should stipulate who owns data and how it will be migrated, if necessary. Partner contracts should also cover dissolution for all aspects of the partnerships, including the return of joint investments, equipment, marketing material, intellectual property, and so forth.

4.2.2.6 Organization and Operations

PartnerCommunity pays close attention to its bottom line. Its organizational strategy is based on building a 21st century company with an external, rather than internal, focus. In other words, it will focus on customers, the market, and its partners. It stresses the importance of adapting to constant market changes, rather than a search for stability. There is an emphasis on focusing on core competencies while outsourcing the rest of the operations, thus creating a more virtual organization.

A flat organization is better for service providers because it is more flexible. If there is a large hierarchy, outsourcing becomes very difficult. People start empire building, and senior management has little control in terms of organizational growth. A flat organization gives chief executives and decision makers a clear picture of what the organization is doing, which enables quick decisions and a nimble company. To create a virtually structured company with empowered employees, service providers need:

- Competent people who know what to do
- Motivated people who want to make things happen
- Accountable people who accept ownership and responsibility

PartnerCommunity's anticipation of high growth affects its expectations of everyone in the company. At PartnerCommunity, an employee will only be able to maintain influence in the company if he or she grows with it. Both employees and managers need to learn things fast and step up to take new challenges and opportunities, or they will fall behind. Those who can't keep up need to move aside so the company as a whole can move forward. This should be clearly communicated to everyone.

Managers need to foster an environment of trust and be clear about expectations and how individual employees are performing. If they are not meeting expectations, management needs to inform the employee promptly so the affected individual can adjust his/her actions. Upper management should give all employees the opportunity to grow. They should explain, via examples, what should be done and what goals are realistic. These might be difficult, but necessary, discussions. The company is a sum of its parts, and the individual can only succeed if the company succeeds. Employees need to understand that unity is needed to make the company a success.

4.2.2.7 Entering the Market

It is much more difficult to define services than products. One can define exactly what a product does. Even when a product does not exactly meet the needs of customers, it can normally be customized to fit a certain need. An Internet service, on the other hand, needs to address a customer's changing needs in a changing environment.

The PartnerCommunity approach to this challenge is to focus on, and segment, customers who are similar—in the same industry and with similar needs. Their service strategy was developed over a period of six months. After understanding customer needs, PartnerCommunity reviewed its core competencies, identified the gaps, reviewed the technology available in the market, and found partners to fill the gaps. Daleen supplied most of the marketing information—it already had customer needs identified as a function of its services.

Following needs identification, PartnerCommunity recruited lead customers who were invaluable because they gave honest feedback and helped to refine service descriptions, pricing, features, and so forth. They were patient and willing to work with PartnerCommunity on ongoing issues, getting some service discount in return. Only after PartnerCommunity tests its services, pricing, and so forth, with its lead customers, does it roll out these services to other customers.

Pricing services is difficult, as the value of a given service varies depending on individual customer's needs. How should service providers price for value? There can be no one best pricing that works for everyone. PartnerCommunity has established multiple pricing models in order to accommodate different customer needs. Whatever pricing is used, PartnerCommunity has a feedback mechanism built into its decision processes.

PartnerCommunity is fortunate it can leverage its parent's branding, customer base, and marketing/PR engines. It hired a marketing consulting firm to help develop messaging for marketing communications. This firm helped with the messaging map, identity, branding, and Web site strategy. PartnerCommunity has found the best marketing method to be customer references; once one member of the community is happy with the service, it wants to bring in its partners. A Web presence has also been one of the most important marketing tools in its arsenal. PartnerCommunity uses its Web site to describe and communicate information about community members, including details about a featured partner, which changes periodically. As a member of Microsoft's Telecom Alliance Program, PartnerCommunity is able to get further market reach leveraging off Microsoft's public relations engine.

Market downturn can be a double-edged sword. It makes life difficult because there are fewer customers spending less money. There are also fewer new companies entering the market, meaning fewer competitors in the landscape. Hiring engineers and operations people is easier in a slow market; finding senior management talent is difficult and challenging, no matter what the market. There may be many candidates, but the risk is higher, both in lost opportunity and in dollars and cents, if the candidate does not work out.

4.2.2.8 Service Delivery

PartnerCommunity service delivery consists of initial integration and ongoing partner chain management. The objective of initial integration is to bring a service provider into the community. It includes requirements analysis, business process and workflow modeling, application integration and testing, and customer acceptance. Because of its network-based hub-spoke architecture, this initial integration process does not need to be repeated for each additional partner for a particular service provider, resulting in significant cost savings.

Partner chain management services are delivered through its Web portal and its hub. Through the Web portal, members can find partners, request information, proposals or quotations, manage contracts and SLAs, and review order and trouble ticket status. Through its hub, these services are integrated in workflows. For example, orders and trouble tickets are validated against contracts and SLAs, and routed according to workflow; contracts and SLAs are monitored based on rules and events defined.

PartnerCommunity uses B2B integration tools from leading technology providers to speed the initial integration when a member joins the community (see Figure 4-4). These significantly reduce the integration time from older methods by up to 75 percent.

The hub-spoke architecture supports back-end applications and helps determine the best way to do the integration. For example: Two service providers work with each other to deliver a new service. If one is a DSL provider that makes a sale of DSL bundled with intranet service to a small business, the data local exchange carrier (DLEC) asks the ASP to provision the intranet service (email, calendar, and file server). This usually occurs by fax. The DSL provider collects information from the small business and puts it into its order management system. That information then goes into the order via an internal workflow management process. The paperwork is faxed to the ASP where an administrator manually types it into the ASP's own order management system, entering the ASP's internal workflow. When the service is provisioned, the service provider manually communicates this to the DSL provider. Finally, the DSL provider informs the end-customer. As one can see, many things—a lost fax, misread data—can go wrong in this manual process.

Figure 4-4 PartnerCommunity integration.

With PartnerCommunity, when the DSL provider puts the order information into its order management system, its internal workflow will ask PartnerCommunity to route the appropriate information to the ASP. PartnerCommunity routes the order electronically to the ASP's order management system, eliminating the expensive, time-consuming, and error-prone manual steps. With the hub-spoke architecture, the DSL provider can partner with multiple ASPs with a single integration, and so can the ASP—both gain true flexibility in their value chains.

Similarly, PartnerCommunity enables service providers to integrate trouble ticket management and resolution. PartnerCommunity also enables its members to more easily meet its service level agreement commitments through effective trouble ticket management between trading partners, meaning there is a lower risk of defaulting on high availability guarantees if a provider fails to deliver as promised.

The service delivery infrastructure needs to be scalable, highly available, reliable, and information carried to the hub must be absolutely secure. These transactions carry vital information for customers and community members, which makes it mandatory that only authorized people should be able to access PartnerCommunity systems, and those who run the systems must follow strict business processes so they don't become the "weakest link." Like a bank, PartnerCommunity personnel can't disclose account details and must adhere to strict guidelines.

4.2.2.9 Customer Care

The key to customer care is to be proactive—reactive customer care is a recipe for failure. In other words, service delivery and customer care must not be separate and independent—they should be integrated. To deliver customer care as a part of service delivery requires an integrated infrastructure.

PartnerCommunity offers specialized service to a small number of service providers, instead of millions of end-users. The users are sophisticated and are contract managers, system administrators, or product managers. These people generally know how to navigate a Web site, so the PartnerCommunity care system is designed for sophisticated users who want to accomplish tasks quickly and effectively. Users are more interested in efficiency and productivity than in exploring the site. PartnerCommunity personalized user environments show relationship partners linked to their company, contracts in place, and other helpful information in the first screen. Since this information is in the top screen, users don't need to go through a lot of menus. This is another example of how PartnerCommunity helps users accomplish their tasks in the shortest possible time.

4.2.2.10 Billing

The last thing a service provider wants to do is bill per byte or per minute, because new services will not align with traditional tariff conventions. Billing for distance will become less common, unless the distance has a regulatory issue-based tariff associated with it. In general, distance billing does not apply in the Internet environment.

There are two aspects to billing—billing customers and billing partners. Customer billing needs to be value-based. Flat-rate and strict usage-based billing does not always work because usage alone does not indicate the real and/or perceived value for the customer. Partner billing requires a strong settlement engine. Both billing and settlement need to be integrated with service level agreement and QoS measurements.

As mentioned, PartnerCommunity aggregates the total transactions with a particular partner and, based on the value, comes up with price. This is not based on a particular transaction, but on a group of transactions, defining the total business transacted while determining its overall value.

When there are multiple back-end partners, accurate billing information needs to be sent in a timely manner so the issuing organization has correct information for the final bill. This is the same situation after the payment is received. PartnerCommunity infrastructure facilitates these processes. It does not provide a clearinghouse function for monetary settlement, but will help providers determine how much money is owed each partner. PartnerCommunity will partner with existing automated clearinghouses.

The main PartnerCommunity billing system used is Daleen's, but it integrates whatever billing system the member would like. Billing is very personal for service providers, and each partner's billing may be different. When offering complex, multiparty services, service providers should realize that each part to the equation might have:

- Different contractual relationships between the partner and end-customer
- Different billing cycles
- Different refund policies
- Different multilateral agreements with conflicting terms and conditions, and so forth

Service providers need to understand how they will reconcile the obligations and policies that might differ between service provider partners. Either service providers need to use software to help solve these issues, or they need to renegotiate terms and conditions with each partner involved. Most will probably try to live with the differences and try to work around these issues in order to get to market in a realistic time frame.

4.2.2.11 Infrastructure

One of the biggest challenges is to make sure all applications, CRM, billing, provisioning, partner management, and network management integrate and work seamlessly. While they can be integrated, such integration usually causes loss of personalization, intelligence, and management capability because they were not designed to share data and intelligence.

Most of the infrastructure in PartnerCommunity is based on Microsoft's .NET platform. PartnerCommunity chose Microsoft because the software helped solve their two main infrastructure issues: system management and software development. Management complexity is directly linked and related to the number of technologies involved. Microsoft offered economies of scale because all their software products worked together, and PartnerCommunity was able to limit the number of infrastructure platform providers.

The PartnerCommunity infrastructure needs to support fast application development. When an industry changes so quickly, a service provider can't wait six months, or a year, to develop a decent application. The basic PartnerCommunity infrastructure must adhere to strict scalability, security, manageability, supportability, flexibility, availability, and dependability guidelines. They use a multilayer defense for security issues, combining firewalls, software defenses, and manual processes. Authentication and access control are used to control manual access to the systems.

4.2.3 Last Words

The number one priority for a service provider is creating the right services for the chosen market segment(s) at the right time. If the services are wrong, it doesn't matter how well customer care, billing, or any other part of the infrastructure works, because there won't be any customers using the service.

Service providers need to have the right people on staff. These people should have the right blend of technology and domain expertise. When this mix is available, they can identify problems and determine solutions that are ahead of the competitors. People with domain and service provider expertise will understand the unique challenges of this business and how to run an operation that needs to work 24/7. The better the management team, the better they are able to execute against a well-written business plan.

Providers must plan for economic slowdowns, as well as the good times. As the economy slows, customers are less willing to spend, so the service provider needs to understand and show end-customers quantifiable returns on investment. The value proposition must be strong and something that is easy to articulate/communicate internally, as well as to customers. The organization must also be nimble to adapt to changing environments.

Service providers need to understand the importance of partnering and how it will become even more important as Internet services become more complex. Service providers will fail if they can't understand how to leverage partner advantages and focus on their core competencies.

4.3 Endnote

1. Content for this case study provided by John Yin, president and CEO of PartnerCommunity, Inc. A special thanks to Lloyd Spencer from Microsoft for making the initial introduction.

CHAPTER 5

Asia Pacific – Acer CyberCenter Services, Inc.

Asia Pacific is a huge region, including Australia, China (PRC), Hong Kong, India, Indonesia, Japan, Korea, Malaysia, New Zealand, the Philippines, Singapore, Taiwan, Vietnam, and Thailand. It is extremely diverse culturally and in Internet readiness. These countries are behind the U.S. and Europe in terms of Internet business trends, but are catching up quickly. The world has an eye on gaining a foothold in mainland China and many foreign firms are positioning themselves to take advantage of this huge market.

5.1 The Asia Pacific Market

5.1.1 Current Situation

Internet business is rapidly getting more of the IT investment dollars as many companies are retooling to support their Internet business strategies. Long-term relationships between buyers and suppliers are highly valued in this region and many companies are looking for better ways to build and share information links through e-procurement and e-marketplaces. Users are interested in sharing their demand and inventory information, as well as product development and design information among partners. There are many opportunities for process and service delivery integration and development. In Japan, many providers are creating consortia to pursue manufacturing portals, online banking, logistics, and other new services. In many places in Asia, companies were focused on year 2000 concerns so they are only now starting to incorporate Internet business strategies into their everyday business. Because the market is largely needs unaware, many are educating themselves to better understand what new technologies are available and how these can be effectively used. Many businesses are considered small or medium-size; most of the projects are smaller than in other regions of the world, and service providers tend to be smaller and more local.

In areas where infrastructure is not developed, some service providers are waiting for wireless technologies to become more advanced and less expensive before offering more complex services. To facilitate Internet business growth, some countries offer government initiatives, in conjunction with private financing, that help small and medium businesses build the infrastructure needed to participate and build Internet connections with supply and demand chain partners.

Foreign firms have the advantage because of their brand recognition and perceived experience in the Internet market. This situation will probably continue until local service providers can prove themselves.

5.1.2 Trends

In this region there appears to be an emphasis on the vertical industry, more so than in other regions in the world. Wireless and mobility services are fueling growth in Japan and convenience stores seem to be the portal for Internet services. These stores support Internet transactions from utility bill payment through travel services and music-on-demand capabilities purchased through onsite kiosks. Internal IT departments continue to be one of the big competitors to service providers.

5.1.3 Going-to-Market

Sales and marketing in this region are very much based on relationships, branding, and references. Because of this, service providers go to market by being successful with a small number of customers that can later be used as references before rolling the service out to other customers or other countries in the region.

Since the market is largely needs unaware, service providers are focusing on educating the public on the value of Internet services. Also important in the region is the concept of the development lab where customers can complete hands-on work and integration, in addition to purchasing more traditional services.

Hierarchy and position are very important and the typical service provider sales team relies heavily on the relationships built between executive managers of both the customer and the service provider. Lower level employees work through the details for initiatives that must be formally agreed to at the executive level.

Target reference customers are usually large enterprises. Notable multinational firms have better branding from the standpoint of being used as a reference, but prominent local or regional companies are also a prime focus. The most advanced vertical industries are finance, communications, and manufacturing.

Finding service provider resources is still a considerable challenge in the region. Many with the needed expertise go to other countries, like the U.S., to get experience and higher salaries. One advantage to the economic downturn is that technical experts tend to stay longer because jobs aren't as plentiful.

Service providers are interested in expanding geographically within the region, especially into the greater China market. The expansion is happening, both organically and via partnerships, as a way to leverage technology, brand awareness, and a customer base.

5.2 Case Study – Acer CyberCenter Services, Inc.

5.2.1 Company Overview

Acer CyberCenter Services, Inc. (ACCSI)[1] was founded in May 2000 as a subsidiary of the Acer Group. The company, headquartered in Taipei, Taiwan, specializes in offering IDC services in the greater China region. ACCSI was founded partly to fulfill needs by companies in the Acer Group for business continuity services due to the unstable natural environment (earthquakes, and so on) in Taiwan. As the IDC data services market began to grow, Acer saw more justification in building IDC infrastructure and supplying IDC services to the Acer Group, as well as to the Asian market at large.

The idea to form ACCSI occurred as a result of the big earthquake in 1999 in the central part of Taiwan. Acer Group CEO Stan Shih wanted Acer to provide earthquake resistant facilities to enterprises in Taiwan so that after a natural disaster, their data systems remained operational. Shih also had the idea to create a server farm—many small servers in one data center, as a way of providing computer services so customers would not need to take care of their overall server infrastructure. This would mean more business for Acer's own line of servers. Acer wanted to prove its capability to offer a full range of services and become a service provider, not just an equipment manufacturer.

Dr. Simon Chang is president of ACCSI and was director general of the Planning and Evaluation Division of the National Science Council (NSC) and founding director of the National Center for High-Performance Computing (NCHC). Jerry C. Huang is associate vice president of the operation and came to ACCSI at the request of Frachard Lung, CIO of Acer Group. Huang was hired because of his first-hand understanding of Acer's Management Information Systems (MIS) and because he understood the philosophy of and how Acer wanted to build ACCSI. At Acer, Huang's responsibility was to create the system and service requirements for all of the company's subsidiaries throughout the world. As of January 2001, ACCSI had more than 40 employees and in late June 2001, opened its main 7,000-ping (1 ping is equal to approximately 3.306 square meters) IDC in Luntang, the largest in Taiwan. This is equivalent to 22,000 square meters of usable data center space. ACCSI's 200-ping IDC in Taipei was launched in January of 2001. ACCSI is planning to expand to the Hsinchu communication hub in July 2001.

ACCSI specializes in offering mission-critical enterprise IT infrastructure operations, providing scalable and highly available data distribution, storage, and backup services. These services include:

- Performance-based dedicated Web hosting
- Application hosting, in cooperation with ASPs, ISVs, and system integrators
- Complex enterprise Internet hosting
- Storage services
- Other services such as IT security and mission critical email hosting.

Because of the large size of the main IDC, ACCSI is considering including IDC hotel services as another business line. An IDC hotel is a way to fill excess IT hosting space with other service providers by offering wholesale services that are based on a high quality IDC infrastructure. These providers are not able to build, or manage, their own IDCs and are searching for a reliable company offering outsourcing services. ACCSI's core competency is its top quality IDC infrastructure and facilities management—offering a one-stop shop to service providers searching for this type of infrastructure.

The major focus of ACCSI's IDC operation for next few months will be enterprise IT outsourcing and storage services, including remote back up and disaster recovery for the banking industry and large enterprises. Basic collocation and Web hosting markets are becoming mature and experiencing downward price pressures so services will not be profitable if ACCSI doesn't add higher value functionality to these services, justifying higher prices. ACCSI will be the hosting provider for all of Acer. It is internal Acer Group policy that Acer, Inc. acts as the benchmark customer (pilot customer) for ACCSI services. Shih intends that, eventually, all of Acer Group will use ACCSI for its hosting infrastructure.

ACCSI's value proposition revolves around alliances, high quality IDC services, and leveraging Acer's trusted brand image. Its alliances with such vendors as IBM, HP, EMC, Cisco, AT&T, and others, ensure customers will always have the most advanced information systems and network management in Asia. ACCSI placed its IDCs far from metropolitan areas, so they are ideal locations for backup storage sites. The IDC infrastructure will survive, even in cases of natural disaster that would destroy normal data center facilities.

Current customers that are expanding to the greater China market are pulling ACCSI into the arena faster than originally anticipated. Initially, ACCSI intended to build more core competencies in Taiwan before expansion, but now market demand may mean entering this market as early as the fourth quarter of 2001 or early 2002. ACCSI intends to leverage Acer's strong brand image and brand awareness when it begins business there. Acer's notebook computer is already in the top three in terms of sales volume, and desktop sales volumes are among the top five in mainland China. More amazing is that these sales volumes occurred so quickly. Acer only entered the mainland China market in 1999. When it enters this market, ACCSI plans to transfer its core competencies to a local partner to offer the best services in greater China. Currently, this market seems to be mainly collocation, but ACCSI still needs to prove its capabilities to offer the best managed services over the communication bandwidth infrastructure locally, in Taiwan, before it can transfer these capabilities to mainland China.

5.2.1.1 Local Market

Currently, the major IT outsourcing market in Taiwan is collocation of which ISPs hold the majority market share. Shared Web hosting is also offered by some ISPs targeting the small Web site market. These services are not the focus of ACCSI.

ACCSI offers a performance-based Web hosting service. Customers are almost exclusively requesting simple collocation, which means service providers offer facility, rather than managed, services. Some providers, including ACCSI, offer content distribution services that accelerate the content access performance from end-user sites.

Application hosting is still not mature in Taiwan although local market analysis firms forecast the ASP market to boom in 2002. Email is usually the only application that can be outsourced now because it is generic in function and operation. This describes a commodity service, meaning low margins. Any high margin services/applications requiring customization would be quite a challenge from the standpoint of current ASP implementation expertise. There are some instances of complex Internet enterprise hosting, but these are limited to interenterprise hosting situations that could develop into future ASP spin-offs. Despite this, or maybe because of it, many Taiwanese ASPs formed the ASP Association as a way of educating the market and as a platform for service promotion. ACCSI decided not to become an ASP, but rather to partner with ASPs and become a wholesale infrastructure provider.

The biggest players, from the standpoint of ACCSI's focus business, are Hinet and eASPNet. Hinet is the largest ISP in Taiwan, owned by the government in competition with private enterprises. Since this is the largest facilities-based ISP in Taiwan, and has the backing of telecommunications firms, it owns, or has access to, a majority of bandwidth resources and is now trying to provide IDC services. It has many internal challenges relating to the organization and businesses of its largest shareholder, Chungwha Telecom. Chungwha locations in the north, central, and south regions are all trying to provide IDC services, in competition with Hinet.

Nortel, along with some Taiwanese enterprises, founded eASPNet. It was launched in December 2000 and its focus is application hosting, making it a direct competitor to ISVs, system integrators, and other ASPs entering the service provider market.

After understanding the competition, ACCSI defined its value proposition and created market messaging differentiating them. For example, ACCSI differentiates itself from eASPNet by stressing its multisite IDC data center expertise that cooperates with ASP/System Integrator (SI)/ISV Internet businesses. Since ACCSI does not offer retail application hosting services, it is not a competitor. ACCSI's core competency is different from eASPNet's since its focus is on managing IDC facilities in partnership with major ASPs and ISVs in Taiwan.

ACCSI differentiates itself from Hinet by offering a more expanded services suite, more IDC management expertise, and better customer care. ACCSI provides managed services, not only for pure collocation, but offers five-star hotel management services. Further, it provides the necessary consultancy services around services management, including system management, capacity planning, storage, and other services. Hinet may have considerable expertise in the telecommunications industry, but ACCSI has core experience with IT departments and understands how to operate a data center, knows the requirements of an enterprise's MIS department, and is more customer-centric.

5.2.1.2 Partnering

In general, ACCSI tries to keep things as simple as possible throughout the partnering process.

ACCSI's partner strategy was developed by first looking internally and understanding the value chain needed to offer IDC services. It then looked externally to define how best to fill the data centers. ACCSI defined general solution vendors it considered important as a part of its IDC value chain:

- Vendors: Acer, HP, IBM, Cisco, Unisys, Microsoft, Intel, BMC, among others.
- Packaged service providers: AT&T, Trend Micro, EMC, ISS, and Storage Access.
- Application or business solution vendors.

ACCSI defined its core competency as IDC operation and management, stopping at the business application layer. In those areas where a gap, or weakness, was identified, ACCSI decided to build domain know-how by partnering with those vendors or suppliers identified earlier. ACCSI put first priority on those vendors that have the knowledge, products, services, and installed base, like HP or IBM, to help start operations as fast as possible. According to Huang, "We don't just want [a] solution provider, [we] need … [a] partner … [to] share risk [either through] revenue sharing or [by] offering high discounts for products—higher than typical channel or customer program discounts." ACCSI wants partners that can adjust prices so that ACCSI can offer competitive pricing in the market without creating a net loss, especially while trying to gain initial market share. In return, vendors get an IDC partner, and the associated trusted brand, to use as a channel into more enterprise sales opportunities. ACCSI plans to leverage joint branding and image to build brand strength outside of the Taiwanese market.

Using such strong and well-known partners certainly has its challenges when managing channel conflict, especially among partners focused on the same market segments with similar products. This is one of ACCSI's major challenges. It was hard to position partners in their data center; however, ACCSI couldn't afford to have one major partner to dominate all the solutions. It wanted a balance and the best way was to try to balance each partner's interest in ACCSI, focusing them, and building some boundaries around their spheres of influence. For example, ACCSI chose BMC as the system management platform and Hewlett-Packard's Openview as the network management tool, so each has a specific role in the data center operations. ACCSI knows the chosen partner products will work together because they already are integrated in customer sites. To work through partner conflicts, ACCSI assigns different solution segments to partners and tries to be open during the negotiation process.

ACCSI uses partner contracts as a way to assure flexibility in partner choice. For example, some contracts are for three years. Essentially, ACCSI has the option to bring in a new partner after the three-year term expires. The contracts further allow for exit if the partner does not fulfill certain jointly agreed upon goals.

ACCSI does have some joint selling and comarketing activities with its partners, but these are rather informal and require no joint investment. Major vendors are willing to work with ACCSI because of its positive brand image and both parties jointly develop the market, seeing each party as a new sales channel. For example, if the partner, together with ACCSI, sells storage to an IDC collocation customer, there may be an analogous sale into the ACCSI data center to handle extra storage needs that result from more backup services required by the customer. This means, the partners sell more than normal because each sale to an end-customer could result in another IDC sale. ACCSI and partners share customer lists and decide on which joint customers to focus. Joint funnel sharing and agreeing on joint focus account lists can be an effective way of managing sales channel conflict. That said, managing partner relationships continues to be a big concern and ACCSI is constantly looking for ways to improve the efficiency and manageability of partnering relationships.

5.2.1.3 Outsourcing

Initially, ACCSI was not going to outsource any part of the operation, but now officials are reconsidering this decision. They are exploring outsourcing functionalities in three areas:

- Non-destructive security (penetration) testing
- Call desk resource management
- First tier Help desk

These are all areas ACCSI decided were important to the business, but building in-house competence would take too long, be too expensive, and requires a shift in focus away from core competencies.

5.2.1.4 Organization

The IDC industry is dynamic and some sort of basic organizational structure is needed to define roles and interactions among different people in a company. For ACCSI it was a challenge deciding whether to have a solution- or product-oriented organization. Solution-oriented organizations allow the grouping of engineers with similar skill sets, making solution implementation easier. This sort of organization focuses on complex technology and makes it more challenging to design new versions of end-to-end solutions incorporating functionality outside of a particular solution's design advantages. In contrast, a product-oriented organization has the benefit of quick end-to-end solution design, but the challenge of complex technology updates. ACCSI decided to build a solution-oriented organization, with senior technical engineers rotating as product managers. This encourages product design that reflects market requirements and trends. ACCSI added an incubator group that continually monitors the market for new trends and builds service solutions to meet new market needs.

ACCSI is trying to reduce possible culture conflicts between ACCSI and Acer as more and more MIS personnel are reallocated between the two companies. Education is the key to the process and ACCSI is trying to do this in several ways:

- By introducing ACCSI to Acer personnel and giving them information about its charter and current solutions
- By educating Acer staff about IDC operations and services, in general
- By educating Acer staff about the differences between IDCs and traditional enterprise MIS operations

Acer staff has a more traditional enterprise MIS mindset and the IDC concept is still new to them.

There is a key personnel issue revolving around people who have worked at ACCSI from the beginning and who expect to be promoted as the organization grows. While ACCSI believes in promoting from within, senior people from outside the company will probably be hired to do these higher management functions. ACCSI hopes if its employees are aware of this policy, it will lessen the expectations mentioned earlier.

5.2.2 Entering the Market

Collocation is the main service offered by IDCs in Taiwan and other services are still quite new. As seen in Figure 5-1, ACCSI anticipates that its customers will give them business in phases, as trust is built. Figure 5-2 shows Acer, Inc.'s outsourcing priorities helping ACCSI to plan its focus on more and different value-added services (services outside of collocation) while treating collocation services as a way to grab initial market share or revenue. It does not anticipate collocation to be a profitable service.

Since ACCSI is new in the market, and focus ACCSI services are not mature in Taiwan, ACCSI is using the following strategy as it enters the market:

- Make strategic alliances with well-known global IT enterprises and communicate these alliances via joint promotion activities like press conferences, public speeches, and other marketing communications venues.
- Leverage Acer's brand image as a way to arrange meetings with top executives of large enterprises to introduce ACCSI's services. ACCSI will use these discussions to elicit high level customer feedback on market needs and if/how the proposed services will fill those needs.
- Partner with ASPs and ISVs and use them as channels to deliver application solutions, using ACCSI as the managed infrastructure supplier. Some second-tier nonfacilities-based service providers may also fall into this category.
- Leverage Sertek's sales channel into the greater China territory. Sertek is a sales subsidiary of Acer Group in the greater China region and it has one of the largest computer sales forces in Taiwan. Sertek will also be able to act as a channel to sell ACCSI's packaged services to small and medium businesses in chosen markets.

1. Outsource the simplest applications first.
2. Platforms are outsourced one by one, each with a dedicated project team.
3. Complicated applications such as ERP and CMS should not be outsourced until the next generation of ERP is launched.

Figure 5-1 The ACCSI outsourcing principles.
Source: Jerry Huang, ACCSI.

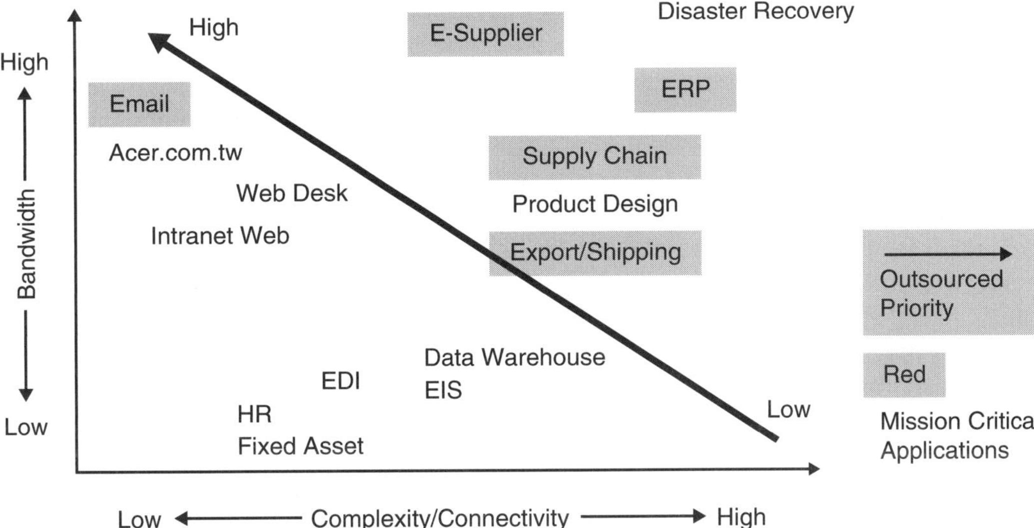

Figure 5-2 ACCSI application mapping.
Source: Jerry Huang, ACCSI.

- Leverage service offerings of other service providers. If an interesting service has been launched by another IDC, review the service functionality to see if ACCSI has capabilities to deliver new value-added functionality. If so, relaunch the service after reviewing the price to see if the margins can be expanded. Commodity services will not be an ACCSI focus.
- Find reference customers for services and publicize them well.
- Test services via a pilot program. During the pilot phase, ACCSI found many new services it could bundle into the main offering. (See the section entitled, "Billing," later in this chapter.)

Since the market is still so new, ACCSI continually tries to understand customer needs and educate the target customer base. Partnerships are important as ways to quickly offer new services in new markets. Customers may also turn to new business channels for service providers. Since these are new markets, potential customers may not know they have a need and it is up to the service provider to show the target customer base how these new services can promote new profits. Assuming the business case is solid, ACCSI will go to market with the service. For example, many customers didn't understand why remote backup was so important. ACCSI showed international trends and customer losses in those cases where they didn't have this type of service available. Further market education venues include press releases, conferences, sponsorships of conventions, and so forth. ACCSI uses these vehicles and slides, such as Figure 5-3, to show why these services are important and why ACCSI is the best choice to provide them.

Educating the sales force is another important aspect of entering the market. As part of joint agreements, ACCSI asks partners to educate the sales force in all aspects of sales including: market segmentation, needs, and competition. ACCSI has an advantage in that its sales force is

- **ACCSI as an IDC Provider**
    - Highly available communication
    - Secured network environment
    - System monitoring and management tools, proactive management reports
    - Capacity on demand
    - A dedicated and flexible development and testing environment
- **Acer MIS as an ASP and ISV**
    - Application services to Acer Inc. internal users on a robust and scalable infrastructure
    - Best practice for external and global ASP and ISV markets

Figure 5-3 ACCSI value proposition.
Source: Jerry Huang, ACCSI.

still small. It can have regularly scheduled meetings that include sales and product development topics to further define service descriptions for standard services. Sales has input into pricing, as well. This process helps the sales team understand the services, pricing, discounting, ordering processes, and other aspects of service marketing making the combined team work as a more homogeneous unit.

5.2.3 Service Delivery

ACCSI is developing standard service delivery procedures, finding that it still needs to learn and update procedures with each implementation. The manual procedures will stay in place until they can be standardized, then they will be automated. At that point, ACCSI plans to introduce a process management system and integration bus as a way to have one end-to-end view of service delivery and the ability to optimize the entire process. Automating service delivery is one of the most expensive investments, yet offers one of the highest returns on that investment.

ACCSI is using a step-by-step approach to service delivery, using actual customer situations for final inputs into the service delivery process definition. It will use these processes as a basis for the service delivery procedural manual. In parallel, ACCSI plans to bring in consultants to help it build and validate initial procedures.

The largest challenge for ACCSI was trying to define the processes. The company decided to align them with phases used for an enterprise IT project:

- Engagement
- Scoping
- Detailed design
- Implementation
- Support

ACCSI then partnered with IT companies that have experience in service delivery, such as HP and IBM, to understand their service delivery processes. In the near term, ACCSI plans to subcontract these services to HP or IBM while building the core competency.

Service integration, logistic support, and after launch support are challenges because value-added services mean, in some way, customization based on customer requirements is necessary. If services are not uniform, an efficient way to define the phases described earlier becomes more important and more difficult. ACCSI strives to create a centralized service delivery organization with senior product managers to integrate all the functional departments, manage the service delivery status, and resolve any production bottlenecks.

5.2.4 Customer Care

Customer care is a philosophy and a system that must be supported by the entire company. ACCSI is considering outsourcing its first tier call center/Help desk service to another service provider, and focus on the second- and third-tier Help desk functions in tracing problems, integrating functional departments, solving technical problems, giving feedback to customers within the required time, and analyzing problem features.

ACCSI has just defined call center processes and has moved into feasibility testing. Pilot customers are used for the testing phase. As they were formulating the call center functions, ACCSI officials considered two options: outsource the call center operation, or keep it in-house. They finally decided to keep the Help desk in-house, but outsource the first-tier call center. ACCSI will implement a system that supports the customer relationship management philosophy, integrating information from an internal management system into a screen for the CSR. By looking at the screen, the CSR will already know, before they pick up the phone, who the customer is and something about the problem. The customer care system will include Internet self-help, allowing customers to check problem status real-time.

Important customers get a dedicated account manager as a focal person for their account. Executive sponsors are paired with important customers, ensuring open lines of communication. Enterprise customers will have a dedicated account manager assigned. This account manager will understand the customer's requirements and concerns, and integrate the internal resources needed to ensure customer satisfaction. Key people from large enterprise customers will probably be resident in ACCSI to further keep the lines of communication open between ACCSI and its enterprise customers.

5.2.5 Billing

During ACCSI's ramp up, the billing function is handled manually. The system works today because ACCSI has a small customer base using services that have fixed tariff parameters with easy billing records. ACCSI is able to leverage the expertise of an Acer Group billing expert who is transferring his knowledge to ACCSI resources.

ACCSI's first pilot showed that, although customers initially only requested collocation services, after their installation, wanted more than what was described in the service bundle. Now

ACCSI can incorporate these requirements into initial offerings for future customers. Billing for these extra services was also defined through the pilot process. For example: pilot customers initially didn't want ACCSI backup services. After installation, they saw the value of ACCSI doing both their system management and backup. At that time the customers gave ACCSI their functional requirements for these services for later inclusion in the basic service package.

Another area of discussion is what billing system to choose. Did it make more sense to choose a billing system with a considerable amount of flexible and intelligent features or to go for a more simple, integrated one? Option one took much more upfront investment, but will probably scale and be flexible enough to support future ACCSI needs. ACCSI chose option two, the simple, integrated billing system without the bells and whistles, because it fit within its financial parameters, filled current needs, and was modular in approach so ACCSI could add on functionality, as needed.

Making the billing system decision was easy compared with collection issues. ACCSI needed to agree on who was responsible to collect late bill payments. In this case, ACCSI decided that customer care would follow up when payment issues arose because that division has the billing information and also interacts with customers on a regular basis, thus understanding their expectations and concerns.

5.2.6 Infrastructure

The prime directive for ACCSI is to build a world-class and robust infrastructure. The challenge has been that the Taiwan market is still developing and is a relatively unknown commodity. ACCSI walks a tightrope between upfront investment, customer satisfaction, and meeting the required financial results. A full-scale investment may be too risky, in terms of corporate financial policy. When requesting a scalable architecture design from partners, ACCSI insists it be in line with their corporate fiscal guidelines. ACCSI requested the architecture be modular so that the minimum phase one design will scale to include all functionality, manageability, security, and other customer needs, as it spreads to other satellite sites to support ACCSI's increasing customer base.

It was a challenge to design a technical architecture to support ACCSI's IDC services. Since IDC services are still a new business in Taiwan, there is little local expertise with the know-how to design the technical architecture for supporting this sort of business. To solve this problem, ACCSI leveraged the experience of consultants from well-known solution providers. Most of the consultants were from countries with mature IDC markets. ACCSI intends to build internal expertise in this area using an on-the-job training strategy.

It is an art to decide how much infrastructure is enough. It is difficult to determine exact market sizes and how much investment to make. When the service provider makes the investment, its officials are concerned about cash flow and want to invest only enough to support anticipated needs, without over building. This, in turn, makes it difficult to determine return on the investment. Network devices are a good example. ACCSI initially wanted to minimize its network device investment, but wanted to have enough to assure that the customer gets the response needed. Storage services are another example—initial investment for this computer infrastructure can be high. If the market size is unclear, it is hard to determine what initial capacity is needed. ACCSI may know potential customer levels, but its officials don't know the timing for when these customers will need the service. On the other hand, customers need to feel confident and trust that ACCSI has enough infrastructure to deliver the services promised within the stated quality assurance guidelines. ACCSI constantly reviews its operation to assess the investment/quality mix, making sure the balance is correct.

Technology is not as important as understanding the potential customer base, where it's coming from, and what ACCSI needs to do to fill its IDCs.

5.2.7 Last Words

Sponsorship, fostering trust, creating a strong trusted brand image, and partnering have been the most important operational aspects for ACCSI's successful business to date.

- Brand Image: Having a strong brand image is extremely important in attracting potential partners and customers. ACCSI has many choices of partners because of the strong, trusted Acer brand, and these partners are more open to sharing their funnels and customer lists, and to develop new markets.
- Create a win-win environment: Service providers should strive to create a win-win environment for both parties. ACCSI strives for this and tries not to limit this to its Taiwan partners.
- Plan mission critical services: There needs to be a solid plan to deliver mission critical services. Service providers might find themselves being a pioneer in the market, defining service delivery in new ways, as does ACCSI in the Taiwanese market.
- Foster trust: IDCs may offer services that appear to be the same, but on closer inspection, they do not compare in functionality, infrastructure and/or ability to deliver. It turns out that these companies are able to offer only words with nothing behind them. ACCSI is developing the actual capabilities before communicating to the market. Partners and customers acknowledge that ACCSI has solid plans to deliver the promised services.
- Executive commitment: ACCSI has a strong commitment from the CEO of Acer Group who has a personal interest in seeing the success of the venture. If the project is not successful, Shih realizes this will affect his entire group of companies. Sponsorship is especially important during market downturns in case cash injections are needed to continue operations. Investment in ACCSI was a turning point for Acer Group.

5.3 Endnote

1. Content for this case study provided by Jerry C. Huang, associate vice president for product design and services, ACCSI.

CHAPTER 6

Europe – KPNQwest

Doing business throughout Europe means having to satisfy at least 15 totally different masters. To be successful, the service provider must conform to local conventions in each European country. For regional providers there is a real challenge keeping central command and control while satisfying local needs. Internet use is pervasive across the region, which, for the purposes of this book, includes all countries in the European Union (EU).

6.1 The European Market

6.1.1 Current Situation

Across Europe, firms are seeing the necessity of investing in Internet businesses. Many of the investments are focused on optimizing and scaling investments in e-commerce, CRM, and wireless technologies. Investments are coming from vertical industries, mostly financial, communications, and retail. Many of these customers plan to work with service providers to complete Internet business initiatives.

6.1.1.1 Customer Needs

European firms are looking for advice on the fastest way to implement, and get results from, Internet initiatives. They are looking for a partner to help transition their firms and get maximum gains from their Internet strategies. Customers are requiring multicountry capabilities because as customer Internet businesses mature, they increasingly look toward multicountry rollouts. They need something more than local language support as they look toward cultural differentiation needed to be successful in local markets.

6.1.1.2 Service Provider Positioning

European providers are positioning themselves as total solution providers, delivering end-to-end services. Many providers may not own all aspects of the value chain, especially the IDC, so they must find partners for this functionality because hosting services are still important. As the business matures, providers are moving away from offering horizontal services toward industry verticals. Those providers with more vertical industry knowledge are well positioned for the consultative selling needed as the industry enters a more mature phase.

6.1.1.3 Special Challenges

European firms are selective when it comes to where their infrastructure is hosted. Many want it hosted in the same country, even if an IDC in another country may be closer. Providers that are regional in scope need to develop umbrella branding, processes, and market messaging, but have local sales managers that own local relationships.

6.1.2 Trends

Service providers want a long-term customer relationship that will last through many business cycles. Sales are focused on business, not IT managers who support the idea that infrastructure must support the business strategy of the firm, and not visa versa.

The majority of service providers are focusing their direct sales forces on large and medium established firms and are taking conservative approaches to building a customer base. Service provider growth throughout Europe is typically done through mergers and acquisitions, certainly the easiest and fastest way to enter new country markets and acquire knowledge of the local language, culture, and an existing client base.

Service providers are keen to develop skills and capabilities around emerging technologies and services. Some of the more popular service trends emerging in the European market include:

- Wireless
- CRM
- Broadband services

6.2 Case Study – KPNQwest

6.2.1 Company Overview[1]

KPNQwest was created in April 1999 as a joint venture between KPN, the leading Dutch telecommunications company, and Qwest Communications, a U.S. alternative carrier. In mid-2001, it had more than 100,000 customers in 15 European countries. Within two months of its opening, KPNQwest raised EUR 800 million in high yield debt and was ready for an initial public offering (IPO) by November 1999.

The company was formed to take advantage of opportunities created by the trend toward convergence of information technology and IP bandwidth. Executives of the two companies thought they saw information technology evolving from the simple running of private proprietary software, through driving the desktop environment via LAN/PC deployments, into a real time environment, running open network software and supporting real time transactions/interactions. The transformation from voice to data, the resultant changes in running/managing information technology networks, and the exponential growth of data networks, added fuel to the fire. These evolutions would require massive amounts of bandwidth and data infrastructure opening a new opportunity for a top quality, facilities-based operator.

At the time the companies came together, Qwest had acquired EUNet. EUNet was one of the first ISPs in Europe with roots in academia and the burgeoning UNIX community. EUNet had 15 different businesses linked under an alliance with a common logo and common look and feel. Qwest brought its high-speed network expertise to the local service providers in the alliance. This was an important addition because at the time KPN was just beginning to build its EuroRings™ and its corporate background was more in the traditional telecommunications markets.

KPNQwest is one of the leading facilities-based, Pan-European providers of IP-based data-centric services. Its facilities are based on 20,000 km fiber-optic networks connecting 50 cities throughout Europe. As mentioned earlier, KPNQwest is one of the largest business ISPs in Europe with operations in 15 countries. It has peering relationships with 170 European networks and 73 U.S. networks. The company has 12 IDCs, called CyberCentres, two mega CyberCentres in Munich and Paris, with a third in London under construction, and plans to roll out more across Europe linked to the high-capacity fiber-optic network. These centers will provide Web-hosting, application sharing, and collocation services. They have been built to support the most secure, reliable, and technologically robust Internet value-added services.

KPNQwest's EuroRings™ are high-capacity OC-192 fiber-optic networks, with bidirectional self-healing SDH rings. The network uses state-of-the-art fiber and routing technology with a minimum of one spare conduit on all terrestrial routes. KPNQwest also owns 15 business-to-business ISPs across Europe. These are companies that were market leaders in their countries under the EUNet, Xlink, and COMM2000 brands—brands that are now integrated into the KPNQwest network. Each offers a full range of value-added Internet services, from dedicated Internet access, unified messaging and firewall management to remote Internet access, IP virtual private network (VPN), and e-commerce services. These are in addition to the services offered through the CyberCentres.

President and CEO Jack McMaster, highly experienced from his time at AT&T and Qwest Communications in the United States, heads KPNQwest. It employs approximately 2,000 people in 15 different countries across Europe, in addition to a sales team in the United States. The core competency of the company can be described as building, owning, and operating the highest quality, lowest cost, macrocapacity fiber optic network in Europe. The company focuses on offering state-of-the-art IP-based services and applications, enhanced through seamless connectivity to the Qwest network in North America and beyond. Its future is based on three variables: continued rise in Internet usage in Europe, increasing sophistication of the applications offered over the Internet, and exponential demand for reliable, secure, high-speed bandwidth required to run those applications. This is why it has built the longest, most modern European fiber optic network and focuses on finding and keeping the best people.

6.2.2 Local Market

KPNQwest integrates its business over 15 widely diverse markets, plus the United States. Cultures vary differently at the customer interface level and the service provider must have a local face. This means, in Italy, business must be conducted in the "Italian way," in Germany the "German way," and so on, and companies can't afford not to conform to local conventions when working in the local market.

This doesn't mean products can't be the same; although some may be localized to address a particular local need. It means that social conventions such as local perceptions of punctuality, contract writing conventions, how business discussions are conducted, how best to interact with and work through prospective customer infrastructures, must be observed.

Addressing cultural differences is extremely important. In the case of dedicated hosting, a customer in one country may not want his/her data hosted in a data center located in another country. Not understanding these issues can make a huge difference in the success or failure of the service provider's business.

6.2.3 Partnering

The world is moving quickly, with many new and ongoing innovations. Service providers are forced to partner to get the best technology in time to make the market and at the best price.

KPNQwest uses both direct and indirect sales channels. KPN is the exclusive distributor in the Benelux (Belgium, Holland, and Luxembourg) and Qwest, the exclusive distributor in North America.

6.2.4 Organization

The organization and set-up of KPNQwest was a stroke of genius by KPN and Qwest during the third quarter of 1998. According to McMaster, "People couldn't stop laughing when I said that [this] was going to be a great company. They kept waiting to see [the] next train wreck like the others that didn't work out." KPN and Qwest studied why other similar ventures didn't work and came to the conclusion that the company needed to be set up as a stand-alone. One reason similar joint ventures failed was people didn't work for a real company—it never actually had any assets or allocated resources. This "company" became, instead, a receptacle for its parent's losses. These ventures represented only expenses, not assets, to the parent company's balance sheets. KPN and Qwest decided to spin off a new company with its own market capitalization, its own assets, its own shared owner base, and its own personnel. It is able to foster loyalty and career progression linked to meeting the expectations of KPNQwest, not as a result of a short term rotation to the spin-off company that might be needed for career progression in the parent company. As a result, KPNQwest has its own corporate culture and established identity. Its innovative structure makes the company different and, according to McMaster, no other joint venture in the telecommunications space has worked as well.

Communication is key and KPNQwest people don't necessarily want to work for a "typical indigenous company." Typical indigenous companies are homogenous, having accepted ways of doing things and KPNQwest people are attracted to the large disparate cross-cultural flavor of the company. In this environment communications can be a challenge. KPNQwest borrowed a convention from EUNet making English its official language. KPNQwest did this because there were no English companies in the EUNet alliance at that time and company leaders decided it was most fair to put everyone at an equal disadvantage. Having an official language drills down into email conventions—all email must also be in English. KPNQwest developed an email-centric culture having some asynchronous results. The communication challenge extends to all communication because the words used may not be exactly what is meant. Employees must instill a subconscious editing function in day-to-day interactions, they need to listen harder and ask more questions. Patience plays a part, as well. If it turns out someone didn't mean exactly what he or she said, they probably were not trying to be difficult. Prospective employees should make a self-assessment and if cross-cultural interaction is difficult, KPNQwest would not be a good fit.

Merging two diverse corporate cultures is an ongoing challenge. KPN has a more traditional telco (telephone company) culture—it tends to be slower moving, more hierarchical, and process oriented. EUNet was based in academia, which fosters a more casual intuitive culture. KPNQwest is working through this by offering rotational assignments, including a headquarters tour of duty. Some people like that duty so well they are reassigned permanently. This has distinct advantages for communications. These people usually maintain their local contacts and they are able to better communicate headquarters policies, initiatives, discussions, and so forth, than "official communications" can. They also give important input to headquarters policy issues.

In meetings people are encouraged to express how policies will affect their specific local environment. If a regional service is packaged for rerelease on a Pan–European level, the local manager may have his/her objectives reassigned to reflect Pan-European metrics, but they will not necessarily be reassigned to headquarters.

KPNQwest stresses a culture of accountability. All employees, from McMaster on down, are made to understand that there is a big difference between input- and output-oriented organizations. Companies go through a shift as they grow from small start-ups to more mature corporations. As the company becomes larger inputs are interesting, but outputs become more important. Following rules can't be a substitute for getting things done and delivering results when needed. KPNQwest went through a cultural shift as people learned upper management was not so interested in *why* a goal wasn't achieved, but was interested in *how* the group is adjusting the business to react, or pro-act, to market signals in order to achieve the goals. People are held accountable for their actions and as people got used to the accountability model they felt liberated, empowered to innovate on the fly.

Now reactions are coming more from a position of security, personnel realizing they can come up with creative solutions when goals become evasive. Every quarter over the last 10 quarters has seen innumerable ways to fail, but the margin for error is quite small. Earlier, people may have passed the blame if results were not achieved, but now employees feel secure enough to accept the new culture of accountability.

6.2.5 Entering the Market

Being facilities-based is a differentiator. By building, not leasing, the infrastructure, KPNQwest is able to take advantage of economies of scale and price accordingly. The company is only two years old. The first year was about building the fiber infrastructure and the operational framework. During this time wholesale customers were targeted as a way to pay for the assets deployed. Year two focuses on building value-added services on top of the fiber infrastructure, while shifting the target market from wholesale to retail, focusing on global multinational companies, major national organizations, and small/medium enterprises (SMEs). Services such as Asynchronous Transfer Mode (ATM) and IP/VPN will be augmented to take advantage of the higher margins KPNQwest can charge for services like hosting and streaming video.

KPNQwest will be consolidating services. There are many diverse services currently offered as a result of the pre-joint venture business, mostly tied to EUNet. KPNQwest plans to centralize service offerings, but not to the exclusion of successful local offerings. There may be some local offerings that are profitable with a large local installed base; these services will continue, and may be packaged for deployment in the Pan-European market. Additionally, some centrally packaged services may need localization for acceptance in the local markets. There are vast regulatory differences between nation states that will affect the services roadmap. Some countries have easier access to DSL; for example, in this case there is no reason to limit DSL-based services, as long as they can be deployed profitably.

In the area of services launch, KPNQwest tries not to get overly distracted by legacy services. Its focus is to get new services to market as quickly as possible and then discuss older services, if applicable. In September, KPNQwest launched the Pan-European version of its IP VPN service and has 104 networks online, including Dell Computer. KPNQwest attributes this success to understanding that the service needs to be competitive in the marketplace and market research is key. KPNQwest used firms like ACNielsen to determine what customers value in an IP/VPN service. It also used other research firms to understand the competitive landscape and offerings. The ACNielsen report uncovered some surprising trends. What customers valued most in an IP/VPN service in Europe was effective customer care. This was ranked eighth in the U.S. KPNQwest attributes this to the increase of global business; foreign multinationals are not willing to waste time with local regulatory problems or poor service delivery infrastructures to get mission critical services up and running. Local access is a good example. U.S. multinationals don't want to wait four months to get simple connectivity because local telco monopolies have never had to offer faster service. Customers are incorporating more global standards than they were just five years ago.

KPNQwest has a dedicated direct sales force of more than 400, and it sells through indirect channels, as well. The direct sales force is more oriented toward traditional telecommunications services. KPNQwest is training them so they better understand the new Internet market and services offered by KPNQwest and their competitors. To do this, they have not only face-to-face training sessions, but a great Web site with vast amounts of information available on their corporate intranet, including sales tools, regional information, and product information. There are dedicated people tasked with making sure the Web site is up-to-date. Most importantly, KPNQwest advises readers not to assume once the training is done, it's done—this is an ongoing process needing some sort of refreshers once a month. The profile of the sales person is changing, as well. Where originally KPNQwest recruiters looked for telecom experience, perhaps from companies like AT&T, GTS, or Global Crossing, they now look for a combination of IT and IP expertise, and might tap companies like Oracle or KPMG.

For its indirect channels, KPNQwest has 40 to 50 partners, but its main outside sales channels are KPN and Qwest.

Pricing is based on market prices, but kept within reason. This means KPNQwest maintains centralized market pricing as much as possible and tries to make sure sales reps and sales channels are selling the right thing. Services are extremely complex and the margin for error is high. Typically, if a U.S.-based multinational extends to Europe, it may become confused because many service providers' prices take into consideration local regulatory tariffs. KPNQwest uses a one-price policy throughout Europe. All the customer has to do is tell KPNQwest where the installations will take place and KPNQwest personnel are able to quote a price that takes into account the different regional pricing vagaries. In generating such a value-based pricing model, KPNQwest tries to understand market price points, then reviews these with the financial department to understand the associated operational costs. Prices are then reviewed each quarter to monitor profit/loss positioning.

The biggest challenge through all this is to stay focused. Service providers must resist the temptation to do everything. Every day there are calls from companies with good ideas. Management needs to screen each call and decide: Is this opportunity within the KPNQwest core strategy? Is there capacity to execute on this opportunity?

Following through on promises makes the difference between KPNQwest's growing customer base and that of its competitors. KPNQwest successfully established a vision, executed it, and is moving on to the next phase—transition from wholesale to retail markets.

In general, customers in both markets are overwhelmed because of the plethora of extremely complex service offerings. KPNQwest market campaigns focus on keeping services open and simple. It experimented with offering select customers the ability to price and buy services online. In phase one, it sent a direct mailing to 1,300 ISPs with a URL and a unique login and password. The site took the user through several easy-to-read screens, allowing the customers to define the service needed, and purchase it online. There was a higher than 15 percent response rate. Most of the visitors were from the U.K. and Nordic countries; responses varied by region and on affinity to the Web. KPNQwest learned that too much emphasis was placed on price, rather than value and product differentiation, and customers were intimidated by having the ability to order the service online. That said, KPNQwest did receive some orders as high as EUR 400,000 during this campaign, all ordered via the Web. Company officials are now able to better understand who visits their site, what the customers are interested in, what they are pricing—both locations and speeds—and which users return to the site.

During the second attempt, KPNQwest added French and German language versions, instituted processes for managing and tracking follow-up, used the Web to describe more service features and advantages, and changed the Order button to "Interested?" This time the direct mailing went to 2,000 potential customers and once again there were lessons learned: It is important to include the value proposition on the Web site, local language helps, and customers value the simplicity of end-to-end pricing. As a result of both campaigns, KPNQwest received 120 qualified leads for IP Transit and 110 qualified leads for its Managed BroadBand Service (MBBS).

Whatever marketing communication (marcom) venue is used, customer follow up is a must for a successful outcome. Communications, in general, are key and most customers are patient if communicated to often. Service providers can get through most problems by being proactive—calling the customer and explaining the situation. Most of KPNQwest's marketing communications are via direct mail, with some targeted advertising in publications like *Business Week*. Venues such as interviews with the press, tradeshows, and white papers, are standard. Because KPNQwest is targeting businesses, not consumers, it tends not to favor billboards. It did, however, sponsor a Finnish mountain climber for its Traveller service and sponsors a motorcycle racer. Television was used for some advertisements, but marketing executives felt the market reach uncertain for the price associated with the venue.

The Web is an important tool when KPNQwest communicates with the market. This is how it developed the Web interface to its advantage:

- Using direct marketing to bring customers to the site
- Providing meaningful content and capabilities at the site for the customers
- Refreshing information to encourage return visits
- Building intimacy with customers online
- Making purchases simple, accurate, and fast

Customers like this venue because the Web site is fast, accurate, intimate, and costs less. KPNQwest likes it for the same reasons. It also frees the sales force to sell more complex solutions that are difficult to communicate over a Web interface.

6.2.6 Service Delivery

It is most important that a service be deliverable as soon as it is offered on the market. KPNQwest has a series of processes to make sure that any new service defined by one department in the company is deliverable by other departments by the time it is pushed to market. Services like their enabler services are sold on a per-seat basis for a flat fee and must be available within 48 hours. Other applications are combined with transport and sold to customers as a complete solution. These kinds of complex services mean service delivery needs to be especially robust and flexible. To add further complication, KPNQwest delivery must support services being simultaneously pushed in all of its markets across Europe.

KPNQwest uses the concept of centralized and decentralized delivery. It is trying not to take the normal European approach of pushing one central set of command and control functions; instead it acts like a holding company, operating 15 smaller companies in each nation state. KPNQwest uses a holding company concept because there are different laws in each country and there needs to be flexibility at the end of the product delivery cycle to accommodate these local differences. By being flexible, the company can accommodate market preferences and react to competitive situations.

The KPNQwest strategy is to get complete ubiquity across its European entities as it relates to processes, tools, and procedures. It is able to take a resource from any CyberCentre and deploy it in another without retraining because each center uses the same platform configurations, processes, tools, and procedures. KPNQwest uses the same front and back office systems (OSS and BSS) and routinely passes network operations control between the CyberCentres as a way of assuring their 24/7 uptime guarantees. This ubiquity results in KPNQwest benefiting from enormous economies of scale, scalability, and high-resource utilization. Stated a different way, consistency is one of KPNQwest's secrets to SLA management and guarantees.

The company is centralizing its operational infrastructure, updating and replacing local applications to conform to central processes. It wants to achieve a ubiquity in operations and in the way individual countries contribute, avoiding the trap of having 15 separate operations. Under this centralization, the company's headquarters is measured on how well it keeps local businesses happy. People located *in country* are measured on their core competency new business volumes. Taking this central approach generates more revenue and frees local engineers to do customer-specific projects.

6.2.7 Customer Care

Technology enables leveraging assets. All KPNQwest's CRM is built on Web-based applications. These applications support CTI and are integrated with voice over IP platforms. By doing this over an IP network, calls can be routed intelligently. In addition, KPNQwest will leverage local call centers for their multilingual operations, but the idea is to reduce the number of operations from 15 to three or four.

6.2.8 Billing

According to Ray Walsh, KPNQwest CIO, billing is nowhere near the differentiator it once was. QoS and responsiveness are most important to business success. If tools allow usage of disparate devices to bill customers, time to market is drastically reduced. The tools used by the service provider need to be flexible and generic. Anytime custom interfaces are used for collection, or anything else for that matter, the implementation process is slower and more expensive. New tools make working through billing challenges easier and less complex.

6.2.9 Infrastructure/Operations

Customers want a service provider that has a reliable infrastructure that is secure, offers transparent operational simplicity, and will support a global reach—all with professional customer care. KPNQwest provides both applications and transport to the customer, with network availability approaching 100 percent.

The joint venture meant starting with the KPN fiber footprint and integrating with 15 EUNet legacy systems. The challenge came with trying to optimize the footprint and creating uniform architecture and processes. There were 15 billing systems, 15 customer care systems, and so forth. KPNQwest decided to first focus on building the new infrastructure—the fiber backbone and CyberCentres—migrate the legacy systems to the new infrastructure and then shut down the legacy. Off-the-shelf packages are used as much as possible before trying any customization, keeping the individual pieces as open and as flexible as possible to integrate with other packages in the core.

Consistency of platform configuration and processes helps keep efficiency up and costs down. KPNQwest believes in using all of its own products wherever possible. Advanced products are supported by complex back office functions and involve human interaction. Entire workflow processes are templated for each service as a way to drive the KPNQwest customer-based activities. These processes can be monitored and measured from an operations center located in The Hague. KPNQwest avoids one-off processes, seeing these as potential trouble spots. The secret to success is to have one overall, highly repeatable back office process and system that becomes rote to its users. KPNQwest relies on vendors to integrate their systems into the back-office workflow to enable direct interfaces, as needed. An example is the ordering process. Cisco and Dell are integrated into KPNQwest's system so it is easier to work with these companies. The two vendors are able to offer higher quality products at a lower price.

One other challenge has been not to treat aspects of hosting services as separate environments. KPNQwest sells hosting and network services together, so it needs to work internally to offer this functionality, plus externally to assure the last mile and CPE configuration are done correctly. Internal processes are controllable and use proven repeatable processes, but the external dependencies are always harder because they can't be controlled. This challenge needs to be invisible to the customer and needs to be treated as one product during the service delivery process.

CyberCentre quality and resiliency is a differentiator in business. Industry leaders in IDC construction use KPNQwest facilities as an example of power resiliency, environmentals, and security. Customers want to house their mission-critical applications and data in a premium facility and brand is tied to the known quality of the KPNQwest facilities.

A service provider must be able to deliver services quickly and so must have teams of qualified people to get customers up and running as fast as possible. By owning both the bandwidth and the CyberCentres, KPNQwest is well positioned to deliver faster and better quality service. It is able to guarantee performance from the network, all the way through business applications, through standard and custom service level agreements that do include penalty clauses for non-performance. To do this, KPNQwest needs tools to monitor critical applications and platforms, guaranteeing service and forecasting failure. It is also able to publish availability reports, network status, and alarms via the Web.

6.2.10 Last Words

In summary, the KPNQwest experience shows:

- A service provider can't take its American Experience and duplicate it in Europe
- People matter more than technology
- A company should do what is promised, deliver what's advertised
- Direct marketing can get customers to the door
- Customers value simplicity and speed
- Providers need to give meaningful, accurate information
- Back-end and follow-up processes are critical
- Learn, improve, and expand
- Build an intimate customer relationship
- Transform that expensive direct sales force to solution selling, using the Web or channels for the simpler sales.

Don't "cookie cutter" the U.S. experience. Business is done differently in Europe and the U.S. examples won't work.

People matter more than technology. Building a corporate culture with the ability to flex is more important than just about all other things when a service provider is building its business. The only sure thing is that business will not go as planned and it won't work out as one thinks it will. The difference between success and failure is often not so much in the planning, but how the organization responds when things don't go as planned. There needs to be flexibility to adjust the plan to market reaction. The right people need to be in the right environment and this is more important than upfront planning. KPNQwest recommends understanding the market well enough to pick the right trends and have about 80 percent of the planning complete, then launch the product/service and be flexible enough to improvise on the way to the target. Reward those who achieve their targets.

Europe is made up of many diverse cultures, each different from those found in the U.S. Each country has its own regulatory body that must be respected.

Do what is promised, deliver what's advertised. This is the year KPNQwest will finish its fiber installation on time and within budget. When the project started three or four years ago, no one believed it could be done. Now, no one is questioning anymore and the KPNQwest brand is identified with this success.

As a part of ongoing operations, service providers can't afford to miss delivering what is promised because missing is equivalent to dying.

6.3 Endnote

1. Content for this case study provided by Jack McMaster, president/CEO of KPNQwest; Ray Walsh, CIO of KPNQwest; Piers Schreiber, senior vice president corporate communications; Bill Fugelsang, senior vice president, products and marketing, KPNQwest; Hans Fransen, director, strategic alliances, KPNQwest; and Ben Lippolt, director, product strategy CyberCentres, KPNQwest.

CHAPTER 7

Latin America – Triara

Internet penetration is relatively low in Latin America, but wireless adoption in the region is one of the highest in the world. This means Latin America could be one of the richest regions for wireless Internet growth as the technology becomes more facile and users are educated as to its benefits. The opportunity for Internet business varies throughout the region, which comprises, for the purposes of this book, all countries south of the U.S.

7.1 The Latin American Market

7.1.1 Current Situation

Brazil is Latin America's largest financial market and has been the country to most quickly adopt business to consumer (B2C) applications, but the best growth opportunity in the short term for Internet services is Mexico because of its proximity to, and large trade balances with, the United States. The population is well exposed to Internet services and the educational programs aimed at potential customers.

Industry expertise is valued in Latin America. Vertical markets most likely to be targets of investment capital are agriculture, energy, financial services, and manufacturing. Business is still based on personal contact and local firms have the advantage of understanding local business nuances. Foreign firms wanting to enter the market would do better to partner locally, or work with multinational clients that have a local presence in the region.

Service providers tend to focus on the large and medium enterprise customer segments, as these firms usually have money and an Internet strategy. Normally these companies at least have a Web site. Often, an executive committee that has final approval for infrastructure projects makes purchasing decisions.

In this region, service providers will spend a lot of time educating prospective customers—taking them from being needs oblivious to making them needs aware and showing what the Internet can do for the future of their businesses.

7.2 Case Study – Triara[1]

7.2.1 Company Overview

Triara was founded in October 2000 as a subsidiary of Telmex and other minority partners. Triara offers IDC services, which include collocation, and shared and dedicated hosting. The concept for Triara came about because Telmex realized basic data and voice services did not provide a sustainable long-term business. As a result, Telmex executives redirected their data strategy to cover everything from bandwidth through end-user market applications, including portal applications. Armed with a new strategy, the company was motivated to start filling in the strategy.

A group was assembled to define new data transport service offerings. Guillermo Güémez, the general manager for Triara, joined Telmex on July 1, 2000, from EDS, during the services analysis phase for the new company. He prepared the original business case and managed the project plan, which was then presented to, and approved by, the CEO of Telmex, Ing. Jaime Chico Pardo, and other top executives. Creating a company inside a large group of companies was an interesting process for Güémez. Normally Telmex creates a separate organization within the main corporate umbrella, but in this case it decided to spin off a separate company. What began as a vision by Pardo is, little by little, growing. Güémez' goal is to make Triara more successful in execution than in the business cases designed in the planning stage.

Triara is headquartered in Mexico City and has 100 employees. Its first 30,000 square foot IDC located in Monterey, Mexico, has been expanded to approximately 80,000 square feet. Triara is also building new a headquarters, together with its primary IDC, in Mexico City. This data center will have 100,000 square feet (net) floor space when completed in late 2001. Triara is evaluating other cities and countries for future expansion based on demand-pull by region. Because its competitors are planning to build from 300,000 to 400,000 square feet of new IDC space over the next 12 months Triara will be doubly cautious when planning future IDC construction, making sure that any new space will be filled.

Currently, Triara's main service offerings are hosting, starting at the bottom with shared and dedicated hosting and collocation services. Managed services are offered in conjunction with partners, but it is not yet a Triara core competency. Although there is a market demand for sophisticated managed services in Mexico, as there is in the U.S., the existing volume does not yet justify the required implementation efforts; therefore, Triara's managed services cover only basic infrastructure management.

Triara's value proposition revolves around infrastructure and market penetration. Triara's parent company, Telmex, already owns a nationwide backbone infrastructure. In fact, it owns the largest backbone in Mexico, approximately 70,000 kilometers. About 60 percent of Internet subscribers in Mexico use the Telmex backbone and Triara is only one router hop away, meaning faster service for end-users. This creates a high barrier to entry for competition, since many cannot afford to build the infrastructure needed to be successful. Triara's attention to detail and testing means it can boast the best security offering for hosting in Mexico. Leveraging Telmex's billing infrastructure and customer care systems means customers get better service and attention in Spanish, making end-users feel more comfortable. Triara expects to fill market demands for the long haul, and has Telmex's commitment, ensuring ongoing investments in technology. The fact that Triara is up and running means it will take awhile for its main competitors, Aventel and Alestra, to catch up. By that time, Triara will already be offering more complex services. Complex services are where market penetration becomes a true added value. Triara's huge potential market penetration makes it an ideal partner for complex services that include elements of logistics, trading, and so forth.

Customers want the security of being able to see a working IDC, a trusted brand, and experienced workforce. Triara has first mover advantage and will define the market going forward.

7.2.2 Local Landscape Overview

The Mexican market still reflects some of the characteristics of having had a monopoly telecommunications provider, meaning a dominant long-distance operator that drives a specific sales model. This dominant carrier, Telmex, has over 60 percent market share for long distance and over 90 percent market share for the local loop.

Being so close to the United States gives the data services market a unique flavor. Mexican enterprises think that the U.S. Internet infrastructure services are easy to obtain and manage. This means Mexico's service providers, like Triara, compete directly with those in the U.S. Other countries in Latin America do not, necessarily, have this problem because of the physical distance between themselves and North America. Mexican enterprises will utilize the hosting services of service providers in the United States because of the perception that U.S. providers offer better quality, faster services, and are "closer to the Internet." Internet infrastructure cost to the provider in Mexico is higher than data telecommunication cost and is about three times the cost of similar infrastructure in the United States. Mexican providers pay U.S. list rates for infrastructure, where American providers are offered discount rates by infrastructure owners.

In Mexico, the Internet is not a pervasive part of society as it is in other countries. The hosting market isn't well developed so service providers need to teach the market about the service, what it is, what its benefits are, and so forth. The big three providers, Triara, Alestra, and Aventel as well as some U.S. firms, are beginning to see competition from small hosters. The newcomers to the market, however, face an uphill battle: they usually have small facilities and are under-financed.

7.2.3 Operational Challenges and How Solved

7.2.3.1 Partnering

Partnering in Mexico is intense—everyone is partnering with everyone else as a hedge. Triara is willing to find partners to fill gaps in sales and operational processes. Everyone wants to partner with Telmex because of its market penetration. Telmex can tap into just about any portfolio, company, or brand in Mexico. In reality, many potential partners talk a lot and do very little. Over 50 companies have approached Triara to discuss partnering possibilities, but few are aligned strategically. Sometimes large companies are worse in this area because politically complex environments mean it's hard to get overall strategic alignments. Executives between the companies may agree, but lower-level managers don't support the higher-level view when it doesn't match departmental goals. Smaller companies have less to leverage when negotiating with a company like Triara with its giant backers. Smaller companies may gain the advantage if they can identify a common enemy and offer unique ammunition against it.

In general, partnering is a complex process with no formal rules. The partnering process is basically people trying to sell things between companies. According to Güémez, "[I am] swamped with people who want to partner with me to sell things. [It is] hard to find partners with the same needs and a willingness to risk. Many prospective partners don't understand [the concept of] win-win nor are they willing to risk anything on the line. [Partnerships should] not just be a supplier/buyer relationship. The decision processes involved in a large company like Telmex make smaller companies scared because they don't understand them. To get through these issues with all partners, I'm straightforward about what I want—trying not to waste time. My advice is don't tiptoe around issues—face them head on. Level playing field expectations as soon as possible so time isn't wasted. If a backup proposal shows the potential partner still doesn't understand, I show them out the door. Build trust through honestly facing what is, and isn't, realistic and what things can and can't be controlled. This allows both sides of the potential partnership to take measured risks. Understand who can sign and tie down details watertight in the partner's organization. Signing a partner agreement is close to signing a prenuptial agreement. The parties talk about all the beautiful things that can happen as a result of the alliance, but all this changes as signing the partnership agreement comes closer."

7.2.3.2 Organization

Small start-up companies may not know how many and what types of resources they need, especially when offering a service that is new to the market. One can do a lot of process mapping and look to what others do, but it's only through trial and error that the service provider can understand what works. Having a majority shareholder creates a unique environment, especially when that shareholder has well-established business models and processes geared toward a different, more stable, type of market. The start-up organization will tend to mimic its parent company, which may not necessarily be the optimal solution.

If the service provider comes from an established company in a stable market with human resource rules, it is more challenging because officials sometimes assume that someone at the start-up firm can provide detailed justification documents and function lists. Creating these documents might be impossible because the service has never been offered and total functions aren't yet defined. In this case, organization also becomes a challenge because processes cannot be defined that will fully support the as yet undefined services. Installation processes, service delivery, and pricing are also good examples of things that are difficult to define and justify with new services.

There are no standard service provider organizational models. Each provider has proprietary models for services, functions, and processes. Triara mapped processes it thought supported the offered products and back office services for the initial operating structure. This turned out to be a living document that went through considerable change. The organization was defined at a late date in the set up process so as not to tax the organization with internal HR approvals, a process which can be time consuming for all concerned. Start-ups without large corporate majority stakeholders probably won't have to consider these issues since there may be fewer oversight procedures.

Another reason for design complexity is the extremely rapid organizational growth. Triara grew from two people during its first month of operation to 50 people after six months. Coping with that sort of rapid growth poses two big challenges for management: Company leaders can't immediately get to know the key personnel and early hires expected to quickly rise in the organization.

Communication is the key during every phase of an operation, whether dealing with new hires or old hands. Management and HR need to constantly communicate what's going on, what they expect to happen, and what actually did happen. Email is a good tool, but should not be overused. The personal side of management is very important—especially in a small company. People still want to talk, sit down with management, and hear from the horse's mouth what's working and what isn't. This also gives a sense of unity to the company.

Communication also plays a key role in dispelling "cultural problems" (such as speed of action and reaction, customer focus, processes, and speed of return on the investment) that can occur between employees of the parent company and its spin off. Customer care is a good example where monopolistic telcos (telecommunications companies) could get away with lack luster customer care; service providers must rotate around customer satisfaction. Employees at the start-up may have to deal with the we've-always-done-it-this-way attitude at the parent company.

Finding talent is difficult because service providers work in a new, hot industry. Employee turnover is extremely high. Company loyalty is weak in Mexico, but not as weak as in the United States labor market, where employees sometimes leave a job within a month of being hired. There is no way to avoid employee turnover, but the best way to limit it is by developing a relationship with employees as a way of finding out when they're unhappy, have other offers, and so forth. Eventually, managers need to develop a plan for how they will manage the employee turnover environment. Fast growth also means that often people are promoted above their abilities. It's not unusual for employees to be promoted quickly from making copies to positions where they think they can run the company, with the added incentive of having offers to go elsewhere for more money. Triara does not offer raises or special retention plans.

With such fast growth, many job roles are not well defined and they change rather dynamically. This is another case where expectations need to be managed through better communications. Since Mexico is such a high context culture, managers in Triara sometimes spend as much as 30 percent to 40 percent of their time talking to people and giving them updates about what's going to happen and what isn't going to happen.

Outsourcing can be an excellent solution to resource problems for those areas of the business not considered to be a core competency. Outsourcing can also be a good solution from the standpoint of processes, and local and federal employment regulations. When a portion of the operation is outsourced, Triara doesn't have to worry about the related process issues, or any payroll, social tax reserves, or employee lay-off/dismissal laws, since these are the responsibility of the outsourcing company that provides the services requested.

To decide what to outsource, Triara followed these three basic rules:

- Identify those basic functions that aren't a core competency, but are necessary for the operation. For Triara these were things like: physical security, cleaning, and telephone services (PBX). There was also no cost advantage to having these functions maintained in-house.
- Identify those functions that are available from the parent company and can be provided at a reasonable cost. This allows the spin-off to leverage off the parent company's economies of scale. For Tiara these were things like financials and construction. For example, Triara's CFO works within the Telmex structure and is able to leverage Telmex's infrastructure, thereby achieving more at a lower cost than creating a new Triara infrastructure, or outsourcing.
- Identify difficult-to-find technical resources needed for operations that will stay in-house, but are not core competencies, and try to find suppliers for these kinds of resources. Sometimes these might be vendors, sometimes part time employment agencies like Volt or Manpower. For example, Triara's core competency is not managing the IDC, but is to offer products used in the data center. Outsource everything that is not a core competency.

It is hard to negotiate an outsourcing contract if the needed functions are not, or cannot be, defined. The good news is that most outsourced services are, by their nature, defined. Triara typically selected three companies for quotes. It was relatively easy to find at least three interested parties because of Telmex's size and reputation. Triara actually uses Telmex's preselection process for RFPs. Outsourcing well-defined services made the process easier. As Triara moves up the value chain, it expects outsourcing to become more complex because the services, their functions, penalties, growth path, and so forth, become more difficult to define. If a service provider is outsourcing on a per seat basis, the provider could end up paying more than what is budgeted due to poorly understood growth issues at the time of negotiation. Negotiations can be challenging, so it's best to find someone who has experience negotiating outsourcing contracts for help.

7.2.4 Entering the Market

Triara's services strategy and roadmap were modeled on current offerings in the United States. This is one advantage of being a first mover in Mexico and a late mover in the international market. Triara used experience from service providers in other countries to understand what works and what doesn't. The same goes for service providers in Mexico; here is where Triara's first mover advantage is also a disadvantage. Triara spends money, resources, and time educating the market, which also paves the way for competitors' services. Since Triara services are new to the market, it means that there is not an educated sales resource pool. Triara ends up training sales people who could leave for competitors, meaning that training investment is lost and competitors gain from the prior training. Triara can move quickly by offering new services popular internationally, but not yet available in Mexico. In this way, Triara is not an innovator, but leveraging off of international experience.

As the dominant carrier, Telmex, has an extremely large customer base, over 60 percent market share for long distance and over 90 percent market share for the local loop. This means, by default, that Triara can take advantage of a huge barrier to entry for competitors. Triara has access to just about any CIO of any sizable company and it has access to a sales representative in Telmex who knows that CIO personally. This makes market reach and the sales process much easier.

Price generation is quite complex. The service provider wants to price to the market leader when there is one. When there isn't, like in Mexico for Web hosting, there is a fragmented market with high prices. The service provider is trapped between wanting to drop the price and ensuring profitability levels. Complex cost analysis is needed, including a full cost allocation model. Triara uses a complex model that takes into account the entire architecture, how it is designed, and all overhead costs. By using a model, management is able to show decision makers the true internal costs and verify the results of price changes on profit/loss. Having such a model has enabled Triara executive management to control pricing throughout the service delivery process because they are able to understand the costs.

A further benefit is enabling testing of new or differentiated pricing schemes. An example was the suggestion of offering a service priced per megabyte (MB). Running the numbers through the model proved this pricing wouldn't fall within financial parameters due to high internal costs. Modeling enables management to understand volume thresholds needed to justify reduction in pricing. If service providers don't have a good understanding of internal cost structure, pricing becomes difficult because company officials can't determine if they'll make money on their per unit cost. Service providers with a nonstandard product base and nonstandard pricing need to be careful when determining profitable sales levels. According to Güémez, EDS has mastered this, others have not—the secret is determining true profitability.

Marketing is a frustrating proposition because it is so subjective and time consuming. Service providers should try to find a reasonable marketing agency and work together to define a marketing campaign, and then go for approvals. Sometimes the approval process can be more complex than defining the marketing plan, especially if many approvals are needed on the marketing copy. For example, if a parent company is involved, there may be an approval process requiring many individual approvers who need to approve the look and feel of any marketing messages. This puts marketing management between a rock and a hard place. Does marketing choose the out-of-the-ordinary marketing campaign that will be seen by more people but take longer to get approved; or the conservative approach that will be easier to get approved, but gets less market response? How does the provider get the right message through to the market?

How does marketing measure returns from TV, radio, or magazine advertising? These are expensive communications options that are often difficult to measure. Other options, like direct mail, don't work in Mexico because of poor quality customer databases.

Some service providers may have market communication venue limitations placed on them by the parent company. An example of this is billboards. Billboards are quite popular in Mexico, but Telmex doesn't support billboards as a marketing communications device.

Triara works through these difficulties by trying to make quick decisions that may be changed later if any management concerns are raised. The concern is that if marketing communications are delayed, the marketing message is delayed and first mover market advantages may be lost.

Defining a service and its delivery is challenging. It's difficult to define exactly what Web hosting means from the standpoint of service functionality and delivery. A service description is more than just a few lines about service functionality. Once the service is defined, implementation and service delivery policies need to be defined. This includes details about policies: what the customers have to do and when, what the service provider will do, and what happens when the parties don't perform as promised. Understanding all aspects of the service implementation and delivery processes can only be accomplished via hard work, but if the details are not ironed out, there will be real time adjustments when the first customers come in-house. To work out these policies, a group of employees at Triara brainstormed and identified, in detail, all the inputs/outputs and processes in service delivery, from customer sale, through turnover, to ongoing maintenance. Even after this exercise, there were shortcomings in the initial implementation processes and the team found other items needing to be defined, priced, and so forth. Once the overall processes were defined, documenting them visually helped the team fill in final details. The final filter before tying down processes was in customer interaction during the pilot phase. Triara offered free hosting services for a short period during the pilot phase to thank customers for their patience while the service provider worked through these final issues.

Sales training and management is more an art than a science. How can service providers train sales people to sell something as complex as an Internet service? How do service providers manage the sales teams and customer expectations? How are they sure that sales representatives and customers actually understand the functionality of the services being offered? Triara has found success by developing *train-the-trainer* programs, but these are difficult to manage. Making sure the trainers truly understand the message is most important in these programs, because as the trainers move further away from their original training, people tend to start making assumptions on services, resulting in misconceptions and misinformation. Training the small sales force for high-end offerings in Triara is an in-person, one-on-one process. The larger sales force receives training via the Web.

To find employees, Triara went through an exhaustive interview process, asking difficult questions, weeding out prospective employees who could not support their claims of success or prove their level of experience. Managers should study techniques to help them determine the right person for the job.

Triara had to find employees who can sell a nontangible service, one that can't be seen, touched, or quantified. When the service is complex, finding people who can understand, and explain in simple terms what the service provider is selling and the service parameters involved is difficult. Service providers need sales people who understand the customer, treat them well, and understand the product and its associated expenses.

To build their initial customer list, Triara took the Telmex customer list and identified those customers that should have a certain interest in the hosting product. Normally this was determined by seeing which customers had reasonable Web sites. During the initial review of the Telmex customer list, which includes just about all companies in Mexico, Triara decided to focus on large customers because they are normally the first to have an Internet strategy.

Customers who can be used as references can be the difference between success and failure and the first customers are critical. Which customers are so important that it's worthwhile "buying" their business? To answer this, service providers must ask difficult questions. They need to be careful they aren't pressured into choosing particular customers. Service providers should consider the customer size, reputation, and the amount of business that will be brought in.

The customer needs to have a large enough presence in the marketplace with the right presence and profile. Güémez likes to use the example of Exodus that was built on one of its first customers, Yahoo!

7.2.5 Service Delivery

Since service delivery covers all aspects of customer fulfillment, details of Triara service delivery issues and goals are covered throughout this case study. One of Triara's competitive advantages is its ability to seamlessly transfer customers using its lower end products from sales, through provisioning, to ongoing customer maintenance. This entire process is automated and seamless to the user. According to Güémez, no one else in the Mexican market is provisioning on an automated basis for these services.

For more customized solutions, service delivery is not yet fully automated because service functionality is still fluid and is, as yet, *unproductized*. Delivering to customers who are not yet able to define their desired functionality also is a barrier to an automated service delivery process, at least initially. For example, in one instance, the customer was more concerned about the software brand than the actual product. In the end, the customer couldn't identify which product of the software brand it wanted, making it difficult to deliver the correct solution.

For services that are highly customized, Triara is still working out ways to streamline the fulfillment processes. Workflow is automated, but fulfillment still requires a high degree of interaction and definition among the customer, sales, and Triara implementation resources that can't be supported by workflow automation. Triara technical resources are trying to document and define a process that specifies, with a lot of detail, what's needed on both sides. In parallel, Triara is developing sales force training so the sales representatives understand the more technical aspects of what they're selling, if the configuration makes sense, and, if the configuration is even possible. Triara is also working out issues around monitoring and response work for these highly customized services. Automation is the key. Technical staff is trying to automate as much of the process as possible, like monitoring and response functionality, so that, unless there are critical time periods involved, the process is handled by a computer.

7.2.6 Customer Care

The biggest question in customer care is: Who does the customer call, especially in the case of a complex integrated service? In a complex integrated service, customers have no way to determine what the problem is, so they need a single number they can confidently call to handle first-tier questions for the entire service offering. Next, how does the service provider route the call on to second-tier support? How is the customer's call classified for routing? Triara's services involve many other vendors and are the ending, or starting point for these other vendor services. The customer should see Triara as a seamless point of delivery. The challenge comes in integrating the different platforms and service levels. Some partners have CRM systems, some have only call centers, and some have nothing. Triara needs to offer first-tier care incorporating all these types of partners for two distinct classes of customers:

- Small hosting customers who are redirected to Triara's in-house self-service call center. These customers tend to be high volume and low margin.
- Large customers with true integrated services. These customers are higher volume/ margin and are routed to the Telmex call center.

The Triara definition of a large company is different from Triara's parent company, meaning that Triara needs to continually validate the quality of the care outsourced to Telmex. Triara management can normally detect a problem faster than its customers. If detected first, Triara reacts immediately. If the customer calls the call center first, Telmex will open the trouble ticket and try to find the problem. The interface between Triara and Telmex allows for sharing tracking numbers and for efficient trouble tracking.

Triara is a small company and problems are communicated quickly throughout the company. Most problems are electronic and are auditable across the company. As Triara grows it will certainly need more electronic and automated means to communicate customer needs across the company. This internal communications infrastructure will be needed, not only for call center issues, but also for other service delivery issues so they are handled in the appropriate offices within the company. Currently, each item generated by the call center is sent to Triara executive management and is filtered from there. This methods gives executive management information about how many customers are calling and generally why.

Customer care begins with sales people and quality customer interaction. Training and monitoring employee/customer interaction needs to be implemented across the organization. Presales engineers need to understand that it's not a matter of squeezing money out of the customer, but of offering the best service for the best price. The most effective way to solve this issue is by communication and training.

Triara outsourced its entire call center operation. This relieves Triara of the burden of finding and training call center resources; however, Triara continues to train Telmex CSRs so they understand the specialized services provided by Triara. This is needed because Internet hosting services are different from the phone services Telmex CSRs usually support. Outsourcing can create issues. For example, how can the service provider guarantee QoS? Distance can be an issue. Since the operation is completed outside the provider, how can results be quantified? Metrics must be subjective and measurable. The service provider needs to precisely define monitoring/reporting systems for tracking purposes. At Triara, every time a CSR finishes a call, he or she must ask the customer one question: "Did I solve your problem?" Any time a customer hangs up on the CSR, the call is audited. Examples of metrics include things like the percentage of calls turned over to second-tier support. Second-tier has percentage limits built into the contract with Telmex. Third-tier is still kept within Triara, because any third-tier problem is an infrastructure problem. The metrics are industry standard, allowing Triara to focus on its specific customer profiles and how they are to be handled.

Outsourcing functions force the service provider to think about the relationship between themselves and the outsource company. It forces the service provider to closely monitor the quality of these services, perhaps even more than if the operation were kept in-house. The cost of outsourcing does rise, but it should still be lower than the cost of a fully implemented CRM or call center solution. Determining the cost of the operation that might be outsourced is more than costs associated with personnel. The service provider should outsource functionality because it is not a core competency. Triara was limited to Telmex as its outsource provider, but shopped around for pricing levels to use from a negotiation standpoint.

When metric results are low, that is an indication to Triara management that they should look at training. If it is a specific individual who does not get good marks from customers, Triara can ask for the removal of that CSR. If there is a pattern not based on a specific subject, a training program is developed to address the issues. If metric results point to an infrastructure service issue, Triara checks these internally. Agreeing with the outsourcing company on changeable metrics is the first step in the contract negotiation process. The Triara/Telmex contract stipulated Triara can have up to four programmable questions to measure quality and that the questions can be changed at any time. This option allows Triara management flexibility, and an element of customization, in designing metrics. It also allows the best way of monitoring customer satisfaction.

Initially, outsourcing returned dramatic decreases in operational costs, but Triara doesn't expect these results to last forever. Normally, operational cost decreases level off, or the outsourcer will go bankrupt and/or the service will deteriorate. According to Güémez, "Outsourcing history is full of these examples, in many cases [if the] rates were initially high and continued to stay high, eventually [the] customer will wise up and find another outsourcer." There is a fine line between pushing pricing down for the services offered, and paying to keep service levels high enough to maintain the service quality the purchaser expects.

7.2.6.1 Customer Retention

The best method of customer retention is through good service and reasonable prices. Before readjusting pricing, Triara management looks carefully at the competition to make sure they offer the same service and service quality. If new pricing is warranted, but makes the service unprofitable, Triara will enhance the service versus offering the service below cost.

Service level agreement penalties are used by Triara to further customer retention. Currently, service level agreements are negotiated on a case-by-case basis. Triara prefers free use periods instead of refunds.

7.2.6.2 New Technology

Triara likes self-care options for smaller customers. These customers receive tools to monitor their Web sites and have an interface with Triara via email and a Web site. The Web site is controlled remotely and Triara monitors these systems to get customer reactions and suggestions. Their reactions are used to continually update the self-help systems for better care.

7.2.7 Billing

Triara outsources its billing to Telmex, which has the largest billing system in the country and is another of Triara's competitive advantages. This allows Triara to bill anyone in the country directly—a huge advantage to Triara as a Mexican enterprise. In Mexico, bills are not always received and if they are, are often ignored. The exception is bills sent by utilities, like Telmex. Billing through Telmex means the invoices will arrive and must be paid.

Negotiation with payment option partners is a jungle. These vendors play off float and have terms and conditions not yet geared to the Internet services market. A good example is the credit card companies. Industry representatives often do not understand that the Internet business is currently not well regulated when it comes to payment fulfillment nor do they understand the advantages of electronic billing. The credit card companies' legal departments add another level of complexity, insisting on guarantees for things that aren't guaranteeable. One example might be insisting that the hosting service will be unilaterally cut off if the credit card is stopped.

Billing and determining billing cycles is an extremely complex process. This means defining:

- When the customer will be billed
- When the accounts receivable will be recognized
- When payments will be posted

These issues need to be understood and resolved before billing. The good news is there are many billing experts in the market to give advice. The bad news is that not all experts understand Internet billing needs. For example, some consultants don't understand that billing doesn't start until the customer is installed and service is being delivered based on the guarantees promised. The service provider needs to get the customers efficiently loaded into the billing system, have a process in place for initial charging, and how/when the customer is added to accounts receivable. All of this means longer accounts receivable times, at least initially. Güémez recommends finding a good billing expert to help with billing implementation.

If billing is outsourced, the service provider needs to have agreements in writing about many things, especially bill collection. The service provider should:

- Agree with the billing company about how collection is handled, and how much data can be collected per device/per user
- Make sure billing devices collect data as intended; otherwise, the provider will pay for devices they hadn't planned on
- Find out if the billing system will support charges for excess capacity usage
- Determine if each price charged is higher than the cost to provide the service

At one time Triara almost considered not charging for excess capacity because cost of infrastructure to do this was more than the revenue from the service. Service providers should make sure they use a billing system that supports their industry; for example, a mobile billing system for the mobile industry, telephone system for telephone industry and an IP billing system for IP services.

Understand early in the process what will be billed, how it will be billed, and how the billing system will react. Exchange rates and other currency policies can affect a company's rating and add a layer of complexity in the credit card clearing process. In Mexico, as an example, all prices must be in pesos.

Interfaces with legacy systems need a lot of testing. This means more than just a couple of billing runs because there are thousands of variations that will foul up the computers even without the complications of legacy systems. Control processes are needed to understand how many records and dollars are received, as well as to follow the myriad of details during the testing and benchmarking phase. Triara ran full production monthly billing cycles everyday in a testing environment for a week and a half. This meant they ran the equivalent of a yearly billing run in the testing environment. Even after this, testing continued for the first few months of production with parallel operational checks by the finance group. Triara doesn't have volume problems due to its small customer base, but backup processes are extremely important.

Because billing is so complex, it is best for service providers without internal expertise to find a good billing consultant for help through the implementation processes.

7.2.8 Infrastructure and Operations

Triara believes that the technology needs to be available and working to offer a service, before the infrastructure is made fast or beautiful. Most service providers sprouting up on the Internet are pushing the envelope, offering new services done new ways. The process from service concept to reality is rather complex and many tend to reinvent the wheel during the process. Triara works to ensure there is an infrastructure capable of supporting the proposed service first. Only after Triara is sure the infrastructure will work, do company officials think about scalability and manageability. Often others focus on the abilities before they are sure technology exists to offer the desired service.

7.2.8.1 Manageability

Manageability is critical, especially when trying to run an efficient operation. The fewer people needed to manage operations, the better. In Triara, programmers usually design processes that enable data center operations. The designers tend to focus on code—this isn't the best quality when trying to communicate processes to nonprogrammers who may be managing the data center. What programmers think of as manageable is not necessarily understandable for those in the data center. As such, hiring a project manager is a good way to manage the process. Project managers serve as a sort of mitigation device between those doing the day-to-day data center management and the programmers working on the basic management processes. Common processes need to have links into all areas of company—not just infrastructure operations.

7.2.8.2 Scalability

The secret to scalability is to build modularly and test, test, test, and then test some more. Testing is expensive and time consuming, but necessary. Triara needed to run a test on its mail system. It took two weeks to set up a benchmark to process 30 million mail messages in one hour. After the test, Triara felt confident rating its system for 1.3 million mail users. Its management now knows the system is scalable and understands the process for doing so.

Regarding the IDC infrastructure, Triara doesn't worry about floor space. If there is a shortage, the parent company will build more. Triara has effectively planned for its IDCs well into the future. All planned sites are situated near power and communications infrastructures. For example, both data centers are located next to primary substations for power and within a mile of Telmex fiber sites. Triara has a guarantee from the utility companies and landowners that growth of its IDC operations will be supported.

The IDCs are designed redundantly and modularly to support twice expected needs. Triara is fortunate in that its parent company has exceedingly deep pockets. While it does worry about return on investment for its investors, like most other companies, Telmex won't turn off the tap if a positive ROI is not immediately realized. While this allows Triara to ride out market fluctuations, management needs to stay within the financial limits set in the business plan.

Currently, power per square meter requirements are such that customers requiring full racks of large class machines need approximately 40 amp/sq/meter, but growth is tremendous. To fill this gap, Triara will build more capacity in new data centers, but try not to move already installed customers. Management plans to slowly increase capacity enabled by the pan-operation redundant design. This means they are able to swap out parts, such as generators, and replace them with more powerful devices. The IDC was designed on a component basis from the beginning to enable swapping out components, as necessary.

Triara doesn't have bandwidth worries because it is linked to the largest backbone in Mexico via Telmex. Externally, Triara's data centers have optical feeds. Internal connections use high-speed Ethernet connections. As a way to address availability issues, Triara has two pair of fiber cables that go out of the IDC by different routes to different central offices. One fiber optic cable could be cut and the other will still work. This procedure has been tested and it works. Hardware and software is also fully redundant and hot swappable.

7.2.8.3 Security

Logical security is one of the most difficult things to achieve in the service provider business. In the Internet space everyone has an opinion on security, but few have an idea of the real situation. Since customer perception is his/her reality, Triara makes sure its huge infrastructure is designed especially to provide a secure logical environment. One of the delays around the Triara service launch was making sure the infrastructure was as secure as possible.

Logical security is never 100 percent achievable and a service provider can plug only those holes that are found. That said, Triara has one person who focuses on finding, patching, and fixing bugs. Being the best service provider is an ongoing effort that doesn't stop at launch date. It continues all day, every day. Service providers need to find consultants who truly understand security, not just talk a good game.

Service providers must be proactive in the security area and not wait for vendors to understand what hackers can—and will—do. Physical security can be taken to extremes, but it's worth the money to find a good consultant to help with the design of protective systems. Security experts can help determine the balance between costs, real security achieved with the investment, and operational efficiency. Physical security doesn't come cheap. Systems normally take the form of 12-inch concrete walls to protect the IDC bunker, behind these another set of 12-inch walls to protect the IDC complex with windows that are bulletproof, meaning they have more than 1.5 inches of glass. Triara's IDC is also protected by more than 90 carefully positioned cameras. These experts helped spot security system gaps, suggested which security equipment is most valuable, and pointed out problems in how people work. Sometimes people can be a weak link in a security system. To protect against illegal entry because of doors left open, Triara installed a spring that automatically closes them.

Security does not necessarily mean secrecy. A security officer at another company implemented a security feature prohibiting any program from executing a certain shell program. There was no error message and the programs constantly failed in production. You can imagine the time and money spent to find the bug. Security needs to be public. If an infrastructure is secure only because people don't know, it will not be as effective a system as one that stands up against proven testing.

The most challenging aspect of security is keeping up-to-date with all possible security problems for each application in the IDC. A good security expert can help service providers with these issues. Logical and physical security are expensive propositions. Service providers must spread the word and communicate frequently with customers about security issues.

7.2.8.4 Availability

Triara IDCs use a modularly designed architecture. All systems are 2N redundant—having doubly redundant systems—meaning that everything has two full backup systems. Building on a modular design allows for high availability, one of the most critical aspects for service delivery. If the systems are not available, customers will switch providers. The only way Triara knows to offer service 100 percent of the time is by brutal redundancy and modularity so there is no planned downtime. Triara guarantees 100 percent uptime for the IDC infrastructure, but this does not include customer applications or servers not leased from Triara. The Triara guarantee covers power, access, and environmentals. Availability levels also depend on what the customer is willing to pay. Not all customers need 100 percent availability.

Currently, the guarantee stops as the fiber cable leaves the IDC, connecting IDC with the Internet. Triara is working with Telmex to extend the SLAs to include double redundancy outside the IDC site. This would expand the availability guarantees to cover the redundant dedicated fiber channels between the IDC and the enterprise.

7.2.8.5 Supportability

Important elements that relate to well-supported operations include: modular design, well written operational processes, superior testing processes, and high-quality human resources. Engineers typically write processes for things going right, not for when they go wrong. Testing processes are important to the supportability of the IDC, not only as a way to test execution, but in how the tests are designed. These issues need to be thought about from the beginning of IDC design.

All Triara computers are remotely manageable, which makes for more efficient support. They have a management console that manages each node on the network, and have multiple consoles so nodes can be managed in parallel, if needed. Engineers need to design from the beginning to support worse case scenarios. Processes and the physical placement of objects in the data center need to support efficiency of movement and resources. Processes need to be in place to support complex services and need to support repair during time of system(s) failure. For example, can components be swapped out simultaneously and what is the process for doing this?

Triara has on-site support, 24/7, with an on-site inventory stocked with all the parts in use. There is a 15-minute response time on all repairs. Since everything is redundant in Triara IDCs, it is difficult for something to fail badly. Service providers need to work with vendors to get this sort of support. Support is usually sold on a per-box basis, in other words, the number of computers multiplied by the number of supported months. This isn't very economical for service providers because of the high volume of computers located in the data centers. If service provider management can guarantee enough volume for vendors, they may be able to negotiate better support programs, like having a vendor technician on site all the time, or a parts inventory on site. Having vendor personnel and inventory on site should mean faster response times and faster time to repair. The number of calls a vendor can attend to can be a limiting factor if only one person is available all the time on site. Service providers may want to try to negotiate a pay-as-you-grow arrangement or other method of support contract as a way to help with cash flow.

Economies of scale should get better over time as hardware/software defects are better understood. The number of people to support the same number of machines on site should decrease as processes become more efficient and as the defects per machine ratio decreases. Metrics should be defined with the vendor so cost structures adjust as break/fix metrics become more efficient per computer. These kinds of suggestions may not be viable to all but the largest service providers.

7.2.9 Ongoing Processes

New service providers will find defining operational processes a challenge because they don't understand which processes are needed and what customers will request. There will be a lot of trial and error in determining the best way to set up the operation. But no matter how much service provider management plans, there is no substitute for a live environment to test how well these processes work.

Everyone talks about the importance of good processes for hiring, billing, and so forth, but few understand the processes needed when employees or customers exit the service provider. These processes are even more important and need to be in place from the first days of operation.

Triara outsources many of its operations, so many processes are already defined. At Triara, the key issue isn't definition of processes, but more integrating outsourcing companies with different processes into one streamlined operation. For example: Triara has three entrances to the call center—the Hewlett-Packard call center managing hardware issues, the Telmex call center managing calls for the other processes and different software, and the Triara self-care call center. Each call center uses different processes and different software. All three need to be integrated and results/troubles communicated throughout Triara. The customer will call whichever number is easier. The only way to convince the customer to use a particular process, is to make it the easiest with the best quality. This means creating processes that are user helpful so the customers find the right solutions, in the right place, within their patience parameters. Only then will customers continue to use the processes requested by the service provider.

Triara is still working through integration issues—an ongoing process as technology and infrastructure change. In the meantime, situations are continually monitored to adjust processes as needs arise.

7.2.10 Last Words

To date, Triara has accomplished a lot with little outside help. This company went from concept to production in just over six months. In this short time, it had to build a data center, hire and train personnel, define initial offerings, get computer systems in-house, and generally get production ready. Personnel built processes and operations that are leverageable to satisfy both short- and long-term needs. Triara was able to find ways to get online tactically, without losing direction and focus on long-term strategic goals.

7.3 Endnote

1. Content for this case study was provided by Guillermo Güémez, general manager of Triara.

PART 3

The Readiness Primer

CHAPTER 8

Introduction to the Readiness Primer

Part 3 concentrates on the details behind the seven operational challenges faced by service providers as they work through the highly dynamic Internet services industry. Each chapter in Part 3 ends with a checklist, allowing service provider management to review their progress as they develop their infrastructure, programs, and processes. Each service provider experience is a little different, so the lists may not address everything that may occur in each case. These chapters should be used as a way to orient the service provider and introduce general concepts that make up a part of each operational challenge. We try to give guidance on how to identify and work through the issues. Examples and case studies are included to show more real world examples of how other service providers are identifying and coping with similar topics.

8.1 The Seven Operational Challenges

As a result of interviewing service providers, I've identified many operational issues that loosely fall under seven categories. They are:

- Organization/Operations
- Partners/Alliances
- Sales/Marketing
- Service Delivery
- Customer care
- Billing
- Architecture/Technical infrastructure

These challenges are similar to what we would expect to see in any company or industry; but, as one of my clients pointed out, it's how the company meets these challenges that "separates the men from the boys." Responding to these challenges needs to be well thought out and efficiently executed. The results need to meet market needs, while staying within the financial parameters required by company management. It is a delicate balance, but a balance that every company faces and is not unique to the Internet. The bottom line is, don't forget the fundamentals of good business. Take the time to understand the market needs, to test offerings and messaging with the market. Make the organization customer focused so the customer has an excellent experience buying and using the services. Offer the best service possible within financial parameters. Try not to give services away unless it can be leveraged to higher margin services in the near future.

The above needs to be balanced with time to market. Don't avoid entering the market because not every *i* is dotted or *t* crossed. Sometimes the service provider needs to get to market when only 80 percent of the service or process is defined. There are ways to mitigate the risk in these cases, for example, go to market with a limited offering including only those functionalities and processes already defined while planning a version 2 release six months down the road. Another idea is to offer an alpha launch when details can be completed before the beta or production phases. Risk sharing or partnering with another company that has the operational experience and infrastructure in place could be yet another way to mitigate the risk and get to market fast.

Think of ways to manage the company's destiny and luck in the market. Be tuned in with market trends and the competitors. Develop the ability to read your chosen customer segments and competitors. As in the game of chess, develop strategies that allow flexibility in light of fickle customers and fast-moving market trends.

Promote a culture of continued quality within the company. Just because a service has been launched, or the company has opened its doors for business, does not mean that everything is running smoothly. Create internal measurements and reviews on an ongoing basis to challenge efficiency and quality standards.

In the final analysis, there is one thing that is difficult to change: that of market perception. Perception is reality and if the market has a good perception, it can be forgiving. Service providers should try to manage the issue of perception as much as possible. Time is the only commodity that cannot be replaced. Don't waste it. Be decisive. Work together as a team to focus on a planned goal and efficiently execute toward the goal. The most important things in the game are keeping customers loyal, increasing market share, maintaining high margin revenue, and decreasing operational costs. The following pages give service providers some tools for reaching these goals.

CHAPTER 9

Partners and Alliances

At some level partners and alliances are used by every service provider as a way to expand market share while decreasing operational costs. Strategic alliances and partnerships are built when a service provider faces strategic gaps in a critical capability that is too expensive, and/or will take too long to develop internally. The business owners, themselves, might be partners, like KPNQwest, where partners KPN and Qwest each own part of the business. Partnerships and alliances might be set up to jointly produce a unique product, or service, like a complex application hosting service. Outsourcing is a form of partnership service providers use when developing in-house resources is too expensive. Sales and marketing partnerships (selling to and selling with) are common ways to reach into new markets, or expand present markets, faster and less expensively.

9.1 Partner Strategy

For any kind of partnership or alliance there needs to be a strategy, preferably a formal, written one. The partner strategy should support the business goals of the company, and be used as a way to fill gaps relating to all of the operational challenges discussed in this book: financial, sales, marketing, operational, and so on. The partner strategy execution can be simplified into six steps (see Figure 9-1).

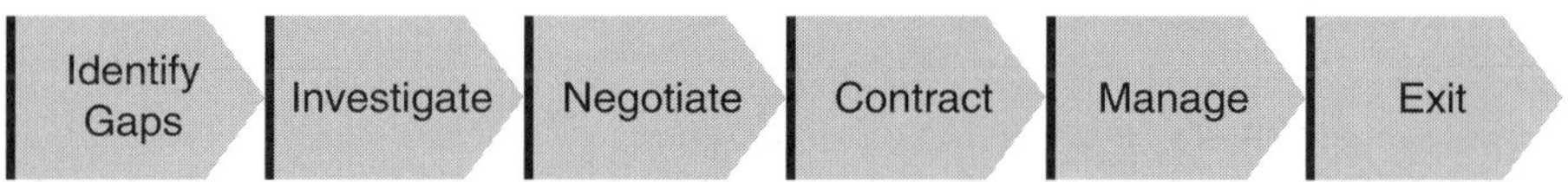

Figure 9-1 The six steps of partner strategy execution.

9.2 Identify Gaps

The first step toward executing a partner strategy is to understand the strengths and weaknesses a service provider has when trying to reach its business goals and objectives. (It is assumed that when the service provider gets to this point, it has at least the beginnings of a working business plan in place). This might be the result of a SWOT analysis (strengths, weaknesses, opportunities, and threats). As the weaknesses and threats are identified, the service provider can start formulating how to fill the gaps in its strategy execution. Once gaps are identified, the service provider needs to identify those corporate profiles that can fill the gaps. Profile characteristics might match those of the competitor(s), something seen more and more often in the industry. "Coopetition" is the term commonly used when competitors ally in working toward a common goal. Examples of this might be virtual warehousing in the airline industry, a concept where competitors pool inventory resources for expensive or hard-to-find parts. The result is more revenue-producing planes in the air.

9.3 Investigate

When the corporate profiles are identified, the next step would be due diligence, seeing not only how well the corporations fit the required profiles, but understanding how they will explicitly be mapped to avoid partner conflict. Typical profiles include tangible and intangible characteristics the service provider needs. Since no partner will have all the characteristics identified, the service provider needs to decide which characteristics are must haves and which are nice to haves.

Here is a sample profile:

- The best in the market for the required technology, market share, brand, and so forth—whatever the service provider has identified as the gap
- Financial stability—will the company be around in the future
- Meets service provider's financial profile (financially stable)
- Invests *X* percent every year in research and development
- Common business goals
- Common business cultures
- Excellent reputation and brand awareness
- Industry knowledge
- Top management expertise
- Sales force experience and reach
- Marketing expertise and budget
- Products are supported at similar levels in similar geographies
- Investment is available for the joint project and the investment levels are similar
- Regulatory and share holder restrictions are similar to both partners

There are many sources to find companies that fit the profile (see Appendix H: Helpful Organizations). The best places are trade shows, word of mouth, trade magazines, venture capital firms, and trade associations. Once the due diligence is complete, it's time to start negotiating.

9.4 Negotiate

Theses are written about the art of negotiation. This section gives high-level suggestions that have helped in the negotiation process, based on personal experience. There should be an understanding of the strengths and weaknesses of any potential partner, as well as of one's own company, as a part of building a negotiation strategy. The service provider negotiation team should understand exactly what its position is before going into the negotiation meetings. It should also understand what is important to the other party, what its counterproposals may be, and what the service provider's walk-away point is. Understanding the potential partner's organizational structure and culture is key. Who is empowered to make decisions? How plugged in is the legal department? Are there partners, such as in a consulting firm, who need to sign off? Negotiating with a Microsoft is different from negotiating with a Hewlett-Packard because the two companies have different cultures and different organizations. An executive level manager might be needed in one company, where a middle manager might be able to make decisions in another. Legal review may occur several times during the process in one company, whereas another company may have one short review at the very end. It is important to understand the opposing negotiation team. Try to build rapport and understand the personal requirements of team counterparts—how can the results help them achieve their goals?

Table 9-1 helps in focusing the negotiation team as it creates its strategy.

Table 9-1 Negotiation Strategy Worksheet.

Overall Goal			
Issue #1	Our position	Their position	Walk away

Try to negotiate in terms of common goals—working against a "common enemy." Try to negotiate from a position of strength; identify gaps in the potential partner's strategy. What does the service provider have that the partner may need to be successful? For example, a service provider needs a partner as a sales and support channel to the small business market. The identified potential partner may be looking for ways to offer new products to its small business customer base as a way to keep it from going to a competitor. Each negotiation seems to have its own speed. Before starting, try to get agreement internally and with the opponent regarding the speed and process for getting approvals/buy-in during the negotiation process. This partnership may be a win-win for both sides, something that should be the goal of any negotiated outcome. It is a good idea to communicate with corporate stakeholders so they also know the status of the negotiations.

9.5 Contract

As the negotiations take place, there will be much discussion about contract terms and conditions. Be as specific as possible in the contract terms. Are there goals, like sales and marketing targets? If so, both the goals and the measurements should be detailed in the contract. Is there investment? How much and when/where will it be paid? Add clauses about what happens if the partnership or alliance dissolves. Put owners and deadlines on the items to be executed as a part of the contract. Sometimes this is easier to do by way of an appendix. Find a good lawyer; advice during negotiation and contractual phases is essential. Getting good advice from an attorney now may save a lot of trouble later on. Try for multiyear contracts that allow periodic renegotiation of key sections. This saves time and frustration in situations where sales/marketing or investment goals will change during the period of the agreement.

9.6 Manage

After the contract is signed, and the celebration is over, is the time when ongoing alliance management begins and the contract terms are executed. There may be someone working full time with an alliance partner, there might be a team of people working an alliance partner, or one person who has several alliance partners to manage. Whatever the situation, there needs to be one single point of contact where the partner can go for help and communication is key. As with many things in life, the better the personal rapport among the channel teams, the better the alliance will work.

As a function of contract execution, both parties should create some sort of plan with more detail about what needs to be done, when, and who owns the action. This is called a channel management plan.

9.6.1 Channel Management Plan

A typical channel management plan would include:

- Common goal and time frame to obtain the goal
- Main contact name and information from each company
- Joint sales plan including joint funnel
- Joint marketing plan
- Joint development plan
- Investment calendar
- Schedule review timetable

Each section should have a time frame and owner, as well as how success is measured. To avoid channel conflict the channel must be focused as much as possible with specific goals. Both parties need to define the escalation policy in cases where conflict occurs. Reality tells us that both parties must be flexible enough to work out unexpected changes to the plans, and must agree on what happens if the association goes sour.

9.6.2 Channel Conflict

Just about every channel or partner relationship goes through conflict at some time. Most important is understanding how the service provider will work through the situation when it arises. Common sense says each situation is different and resolution depends on the details. Here are some guidelines:

- Determine the root cause of the disagreement. It might not be obvious what the problem is.
- How important is the partner in the service provider's overall goals? It could be the service provider is now moving directly into a space that was handled through their partner and maybe it's time to initiate the partner exit strategy.
- Buy time. It's tempting to try to solve everything right at the moment, but try to buy time to understand the entire scenario. This might not be apparent during the initial call.
- Decide how this situation can be rectified so it doesn't happen again with this, or other, partners.
- Before a conflict happens, map the partners to the operation (see Figure 9-2) and share the map with them so they understand how they fit into the total scenario.
- Communicate as much as possible to avoid misperceptions.

9.7 Exit

Like a marriage, there are times when partnerships or alliances need to end. Rarely is it totally one party's fault. Normally there are contributing factors: maybe the common need of both companies changes, the underlying technology goes through a shift, or the required investment is no longer available. The most important thing to remember during this phase is trying not to burn

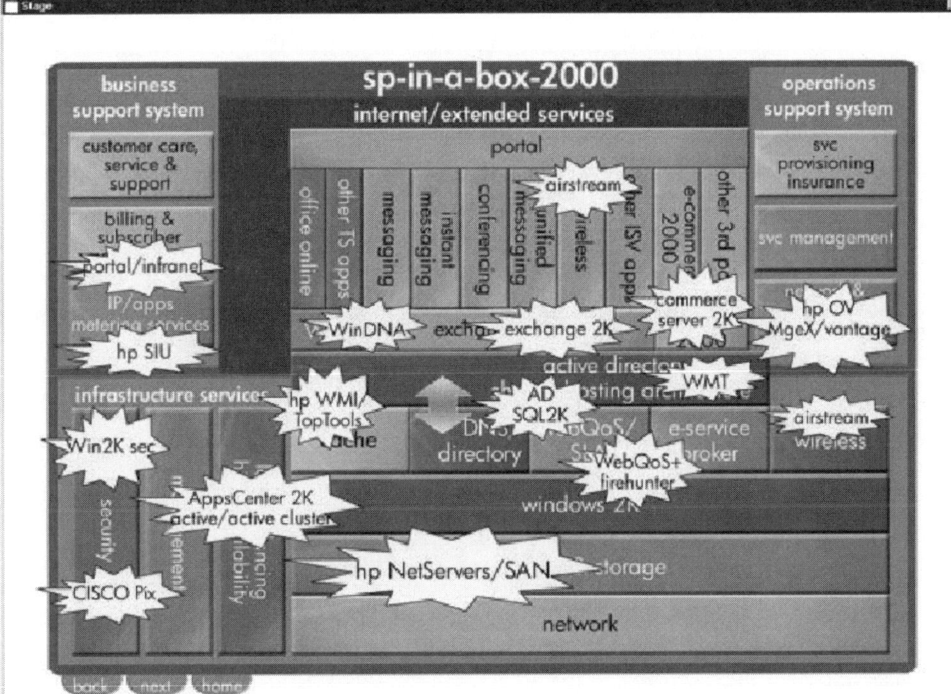

Figure 9-2 Example of partner mapping for a product.

Published courtesy of Hewlett-Packard Company.

the bridge. The company that can no longer fill today's gap, may fill tomorrow's. People from today's partnership may join tomorrow's. The service provider space may seem large, but the same people, if they're good, keep reappearing.

9.8 Case Studies

Partnerships are inherent to a successful service provider. This section contains three examples of partnering: Jamcracker, Inc., Avaya, and HP's Partners on Tap. Jamcracker is an example of a unique Value-Web model, Avaya shows partnering from the point of view of a vendor selling to/through/with service providers, and HP is an example of how vendor programs can extend the normal sales channels in unique ways.

9.8.1 Jamcracker, Inc.[1]

9.8.1.1 Background

Jamcracker, Inc. was incorporated in July 1999 and brought forth a new model for partnering and offering services in the market.

Jamcracker provides customers with unique Web-based IT applications, services and, support—all from a single Web-based workspace on the Internet. It selects, tests, aggregates, and integrates Web-based IT and business services, applications, and tools from best-of-breed ASPs and other service providers. Jamcracker delivers services via the Internet and enables users to easily access them through a single, secure workspace. Customers login once and gain access to a growing menu of services, including human resources, sales force automation, expense management, email, remote access, 24/7 IT support, and more.

To be a leader in the Web-based services market requires a commitment from both the service provider and its partners. Jamcracker is focused on ASP, technology and channel partners who can help deliver the total solution that customers demand. In turn, Jamcracker will provide a unique level of commitment to its partners, ensuring they have the training, support, and superior business opportunities they need to succeed. This way a true win-win relationship is created among Jamcracker, its partners and their mutual customers.

9.8.1.2 Jamcracker Business Development Team

The Jamcracker business development team has two distinct yet highly related and leverageable areas of responsibility:

- ASP and technology partner recruitment and management
- Channel/go-to-market partner recruitment and management

Technology partners play the same role as traditional component and tool suppliers to a manufacturer. Their key technology components are used to build the Jamcracker cosourcing platform. The end-users may not necessarily know or have visibility into these technology components as long as they know that Jamcracker does its due diligence in selecting and certifying these technology partners.

The role of ASP and technology partners are similar, differing only in that customers may select from a list of partner applications in each service category. Jamcracker does not hide the brand of ASP partners since it is proud of selecting and certifying only what management considers to be best-in-class partners.

Channel partners help extend Jamcracker's geographic, or segment, coverage. They can introduce Jamcracker into existing accounts, or take Jamcracker into new and untapped market segments and territories.

In the Closing the Loop section, it becomes clear how Jamcracker strives to make the most of each partnership. This is achieved by leveraging the multidimensional nature of each partnership, and by creating an alliance advantage that benefits the entire ecosystem of Jamcracker partners and customers.

9.8.1.3 Jamcracker ASP and Technology Partner Program

Jamcracker selects, tests, aggregates, and integrates Web-based IT and business services, applications, and tools from best-of-breed service provider partners. By delivering its partners' services via the Internet, Jamcracker enables its users easy access through a single, secure workspace called Jamcracker enterprise. Customers login once and gain access to a growing menu of services, including HR, sales force automation (SFA), CRM, professional services automation (PSA), travel and expense management (T&E), email, e-procurement, remote access, and 24/7 live IT support. In addition, Jamcracker selects and integrates best-of-breed technologies from partner companies to build out its core workspace and cosourcing platform.

Partners see the following benefits from the Jamcracker Partner Program:

Increased business volume Jamcracker provides effective and integrated all-channels go-to-market mechanism for partners to quickly acquire new customers. This includes the sales efforts of Jamcracker's direct sales force and its growing network of channel and referral partners.

Shortened sales cycle and lower selling costs Since ASP partner services are pretested and incorporated into the Jamcracker platform, customers can reduce the time spent selecting and purchasing services. Everyone benefits from a shorter sales cycle—less time translates into lower cost.

Improved, cost-effective support model Partners benefit from Jamcracker's proactive support model—preventing problems before they occur. Jamcracker is the first line of support to end-users. This model reduces the support that partners provide and enables partners to leverage an infrastructure shared by Jamcracker's many partners.

Simplified, consolidated billing and collection Jamcracker simplifies billing and payment collection for xSP partners. It manages billing and collection with customers and provides each partner with a single, consolidated periodic payment.

Rich integration through Jamcracker platform Jamcracker's technologically advanced platform allows for single point applications to achieve data integration and participate in integrated business processes through XML-based integration.

Membership in an advanced partnership ecosystem Partners enjoy membership in an advanced and exclusive community of best-of-breed technology and service providers. Members realize a wide variety of benefits, including opportunities to take part in valuable business collaborations. In addition, Jamcracker actively participates in advancing the market and technology in the xSP space. Avenues of participation include authoring, speaking at conferences and participating on key standards-making organizations, such as the ASP industry consortium (ASP-IC) and Internet Business Services Initiative (IBSI). By joining the Jamcracker partner ecosystem, partners will gain access to the efforts and activities delivered through Jamcracker's participation.

Comarketing Partners can participate in Jamcracker's comarketing activities, enabling them to extend their market reach and image.

9.8.1.4 Innovator Program

Jamcracker's branded program for ASP and technology partners is called an innovator program. Jamcracker segments innovator partners into three main solution areas: business services, collaboration and communication services, and core IT services.

Jamcracker business services help improve the effectiveness of functional areas or departments within companies. Using the service, line of business (LOB) managers and their IT counterparts can work together to choose LOB-specific service solutions that integrate seamlessly with core IT functions. Jamcracker continues to develop partnerships with both pure-play or single application ASPs, as well as partner with ASPs that offer a complete suite of preintegrated business application services.

Jamcracker's collaboration and communication services provide companies with best-of-breed Web-based applications, services, and tools that can be used by their entire workforce. LOB managers and their IT counterparts can choose from these more pervasive services that improve personal productivity, collaboration, and connectivity. IT professionals will benefit from network and desktop management tools.

Core services are the foundation for the high performance, security, integration, reliability, and intelligence of the Jamcracker solution. IT professionals and end-users in companies will benefit from Jamcracker's core IT services immediately. Jamcracker core IT services are deployed in days, not months. As with all Jamcracker services, the core IT services are available 24/7 via Jamcracker enterprise, email, live chat, or phone.

Jamcracker has achieved great success in partnering to create virtual businesses that provide the complete solutions that target customers require. Jamcracker strongly believes that successful partnerships are built similarly to new businesses. The impetus for a viable partnership includes a market opportunity, a joint product or service which matches that opportunity, and a strategy to market, sell, and service the joint offering. The Jamcracker ASP and technology partner program is built on this model and includes programs and activities centered around three key business components: technology, marketing, and sales.

In any new business, the investors must decide what level of investment is appropriate, and the Jamcracker ASP partner program is no different. This program includes three different levels of investment within each partner category: partner, premier partner, and strategic partner. Partners can determine what level of investment, and corresponding partnership level, is appropriate for them.

9.8.1.5 Jamcracker Channel Partner Program

The Jamcracker channel partner program focuses on partnerships that complement Jamcracker go-to-market plans. There are three main categories: explorers, integrators, and syndication.

Explorer partners comprise a networking community that understands the Jamcracker value proposition and wants to be involved in the Jamcracker ecosystem. Explorer partners, who identify and refer qualified opportunities, receive a percentage of the monthly recurring revenue for one year once a deal is closed and implemented. Explorer partners enjoy the benefits of training and education, learning about Jamcracker and the ASP market. They receive internal and external visibility through press releases and document releases on their offerings. They are invited to participate in Jamcracker events and activities that introduce new prospects and partners to the Jamcracker ecosystem.

Integrator partners provide an extension to Jamcracker consulting and professional services. They bring to the table a set of deep consulting and implementation skills offering customization and integration of customers existing environment into the Jamcracker IT and business solutions. Integrator partners are invited to join the explorer program to ensure maximizing their involvement and gaining even more benefits from the Jamcracker ecosystem.

Syndication partners extend Jamcracker's market reach into a specific segment of the market, such as a vertical industry. These are areas that Jamcracker is not directly focusing on and does not intend to invest direct time and resources to penetrate. These partners bring domain expertise and may decide to mass customize the Jamcracker solution to fit the needs of their particular segment.

The benefits of the Jamcracker channel partner program are:

- Earning substantial revenues for each Jamcracker sale
- Expanding service offerings and entering the fast-growing ASP market
- Leveraging the Jamcracker solution to increase sales of partner value-added services
- Gaining access to a broad community of Jamcracker partners
- Using best-of-breed tools to enable channel communication, sales, and opportunity flow
- Participating in comarketing efforts to drive additional business opportunities

- Dedicated account managers supporting partner sales, implementation, and on-going needs
- Receiving the Jamcracker suite of services at a reduced cost

9.8.1.6 Other Partner-Related Programs

Channel Advisory Board Jamcracker established the Channel Advisory Board in June 2000 to make suggestions about how to structure partnership contracts and compensation models and to help the company evolve its channel strategy to best serve its partners and customers. The board is made up of top executives from selected companies in Jamcracker's channel partner community. The Jamcracker partner programs are unique in that they were built for the channel, by the channel.

The Jamcracker advisory board meets every quarter and communicates regularly with Jamcracker executives and channel partners. Jamcracker executives and the business development team select the board members.

Jamcracker ASP/Technology Partner Advisory Board It has become increasingly important to Jamcracker to communicate and exchange feedback with its partners, to understand how well Jamcracker is meeting its partners' needs and to plan for the future.

Jamcracker has created the Innovator Partner Advisory Board as a forum for its strategic innovator partners to meet with the Jamcracker team and focus on how they can raise the partnership to an even higher level. The board will provide partners the opportunity to meet with key Jamcracker decision makers from support, operations, marketing, and engineering organizations and provide input and exchange ideas on how Jamcracker, in conjunction with the innovator community, can exceed customer expectations.

The ASP/Technology Partner Advisory Board is an invitation-only group with members from the Jamcracker innovator partners. It meets quarterly. Jamcracker chairs the board and encourages direct feedback to impact future service delivery roadmaps and partner marketing programs.

Industry Consortium Participation Jamcracker is active in industry consortia focused on the ASP market and key technology innovations. It is currently active in the following organizations:

- ASP Industry Consortium as an executive member and director on the best practices committee
- Internet Business Services Initiative sponsor member
- UDDI adviser
- S2ML coauthor
- W3C
- Oasis as a sponsor member and active in many working groups
- BPMI.org

Through becoming an innovator partner, Jamcracker invites each partner to participate on key consortium-driven initiatives such as defining specifications and best practices. Jamcracker also will introduce partners to influential working groups, and individuals, to learn more about technology and marketing efforts.

Strategic Technology Partners Jamcracker extends its innovator partner program to encompass strategic technology partners as well as ASP partners. Strategic technology partners are those whose technology is used to build out Jamcracker's workspace and platform.

Jamcracker looks for the following attributes when selecting its strategic technology partners:

- Best-of-breed technology in a particular space
- Technology based on Java/J2EE and XML standards
- A modular and extensible architecture for seamless integration
- Open and documented APIs with an SDK for ease of integration
- Highly scalable architecture
- Reliability built into architecture
- Manageability encompassed in architecture with support for SNMP and JMX
- Technology designed, coded, and tested for high security
- Licensing model that allows for rapid customer growth and scalability
- Willingness to allow for channel support via reselling and OEM of technology
- Corporate executives committed to current and future innovation of such technology
- Strong corporate financials for continued market leadership

Jamcracker expects its strategic technology partners to provide:

- Proof of concept prior to licensing and implementation to ensure fit with Jamcracker workspace and platform architecture
- Joint engineering and willingness to incorporate Jamcracker feedback into current and future releases
- 24/7 business critical support
- Developer support and on-site professional assistance available in a timely manner
- Direct feedback between Jamcracker and technology partner product management team on future product/technology requirements
- Joint marketing and awareness building of strength of Jamcracker's solution and partner's technology
- An agreement to engage in channel development activities, including sign on as explorer partner if sales organization is in place to support

In return, the strategic technology partners receive:

- Direct access to Jamcracker engineering resources and product management resources to provide feedback and technology IP to early releases, betas, and product development roadmaps
- Direct access to Jamcracker ASP partners to get feedback on technology development and product features/functions
- Access to Jamcracker ASP partners for potential technology adoption by an ASP
- Access to Jamcracker customer base via channel partnership
- Access to Jamcracker personnel working on industry consortia and standards efforts
- Joint marketing and awareness building through cooperative marketing communications efforts

Strategic technology partners are included in Jamcracker's innovator partner program, and, as such, can take advantage of marketing, technical, and business development resources available to them.

9.8.1.7 Partnering Recruitment Process

The Jamcracker organization is committed to developing successful partnerships (see Figures 9-3 and 9-4). To begin the process, Jamcracker determines which product categories represent strong additions to its platform. To be considered, partners must prove their products command a strong customer demand, and a product consistent with the Jamcracker value proposition. Based on the initial market assessment, a short list is made up of partner companies fitting desired product categories. Jamcracker contacts each company on the short list and engages in discussions to determine business fit.

For those companies with a strong business fit, Jamcracker proceeds on to functional reviews. In this step, Jamcracker works with the company to assess how a potential partnership might work from an operational perspective. Product customer support, integration, sales processes, and competitive positioning are discussed in detail.

Upon successful completion of the functional reviews, Jamcracker and the company work on the terms and conditions of partnership. After reaching agreement, Jamcracker and the new partner work together to integrate the offering into the Jamcracker platform. Provisions for single sign-on access, unified billing, customer support, and intercompany communications are carefully executed at this time.

The new offering is then launched, with appropriate marketing and sales support. Although the product is now officially available, the partnership efforts are by no means complete. Jamcracker and the partner continue to work closely together to ensure success by promoting, selling, and enhancing the service partnership.

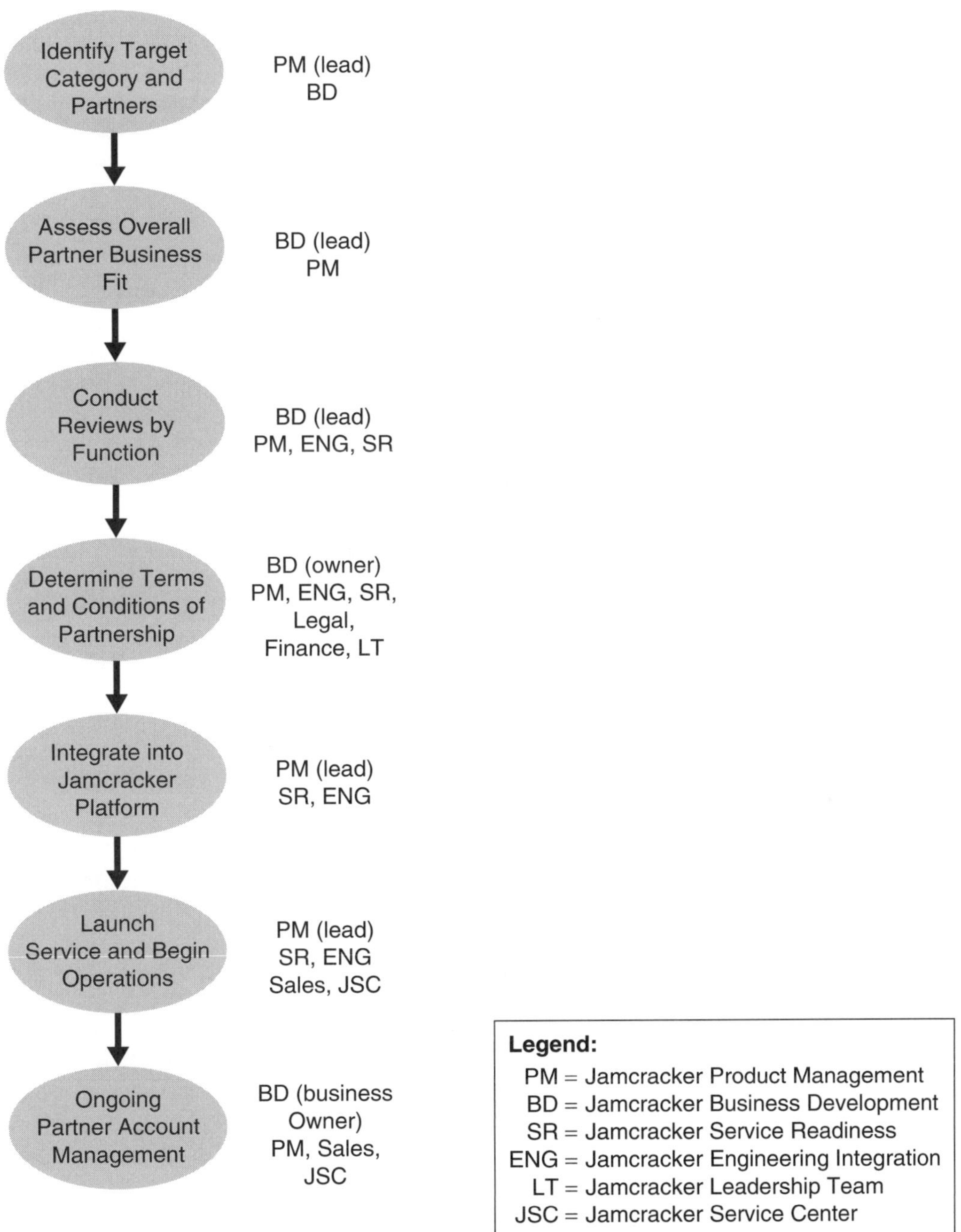

Figure 9-3 Jamcracker, Inc. Process flow of ASP and technology partner recruitment.
Reprinted courtesy of Feyzi Fatehi, JamCracker, Inc.

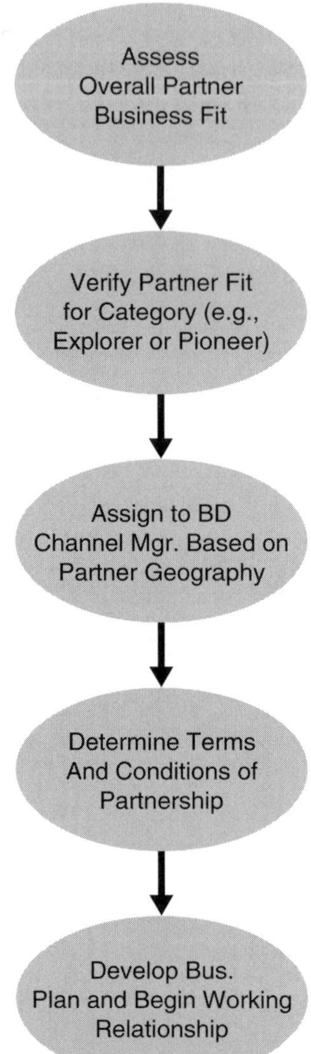

Figure 9-4 Jamcracker, Inc. partner recruitment process Flow.
Reprinted courtesy of Feyzi Fatehi, JamCracker, Inc.

9.8.1.8 Closing the Loop

Jamcracker looks at each of its partnerships from a multidimensional perspective. It tries to maximize the alliance advantage generated as a result of each partnership, and extend it to offer benefits to the entire Jamcracker ecosystems, its partners, and customers.

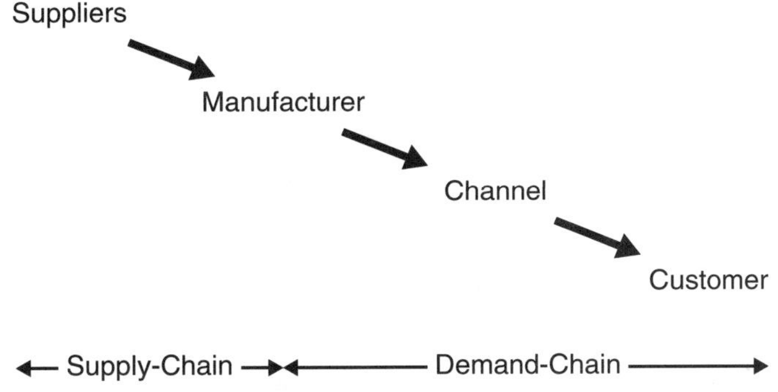

Figure 9-5 The traditional value chain.
Reprinted courtesy of Feyzi Fatehi, Jamcracker, Inc.

For example, in the traditional manufacturer-centric value-chain model, each participant had a well-defined and delineated role in a sequential chain that created an ultimate, and hopefully unique, value proposition for the customer (see Figure 9-5).

Each node in this model was one-directional and one-dimensional, based on pervasive supply and demand-chains. In the xSP space, this traditionally serial/consequential model is shifting to a new and emerging value Web as seen in Jamcracker's strategy.

In the Value-Web model (see Figure 9-6) created by Feyzi Fatehi, participants' roles and relationships move away from a sequential and one-dimensional structure toward a parallel, real-time, and multidimensional paradigm. The resulting ecosystem of partners increases the effectiveness and efficiencies of a real-time, virtual enterprise in an exponential fashion.

An ASP that is a supplier as defined in the traditional model, becomes a customer as well as a channel in Jamcracker's offerings. Additionally, by being a member of Jamcracker's ecosystem, the supplier benefits from latent and existing dynamics (supplies and demands) created by the entire membership community. The same is true for Jamcracker technology providers and channel partners.

9.8.2 Avaya Communication[2]

9.8.2.1 Background

Avaya was founded October 1, 2000, as a spin off from Lucent Technologies and has offices in more than 90 countries. Its headquarters are in Basking Ridge, New Jersey. It is one of the leading providers of communications systems and software for service providers. It offers voice solutions, converged voice and data solutions, customer relationship management solutions, messaging solutions, multiservice networking, and structured cabling products and services. Avaya supports its customers with comprehensive global service offerings, including remote diagnostics testing of Avaya advanced systems, product installation, on-site repair, and maintenance. Its global service organization is a competitive advantage for Avaya and a source of sig-

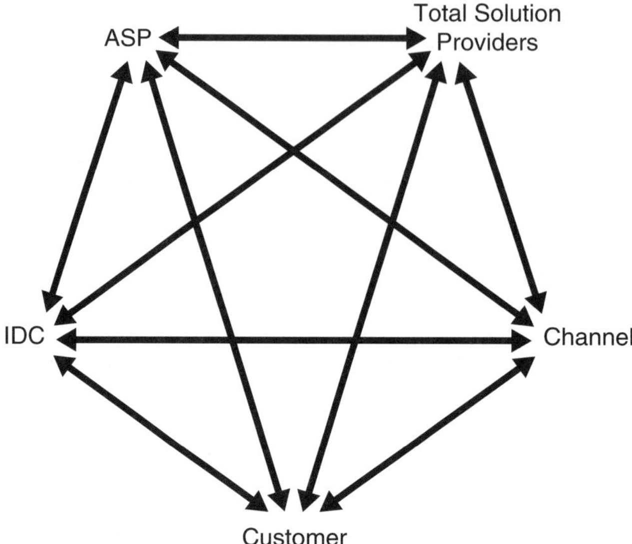

Figure 9-6 The emerging value Web.
Reprinted courtesy of Feyzi Fatehi, Jamcracker, Inc.

nificant revenue, especially from maintenance contracts. Avaya also offers professional services for customer and enterprise relationship management and value-added services for outsourced messaging and other portions of a company's communications system.

Avaya intends to use its leadership position in communications systems and software products, broad portfolio of products and services, and strategic alliances with other technology partners and service providers to offer customers comprehensive e-business communication solutions. e-business is the internal and external use of communications tools and electronic networks to interact, collaborate, and transact business with customers, suppliers, partners, and employees.

Avaya sells to, through, and with service providers. Its solutions are bundles of hardware, software, and CPE integrated to offer service providers a rapidly deployable infrastructure to build up their service offerings. It also offers attractive business models for service providers, including vendor financing and ASP renting models for software. For example, an ASP can rent the Unified Messenger product and pay Avaya per user per month. They use service providers like British Telecom to gain greater market share in target markets. Avaya sells its hosted Unified Messager product to service providers, and encourages the provider to be a reseller and to build services around this product as a way to increase the service providers revenue margins. Avaya goes further to partner with third-party vendors to offer similar options with the service provider for the hardware contained in the bundle.

9.8.3 Organizational Partners

Avaya keeps all functions in-house except for facilities management and payroll. Facilities management includes managing the office space, CPE, and cleaning crews. These functions are outsourced because they are not Avaya core competencies.

Partners are relatively easy to manage because the facilities management has an office in the same building and the Avaya payroll is done electronically. In the U.K., expenses are outsourced to a company called Ossys. The Ossys application allows automated means of claiming expenses. Avaya employees in the U.K. receive an Ossys e-net number. Once the Microsoft Excel spreadsheet-based expense forms are filled out, the employee dials a toll-free number and inputs special e-net numbers plus a security number. The system then prompts the employee for all the subtotals for each of the numbered boxes on the spreadsheet. The system adds up all the figures that must be exactly the same as the totals on the spreadsheet. If everything matches, the system issues an audit number that has to be recorded on the form. Then the employee sends the form to his/her manager who dials into the same e-net system, but with higher privileges so the system will prompt him/her to authorize the claim. The manager then inputs the audit number and, hopefully, authorizes the claim. Funds will be credited to the employee's account in three working days. The e-net system has an interface that is integrated with Avaya's bank account. The signed hardcopy paperwork is sent through normal expense claim department channels that can take up to two to three weeks to process. Partners are measured on task completion times, accuracy, and their ability to keep expenses within the budget.

9.8.4 Core Product: Production Channel Partners

Avaya has several products that have third-party products included, like unified messenger where Microsoft Exchange Server plays an integral part. Some development of these products is done together with Microsoft. Microsoft products were chosen as a result of the due diligence process on the part of members of the alliances team.

Avaya continues to develop processes for partner management and much of the partner management is initially done informally. When business is realized out of the partnership, Avaya and the partner enter into a more formal arrangement. A sales team is responsible for alliances and partnerships called the global system integrators (GSI). Most partners are vendors, but a portion of this team focuses on service providers who are Avaya partners. The partners are tiered, based on business potential. Those partners with the greatest business potential will be assigned more Avaya resources. For those partners in the top tier, joint marketing programs are available. These programs include joint sales calls, funnel sharing, presenting jointly at events, best practice sharing, and joint customer presentations. Partners are measured on the number of leads a week.

9.8.5 Sales Channel Partners

Avaya has GSI like HP, IBM, Accenture, and KPMG that make up their top tier of partners. These partners are managed by a global team, also called GSI, that coordinates local teams worldwide. Partners are not particularly mapped to a single vertical market or region, but, as a lead occurs, Avaya reviews its partner list to see which partner would be the best fit with each lead. These top tier relationships are also those that have joint investment and joint development work.

More important for those interested in using partners as sales channels is to "walk the walk." Each side of the partnering arrangement must see that it is getting something positive back. Avaya has partners with formal agreements but the relationship has yet to produce any revenue for either side. It also has relationships with no formal agreement in place that are producing half a million dollars of revenue based on initial lead swapping. This trend is what led Avaya to its policy of not getting into formal relationships until there is proof of joint revenues.

Good personal relationships are key to any solid partnership. People buy from people. When the personal relationship works, the professional relationship will develop and the business will grow. The examples prove the point. In the first instance, no personal relationship is developed at the field level—the relationship came about because of the partner's position in the market. The second example was built on a good personal relationship at the field level.

9.8.6 Channel Management

When Avaya wants to build—and manage—business, it first tries to understand the partner's business model. Do the business models fit together? Are both partners after the same markets and customers? Avaya management then decides to build the business one step at a time—trying to find short-term, obtainable goals to use as building blocks to the next steps. Too much activity will destroy the focus of the relationship and demolish more than it builds.

Avaya tries to create shared, measurable goals—timelines, revenue goals, and marketing activities—with its partners, even if on an informal basis. For example, they may decide with a partner to capture x percent of market share by the end of Avaya's fiscal year. In Avaya's case with Microsoft, they are jointly selling Exchange Server and Unified Messenger in a hosted environment. The benefit for Avaya is that it has access to Microsoft's service provider channel and customers, offering additional value to Avaya's customers.

Partnerships are reviewed informally on a frequent basis. Avaya uses customer appointments, trade shows, or other events for this. Any function, in other words, to give the sales people a chance to talk to each other. Tier 1 partners also have formal reviews, but these are more for strategic purposes than for plan execution.

Avaya doesn't have any formal exit strategies with its partners, believing that frank, open communication is most important. If the partnership does not work out, it is dissolved. The dissolution of joint investments and copyrights are carried out based on agreements reached when the partnership was formalized.

9.8.7 Hewlett-Packard: Channels on Tap[3]

9.8.7.1 What is it?

Channels on Tap, a new business model for HP, was announced in April 2000. HP acts as a virtual distributor for hosted solutions that service providers want to take to market via a channel. HP will offer those that are eligible to participate access to the HP brand and channel as a sales vehicle and help them navigate the new e-world.

First, HP does solid background due diligence on potential entrants to the program. Only those companies HP is convinced will weather the ups and downs of the Internet world will be invited to become a member of the select community.

Second, HP has created an infrastructure that will support creating and maintaining relationships between the service provider and prospective sales channels.

Third, HP includes its channel partners that understand the HP products and can help act as a go-to-market conduit for service provider services.

The program is made up of two key service types: AgentDepot and AsktheDepot. AgentDepot provides services and information about the service provider to prospective channels selling the hosted solutions. In addition, AgentDepot offers the following added value to its membership of service providers and agents:

- Order processing
- Customer invoicing
- Collections
- Channel recruitment and management
- Channel authorization and training

HP, through AgentDepot, acts as a settlement engine. Channels receive payments from HP, not from the service provider, reducing risk on both sides. Channel leads are distributed, via AgentDepot, to the agents according to authorized solution sets. There is also a mix-and-match function that enables service providers and partners to search and find needed components to provide full solutions to end-users.

AsktheDepot is end-customer focused. Services available to customers include:

- Research center
- Solution mapping
- Member community
- Fulfillment options
- Personalized accounts

This element is designed to allow customers to define their current business problem online and receive potential solution suggestions. Customers also can request a trained agent for help in facilitating their final decision. HP is targeting primarily mid-market customers defined as those firms with $250 million to $500 million in yearly revenue, or a payroll of up to 1,000 employees. In addition, HP will create an environment to foster communities of interest for end-customers, enabling linkages to service providers and other customers, as a means of sharing experiences.

9.8.8 Screening

HP screens prospective service provider community members, looking for companies that are financially viable, that might already have an association with HP, that have exciting or unique value propositions, and that operate in areas that will round out the overall HP portfolio. Financially, HP prefers service providers that have achieved round 2 financing and have at least six months of cash on their books. Following this, HP reviews the service provider's SLAs and customer satisfaction record. Only those with the best customer satisfaction history will be eligible for membership.

Authorization is required for agents to sell service provider services. This authorization comes directly from the service provider. HP will track channel training progress and manage it on behalf of the service provider, but the service provider is responsible for any content and authorization requirements.

9.8.9 Why Are Channels Interested?

Channels on Tap enables an agent, or channel partner, to extend the portfolio of solutions they're able to offer to their customers. In addition, channels are paid for their sales efforts. Using HP as the clearinghouse reduces the risk to channels for receiving their payments. HP and the channel get a percentage of every subscription fee paid by an end-customer. These payments are annuity based and dependent on the customer billing cycle, but normally are paid monthly. Typically the subscription period is from one to three years assuring all parties some sort of basic revenue for the period.

9.9 Summary

Partnering and alliances are important in any business, but especially so for service providers. Partnering is a way to quickly gain entrance to markets, increase product/service functionality, and decrease operational expenses. Partnering may be strategically agreed at high levels between companies, but must have good relationships at the field level in order for the partnership to be executed successfully. Alliances, like marriages, have lifecycles. The alliance lifecycle has six phases: gap identification, investigation, negotiation, contract, management, and exit. The service provider must understand its goals in each of these phases and keep the focus as the relationship progresses. Sometimes, as seen in the case studies, formal relationships are not built until initial success is achieved. Sometimes formal relationships are needed immediately, especially when investments and joint development is involved. Exit strategies must be considered early on in the relationship so that parting can be more equable—one never knows when future relationships will be desirable.

9.10 Endnotes

1. Content for the Jamcracker case study was written by Feyzi Fatehi, Jamcracker's area vice president of business development for North America, with significant contributions from multiple members of the business development team, specially, Amede Hungerford, Kelly Emo, and Robin Singh, all business development directors for Jamcracker, Inc.
2. Thank you to Jorg Kampers, director, Global Service Providers, who provided content for this case study.
3. Content for the Channels on Tap case study provided by Rod Hardman and Lynn Sauder from HP.

9.11 xSP Strategy Checklist for Partners and Alliances

- ❑ Do a SWOT analysis.
- ❑ What do the weaknesses, opportunities and threats say about strategy gaps?
- ❑ Identify strategy gaps.
- ❑ Define ideal profile for company type to fill each gap.
- ❑ Further identify must have and nice to have traits.
- ❑ Scour the market for companies that fit the profile.
- ❑ Do profile companies fit within service provider guidelines for finance, resources, support, global reach, and so forth?
- ❑ Is there a win-win proposition for both companies? Common goals, investment approval, and so forth.
- ❑ Is the negotiation team aware of the overall goals, service provider position and walk away points?
- ❑ Does the negotiation team know details of the potential partner goals, organization, opposing negotiation team?
- ❑ How long will it take, and what is the process, to get approvals during each stage of the negotiation?
- ❑ Communicate with in-house stake-holders during each level of the negotiation.
- ❑ When should the legal department or corporate attorney be involved?
- ❑ Who signs the agreement?
- ❑ Does the agreement include: general tasks, owners and dates? Investment levels? Exit clause? Renegotiation clauses?
- ❑ How often will the main contacts meet and review execution status?
- ❑ Is there a partner management plan? Does it include specific execution with times and owners of those general tasks identified in the contract?
- ❑ Is there an escalation plan?
- ❑ On exit, is there still good rapport between the two companies?

CHAPTER 10

Organization

There is no secret formula for service provider organizational structures. The structure is dependent upon process design and people effectiveness, as well as profit targets and overall customer support levels desired. This chapter contains guidelines for organizational roles and titles, organizational structures, and estimates for resource numbers, as well as a list of processes needed to begin effective operations. Organizational models are included for ramp up and ongoing operations.

There are no definitive in-depth resource plans in this presentation. To create such plans the service provider needs answers to the staffing questions set forth in this chapter, which are then offset by issues of cost containment and productivity.

10.1 Services Strategy

Any organizational structure should support a company's cost containment policies and productivity goals as they, in turn, support the business objectives. The service provider should first decide on its services strategy—what it would offer, with approximate dates. This is covered in more detail in Chapter 11, "Entering the Market."

The services strategy normally takes into account a services roadmap (see Figure 10-1) and includes today's and future services. To build the organization most effectively, the services should build on each other to avoid random, disparate resource investments. When the service provider decides on its roadmap, it can also decide on its core competence—what it wants to be famous for and when it will be, or needs to be, profitable. After this, the service provider can better decide how it will partner and what it will outsource. Partnering is discussed in Chapter 9, "Partners and Alliances." Resourcing plans normally are developed in conjunction with the detailed sales, marketing, and operation plans.

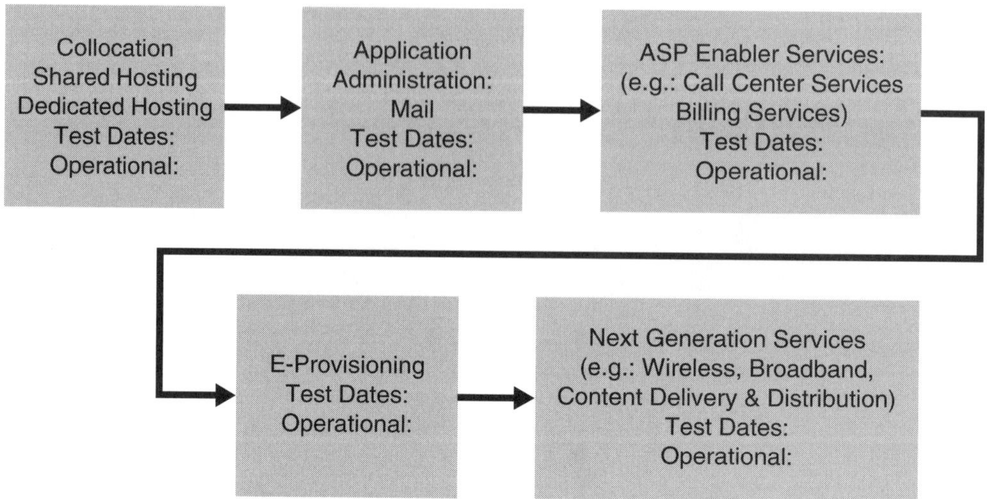

Figure 10-1 Sample services roadmap.

10.2 Organizational Model

The organizational model presented here assumes the service provider does not outsource any of its IDC operations. This model will generally support the service offerings shown in Figure 10.1. It also includes high-level functions and key responsibilities of each part of the organization:

General manager

- Command and Control

Finance and Administration

- Accounting department
- Accounts receivables and payables, payroll, and so forth
- Logistics
- HR
- Quality assurance
- Change and process management
- General services

Sales and Marketing

- Direct sales
- Presales support
- Channel partner management (indirect sales)
- Portal management

- Product management
- Marketing communications
- Sales force education and training
- Product R&D

Data center operations

- Systems administration
- Network administration
- Overall center performance tuning/benchmark testing
- Media administration
- Production engineering (R&D for new products/services)
- Operators
- Facilities

Service management

- Security
- Front office customer support (Help desk, call center)
- Billing infrastructure
- Capacity planning and procurement
- Technical support

Consulting

- Delivery
- R&D

10.2.1 General Manager

10.2.1.1 Key Responsibilities

- Set overall corporate strategy and direction including:
  - Key strategic partnerships
  - General oversight of business and strategic direction
  - Overall success or failure of the venture

10.2.2 Finance and Administration

10.2.2.1 Key Responsibilities

- Run corporate operations including:
  - Accounts receivables and payables, payroll, and so forth
  - Logistics

- Human resources
- Benefits
- Quality assurance
- Change and process management
- Office facilities management and general services
- Licensing
- Legal/Contracts
- Education

10.2.3 Sales and Marketing

10.2.3.1 Key responsibilities:

- Increase market penetration and brand awareness
- Communicate product value
- Manage the customer and partner experience
- Manage the product lifecycle
- Ensure the sales force understands what they have to sell, how to sell it, how target customers do business, what their needs are, the competitive landscape, and so forth including:
    - Understanding the market
    - Understand customer needs (includes domain-specific knowledge)
    - Understand competitive landscape
    - Acquiring and retaining customers
    - Manage customer relationships, online and offline
    - Manage the make/buy decision
    - Acquiring and retaining partners
    - Understand partner needs
    - Manage ongoing partner relationships
    - Product management
    - Determine product features and pricing
    - Discover, market, and test new product ideas
    - Articulate product value propositions
    - Manage the production and distribution of all sales and marketing collateral
    - Managing sales and marketing campaigns
    - Manage sales and marketing training

10.2.4 Data Center Operations

10.2.4.1 Key responsibilities:

- Smooth and cost effective operation of the data center
- Meet *internal* service level objectives including:
  - Meeting system availability response times and objectives
  - Data recovery (historic granularity, data granularity, and request turnaround parameters)
  - Assuring data integrity (physical access security, logical access security)
  - Facilities management (all physical aspects including: power, environmentals, installation, decommissioning, relocation, upgrades, maintenance, physical configuration, cabling, and so on.)
  - Customization, monitoring and maintenance/administration of production operating systems and networks
  - Administration: customization, monitoring, and maintenance of test facility for new services/products
  - Managing change (nothing is allowed to impact production facilities without passing through this)
  - Overseeing all nonautomated operator tasks
  - Overseeing automated operator functions

10.2.5 Service Management

10.2.5.1 Key responsibilities:

- Meet *external* service level objectives
- Manage capacity including:
  - Meeting customer request responsiveness objectives
  - Measuring and reporting of all customer facing service metrics
  - Supporting the front and back office
  - Billing

10.2.6 Consulting

10.2.6.1 Key responsibilities:

- Develop and deliver new consulting products including:
  - Developing new products specified by product management and marketing
  - Acting as a paid resource to other xSPs that want to outsource their consulting services
  - Training end-users

10.3 Resource Sizing

This section contains suggestions and areas to consider when staffing an organization. The principal profit drivers of a service provider are cost containment and productivity. This, in turn, is driven by two key factors:

- Process
- Cost of ownership

There are no industry parameters; guidelines contained in this section uniquely characterize the effectiveness of a single organization. For a service provider, these parameters determine whether, or to what extent, the organization is profitable. From a structural perspective, it is critical to design world-class processes with a clear focus on quality. This is not only about customer service, but is directed at operational efficiency. It is also important to distinguish between process and procedure, particularly in customer facing roles.

The structure outlined in the previous section does not necessarily align with specific jobs and head count. The hierarchy describes functions that are needed for an organization to operate effectively. In a lean organization, one person might take on several functions. In a large organization, many people might have the same function. Not all functions need to be owned in-house, and it may make sense to outsource many of them.

As mentioned previously, the numbers of people within the organization performing functions is not the product of any formula; rather it is dependent upon process design and people effectiveness. Resource allocation is based on the following, offset by issues of cost containment and productivity:

- Servers per operator
- Servers per systems administrator
- Factors determining numbers of network administrators
- Customers per sales person
- Partners per partner manager
- Sales people per presales support person
- Products per product manager
- Customers per technical support person
- Customers per call center person

For example, considering servers per systems administrator, some providers push this into the hundreds (or higher) of servers per systems administrator by deploying many identical, standardized uniprocessors. In contrast, other service providers might only manage three or four servers per systems administrator, because each server is customized.

A continuous quality improvement culture seeks to identify these parameters and relentlessly improve upon them.

10.3.1 Management

There are many options for managing a company. Many decisions may be carried out by an executive committee (in addition to a board of directors). Examples of executive committees include:

- Compensation committee: Reviews overall corporate compensation.
- Nominating committee: Makes and reviews nominations for executive positions.
- Finance committee: Sets and reviews annual budgets and spending.
- Audit committee: Reviews internal corporate processes and/or books for compliance with corporate guidelines.
- Technology committee: Reviews and approves proposals for technology upgrades over a certain amount.
- Employee review committee: Reviews employee performance and makes decisions on corrective action.
- Purchasing committee: Approves purchases over a certain amount.

10.3.2 Operational Processes

Related to organization, in order for a service provider to open its doors there are many operational plans and processes that need to be in place, either formally or informally. These plans and processes directly link to, and are the grease for, the service provider organization, making it function overall as one unit. Formal planning and procedural documents are best as a way of documenting a plan of record, giving employees a written reference to use in day-to-day operations and training situations. Here is a partial list of the plans and procedures needed:

- Business plan
- R&D processes
- Marketing plan (detailed per service)
- Marketing communications plan
- Sales plan (detailed per service)
- Direct sales qualification
- Channel policies and focus
- Resource (staffing) plan
- Financial plan
- Channels plan
- Implementation plans/guidelines for IT implementation
- Data center operational plan
- Floor plan (for utilities and staff deployment)
- IT user guidelines
- IT administration guidelines
- IT operational guidelines

- IT configuration guidelines
- Employee training plans (overall orientation for company, then by department)
- Change/Approval processes
- Escalation processes (in case of disputes)
- Capacity management guidelines
- Service request processes
- Provisioning process/guidelines
- Safety guidelines
- Security implementation guidelines
- Project office process (a project office is used to determine which service provider projects will be implemented, when, and how. These are normally internal projects like implementing or upgrading the billing system.)
- Billing process/accounts payable/accounts receivable guidelines
- Credit policies and checks
- Bill format
- Customer care process/guidelines
- IT support process/guidelines
- Facilities support process/guidelines
- HR policies/guidelines (hiring/firing, salary)
- Code of conduct
- Legal guidelines
- Administration guidelines
- Travel guidelines
- Purchasing guidelines
- Audit guidelines

10.4 Organization and Resourcing Models

This section shows sample models for ramp-up and ongoing operations with sample resourcing levels for each. As mentioned, some of these functions may be outsourced and staffing levels depend on service provider cost containment and productivity goals. These organizational charts are based on experience working with service providers that own their own IDCs, but are partnering for any fieldwork needed outside of the data center.

Planning the organization is usually done in tandem with the business planning function. The business plan should also include information about the organization's core competency, sales, marketing, and resource planning. Based on these and financial input, plus any external input, the executives can review, and agree upon, the organizational set up. External inputs would include any sort of parent company or stakeholder preferences.

10.4.1 Sample Organization Models

Figures 10-2 and 10-3 are samples of service provider organizational models. There are no hard and fast rules about organization for service providers, but these samples illustrate what is working for providers doing business today. Guidelines relating to productivity, financial restraints, outsourcing, core competency, corporate politics, and so forth, will effect how the service provider is organized.

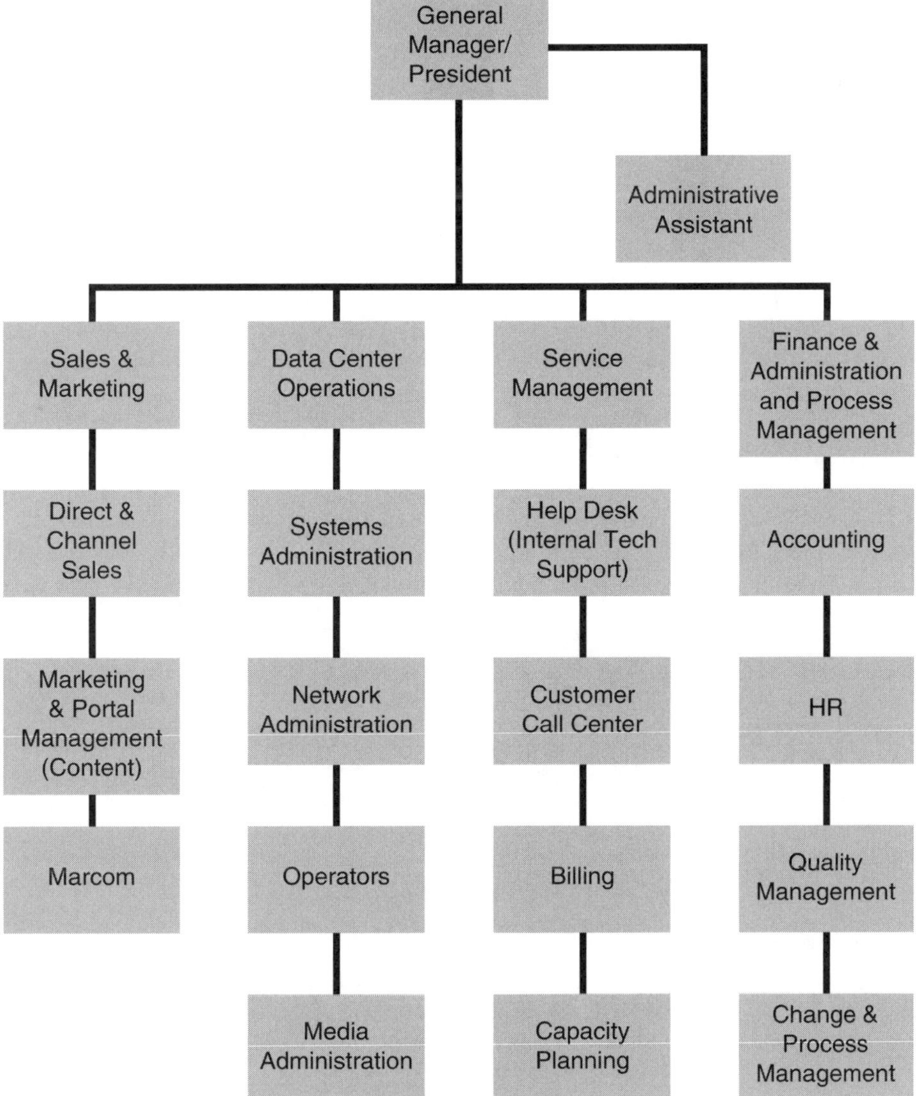

Figure 10-2 Sample ramp-up organizational model.

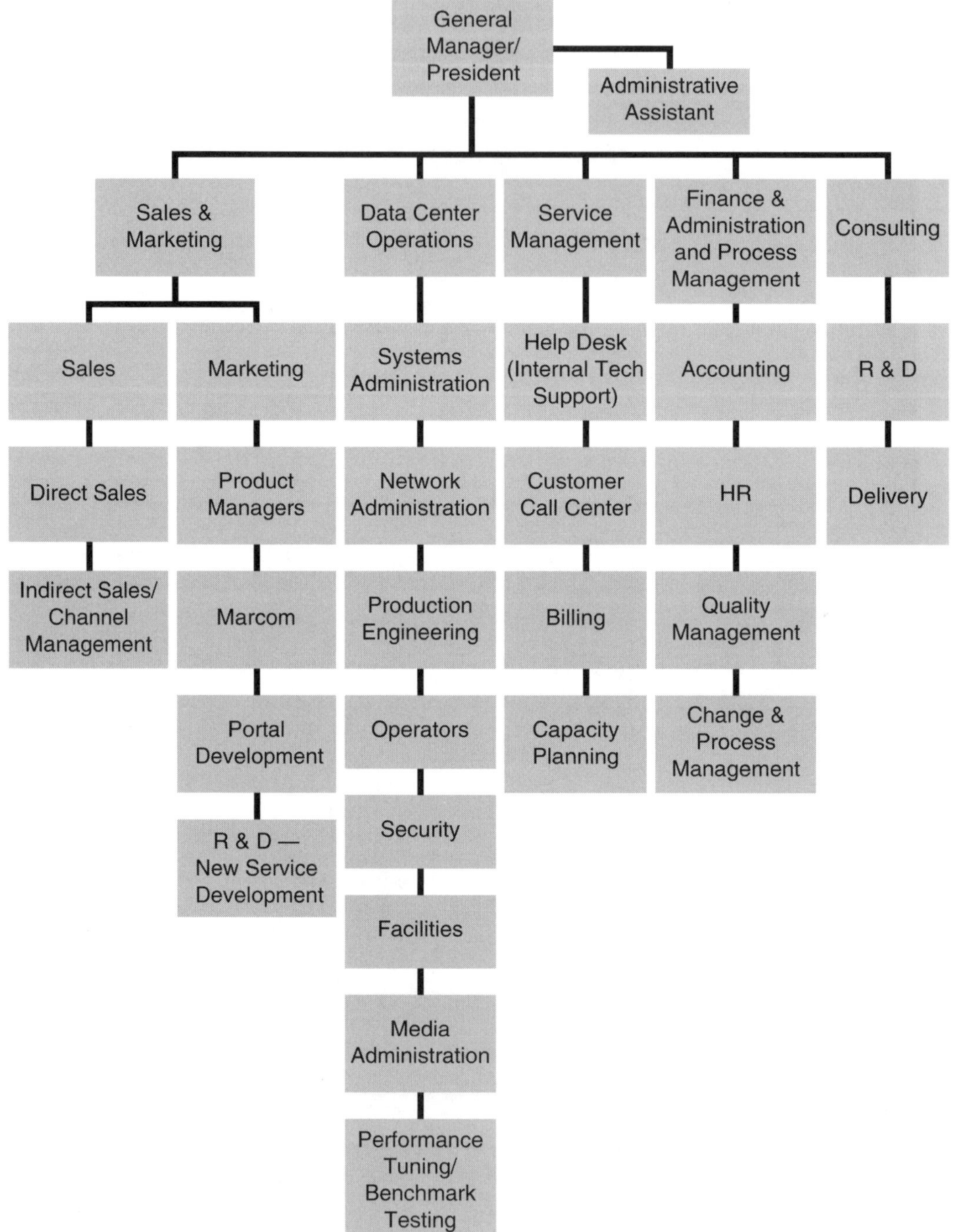

Figure 10-3 Sample ongoing organizational model.

10.4.2 Sample Resourcing

Resourcing for the ongoing operations is dependent upon process and cost of operation guidelines of the service provider. For example, a direct sales force is quite expensive, but easier to direct. An indirect sales force is less expensive, but more difficult to direct. The service provider needs to analyze its "must win" customers and consider having a direct sales person assigned to each key account. Other accounts might go through channels and channels, further, might be split into tiers. Top-tier channels would have a dedicated account representative. Second-tier would have a shared representative and third-tier would be grouped together under one account representative. Marketing normally has a program or product manager assigned to each service.

Staffing for data center operations depends on economies of scale and processes based on specific guidelines. Service management staffing depends on the amount of automation and coverage desired per customer. Consultancy staffing depends on the types and level of consulting desired. This chapter attempts to give the novice an idea of starting staffing levels (see Figure 10-4), but exact staffing numbers for an ongoing organization really cannot be addressed in any meaningful way. Guidelines were presented earlier and the good news is the service provider should know the correct ratios based on actual experience by the time it ends its ramp-up stage.

10.5 Outsourcing

Outsourcing is the act of removing certain necessary, but noncore competency, operational functions from a firm's internal organization and contracting to receive the functionality from another company. Outsourced functions normally require special expertise, take a long time to implement, and/or involve a high capital investment. Examples are data centers, call centers, facilities management, and billing functions. Another reason to outsource is to supplement in-house resources, something to take into account when building a channel strategy (see Chapter 9).

There are advantages and disadvantages to outsourcing. Advantages include:

- The ability to concentrate on corporate core competencies
- Better quality
- Faster functionality implementation
- Lower capital expense/better cash flow
- Better control

Disadvantages include:

- Loss of customer control (depending on what's outsourced)
- Eventual prices for outsourcing could overshoot the cost of implementing the functionality in-house
- Ongoing management issues
- Functionality development may not keep pace with service provider's needs

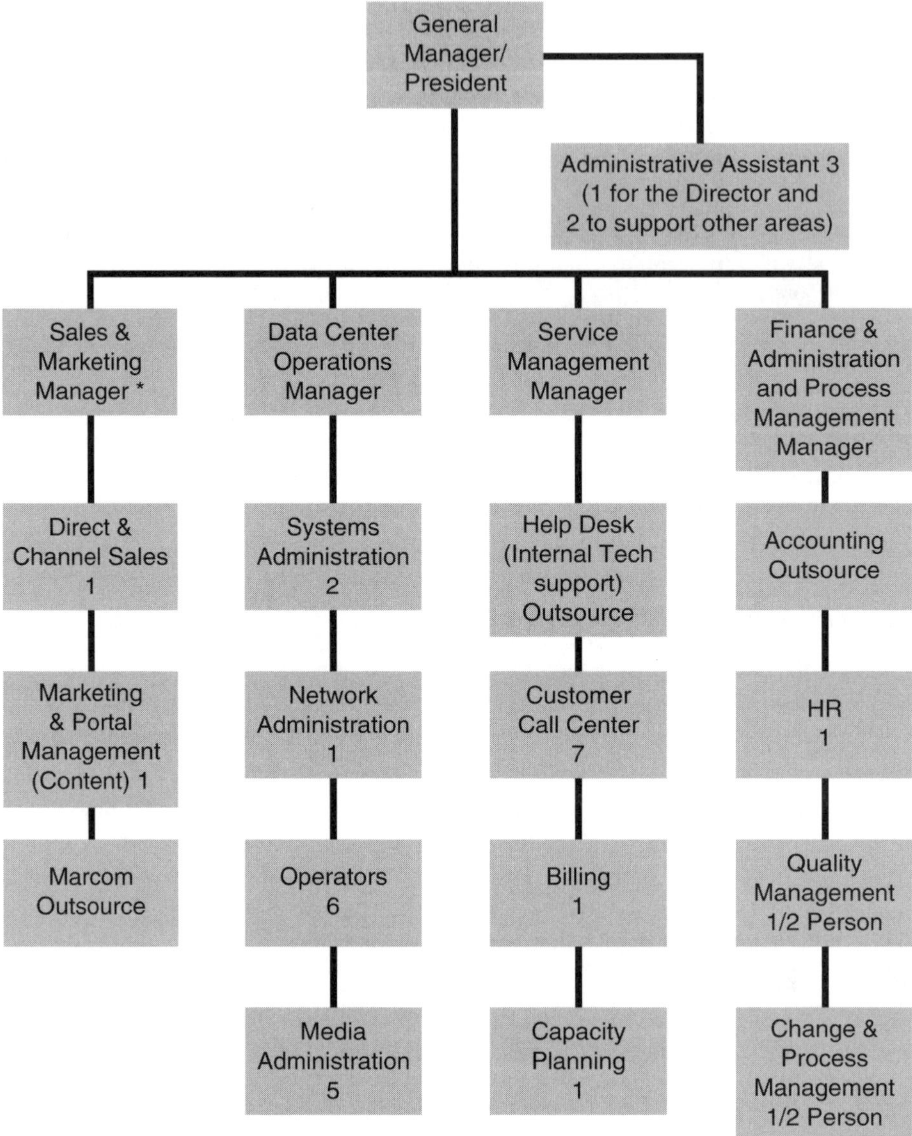

Figure 10-4 Sample ramp-up resourcing model.

When outsourcing a portion of its operations, a service provider must perform rigorous due diligence and manage these associations carefully for quality performance. The outsourcing decision should make good business sense, supporting service provider business and financial objectives. The service provider should understand exact service functionality offered. It should analyze the outsourcing service companies for:

- Financial stability
- Quality of service
- Service functionality and technology roadmap
- Ability to carry out the technology roadmap

How do these align with service provider requirements? What functionality is provided now? What will be provided in the future? Will there be penalties if these functions aren't introduced when promised? How is the service billed? What technology/applications are used? What's the outsourcing service company's roadmap for technology investment and when? Can the service provider leverage the outsourcing service company to increase market penetration through brand, customer base, sales force, and so forth?

The service provider must understand the pricing and contracting structure and restrictions. It must check the outsourcing service company's references: Are they happy customers? Did the outsourcing service company deliver what it promised? It must visit the outsourcing company's premises—are they up to standards? What happens if the company goes bankrupt? What are the switching costs if the outsourcing service provider doesn't satisfy the service provider and it is necessary to change companies? What are the escalation procedures? Are there service level guarantees and what happens if they are not met? The more a service provider knows before entering into the outsourcing relationship, be better it will be in the long run.

Here are a few guidelines to be considered when outsourcing a part of the business:

Do:

- Check several references. Choose references that are currently using the services. Question them carefully and ask to see their operations
- Define exact terms and service levels you expect in the legal agreement between your two companies
- Consider outsourcing nonmission-critical services first, then move on to more important services
- Set up and test a disaster recovery plan with the outsource service provider

Don't

- Outsource anything that forms a part of the business' core competency, or represents a large part of the business value that is being sold. The service provider could become a reseller if it starts to outsource core parts of its business
- Outsource services without an agreed and tested way to review and audit the services
- Be wholly reliant on one outsourcer for all needs

10.5.1 Summary

There is no secret formula to set up an organizational structure for a service provider; rather it is dependent upon process design and people effectiveness, as well as profit targets and overall customer support levels desired. This chapter gave suggestions for organizational roles and titles, personnel organizational models and estimates for resource numbers, as well as a list of processes needed to operate effectively. When the service provider decides on its services roadmap, it can also decide on its core competence—what it wants to be famous for and when it will be, or needs to be, profitable. After this, the service provider can better decide how it will staff, partner, and what it will outsource. When outsourcing a portion of its operations, a service provider must perform rigorous due diligence and manage these associations carefully for quality performance. Resourcing plans normally are developed in conjunction with the detailed sales, marketing, and operational plans.

10.6 xSP Strategy Checklist for Organizational Structure and Resourcing

The information collected from this checklist gives the service provider the information needed to define its organization and staffing needs. If any information is incomplete, the provider will find it more difficult to create its operational infrastructure. It assumes that the service provider will have its data center in-house, but that it will not be performing any customer premise functions. Also included is a separate checklist for outsourced functions.

- ❑ Is there a business plan containing at least those elements outlined in Appendix B?
- ❑ What is the service provider's core competency? (What will it be famous for?)
- ❑ What will the provider outsource?
- ❑ What is the detailed services roadmap, what service levels need to be supported, and what happens if these service levels are not met?
- ❑ What are the detailed sales, marketing, operational, and financial plans?
- ❑ What are the financial and operational guidelines of the service provider as they relate to the following:
    - ❑ Number of servers planned per operator?
    - ❑ Number of servers planned per systems administrator?
    - ❑ Number of network administrators planned?
    - ❑ Number of customers per sales person?
    - ❑ Number of partners per partner manager?
    - ❑ Number of sales people per presales support person?
    - ❑ Number of products per product manager planned?
    - ❑ Number of customers per Technical support person planned?
    - ❑ Number of customers call center person planned?
    - ❑ What is the plan to profitability for the business?

The following is a checklist for outsourcing:

- ❑ What will be outsourced and why? (Does it make business sense?)
- ❑ What, exactly, are the services offered by the outsourcing company?
- ❑ Can quality be guaranteed and measured?
- ❑ Can the outsource company scale to meet the service provider needs?
- ❑ In case of disagreements, what are the escalation procedures?
- ❑ Can service levels be maintained and measured?
- ❑ If not, are there penalties?
- ❑ Can the service provider leverage the outsource brand?
- ❑ Is the outsource company using the most up-to-date technologies?
- ❑ Does the outsource provider have the technology roadmap and capital to support infrastructure enhancements as new technologies come to market to keep the service provider's services at the forefront?

- ❑ How is the service priced?
  - ❑ Are there volume discounts?
- ❑ Are there clauses in the contract so the service provider can switch outsourcing companies if the service is not meeting expectations?
  - ❑ Is there an exit, or transition, plan if the service provider needs to change outsourcing services?
  - ❑ How many, and which, services will be offered by the outsourcing company and when?
- ❑ Do a reference check.
- ❑ Visit the outsourcing company's premises.

CHAPTER 11

Entering the Market

There are no hard and fast rules on how to enter a market offering Internet services. This chapter contains guidelines in formulating a go-to-market strategy and plan as ways to optimize sales and marketing processes. Webster defines sales as "relating to or used in selling...to persuade or influence...a course of action...." He defines marketing as, "the act of selling or of purchasing in a market," in other words, the art of communicating the value of goods or services to a target market in a way that will convince potential buyers to purchase because the perceived value is worth the price.

11.1 Go-to-Market Strategy

A strategy describes the choices made in how objectives will be achieved. A plan is the specific action(s) necessary to achieve those objectives (strategy execution). There are many plans involved in bringing a new service to market: sales, marketing, marketing communication, staffing, and so forth. These plans should be included in the service provider's overall business plan to show how corporate strategies will be executed. Appendix B shows a sample business plan and how sales, marketing, and resource plans are used to support the overall business strategy.

A go-to-market strategy is primarily concerned with the four Ps of the classic marketing mix: product, price, place, and promotion. For service providers, a product can be further defined as a Service Offering.

11.2 Building a Service Offering Strategy (Product)

11.2.1 Introduction

Each customer segment, its associated market drivers, and the proposed service offering have symbiotic relationships that need to be defined. To complete the strategy and planning described in this section, the service provider must continually review, test, and update this relationship as more information is gathered, adjusting the definition of each component as necessary (see Figure 11-1).

Every service provider, no matter how quickly they need to get to market, does the initial component definition and ongoing updating process, consciously or subconsciously. Figure 11-2 illustrates an attempt to break these processes into a series of steps so service providers can consciously, or semi-consciously, review them for missed information.

At a high level, this means:

- Determining a customer segment(s) and its fundamental needs/consequent problems
- Defining a service to fill these needs
- Defining the subsequent plans and programs to reach the strategy's objectives

Needs identification is critical to the formulation of strategy because the value proposition and messaging are mapped to the priority needs of the target customers. (See "Testing" later in this chapter.) In cases of ego, or time-to-market issues, a service provider might start with a fully defined service description and try to force fit it into customer needs. That's not to say that a service provider won't have some idea of what it wants to offer while understanding the market drivers. Service providers normally approach this stage with an innate ("gut") feeling of what's needed because they come to the business with a strong industry knowledge. In the rare cases of

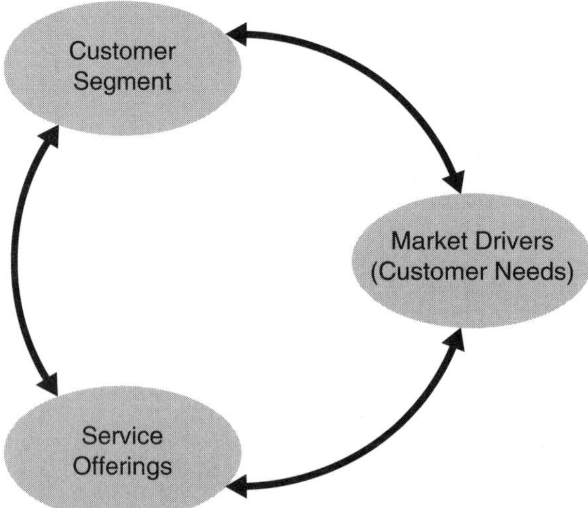

Figure 11-1 The services/market ecosystem.

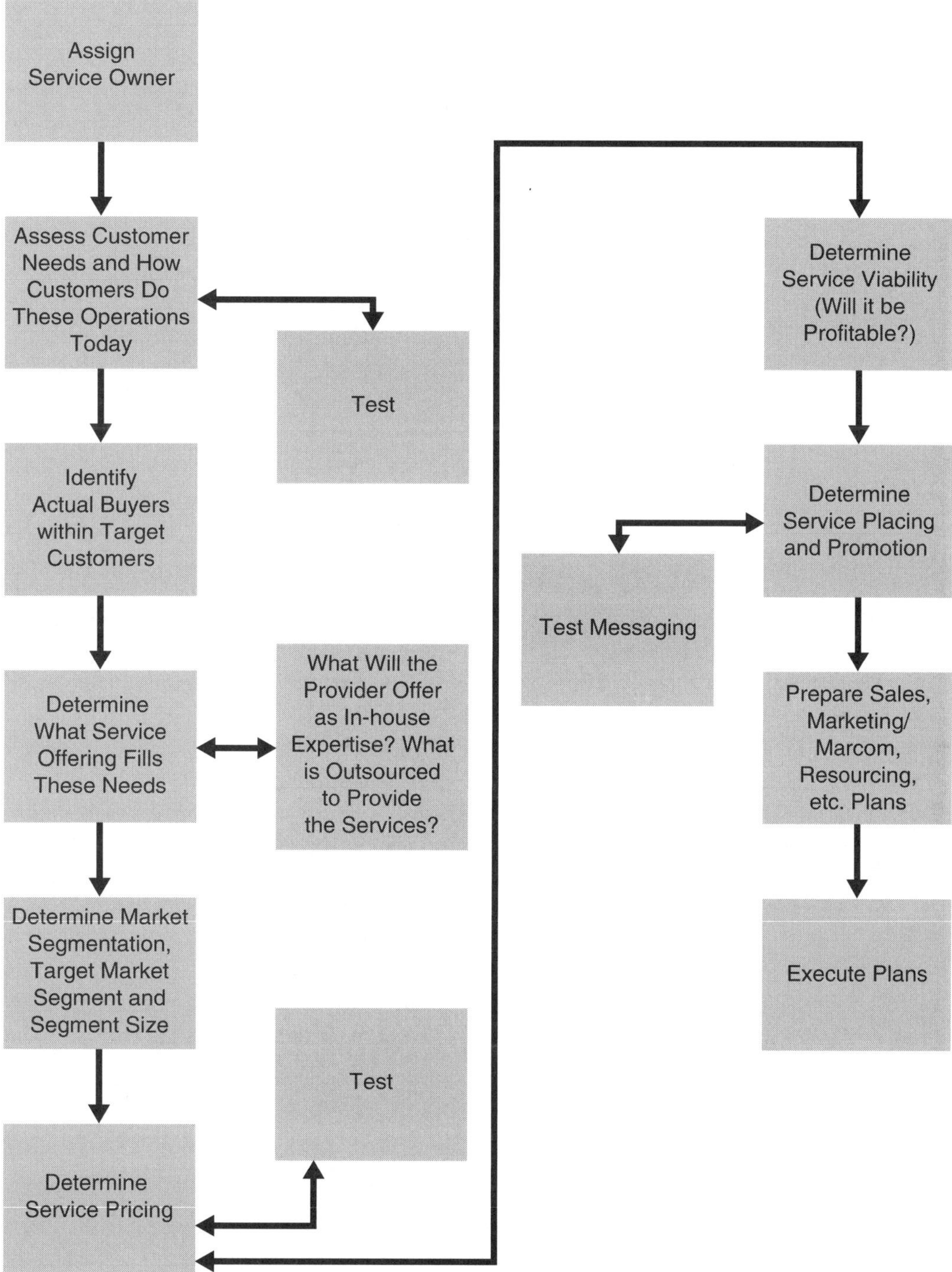

Figure 11-2 The service's initial component definition flow.

a service offering containing a disruptive technology, a service provider might bring a fully defined service description to the market because it needs to educate a largely needs unaware customer segment.

11.3 Determining Customer Needs and Market Drivers

The best way to determine customer needs is to understand the potential target customers' business. For example, how does the business operate? How does it purchase? How does it hire? What is its accounting system? How does it run its IT? What problems keep the owners awake at night? What expertise could my company have that might fill the gaps? There are many publications and surveys available to start defining a focus and to understand potential customer needs. (See Appendix H: "Helpful Associations, Organizations and Publications.") Once the service provider has an idea of where to focus, it can start doing more detailed drill down and due diligence further defining the target customer needs and service offering.

At one level the prospective client is a business, but at another level, the buyers are actually people within the business. These buyers will influence the purchasing decision and it is important to understand their personal needs, interests, and goals when developing a service offering and execution plan. One way to identify the best potential customers/buyers is to ask, "Who in the organization stands to benefit most from a product/service?" Since many service providers' offerings are areas that will be outsourced by the target customer segment, there is little point in spending money and time targeting the people who perform this activity within the target companies. It is better to aim at those within target companies who have problems with the current environment. This might be an IT manager or a business manager, a CEO, or a marketing manager, not necessarily a CIO. It is a good idea to perform test interviews, or purchase research that helps identify the right buyers within potential customer organizations. The test interviews and research can also give the service provider an indication of how needs aware prospective customers are.

Sometimes, when a new technology is available that is revolutionary (versus evolutionary), a service offering is created first and then tested against the market. In this case, the target customers, or their needs, may not be well understood and assumptions or guesses are made.

In doing research and due diligence, many service providers purchase market information from organizations like Gartner Group or International Data Corporation. Some service providers can get a good indication of market needs via their current installed base, which is one of the best sources. Some companies prefer to do their own research via prospective customer interviews or partner information. One thing is sure; it is best to gather information from as many sources as possible as time and finances allow.

A final note on understanding customer needs. The service offering will affect a chain of interested parties—the "customer's customer"—and the needs of these parties must be understood as part of this investigation (see Figure 11-3). For example: A logistics offering will affect the direct purchaser, but might also affect those interacting with the new processes. Another example is a service offering focused on the wholesale market, such as billing services. The service offering should take into account the needs of the retail purchasers and the customers to whom they send bills.

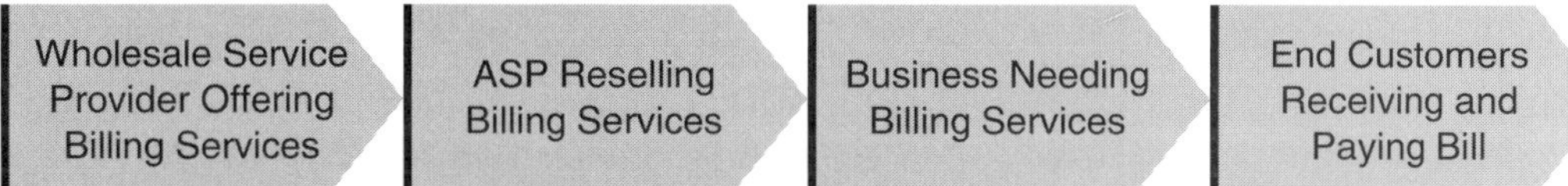

Figure 11-3 Understanding the "customer's customer."

11.4 Determining the Service Offering

When defining service offerings, service providers should consider not only today's market needs, but look to future market trends. Defining future services is sometimes called a services roadmap. This roadmap should be a living document. It will change as the company changes its services to adapt to market needs through time, but it still gives the service provider a way to proceed and focus for marketing communications, in building infrastructure, when hiring and educating the sales force, and so forth. The reverse is also true. The service provider can use future services defined in the services roadmap to better focus present day services; in other words, what resource expertise, core competencies, and outsourcing/channel partnering strategies are needed to support the future, complex service offerings.

Using the roadmap in Figure 11-4 as an example, this company wants to be famous for IDC operations. It uses collocation, shared, and dedicated hosting services to build and prove its IDC expertise, a core competency, adding application management, ASP enabler services, and e-provisioning into the roadmap (see Figure 11-5). By defining e-provisioning now, realizing this may need redefinition as it comes closer to implementation, the service provider is better able to define today's services to support that offering. Providers run the risk of offering simple initial services that will experience, or are already experiencing, commoditization. This is most apparent when the provider doesn't have first mover advantage in the market. That said, simple initial services are encouraged because they can be the key to:

- Getting the provider's processes working efficiently
- Testing mission critical processes like billing and customer care
- Attracting initial reference customers

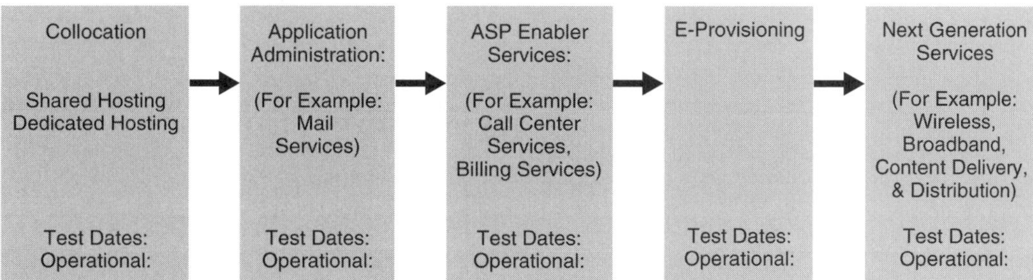

Figure 11-4 Sample services roadmap.

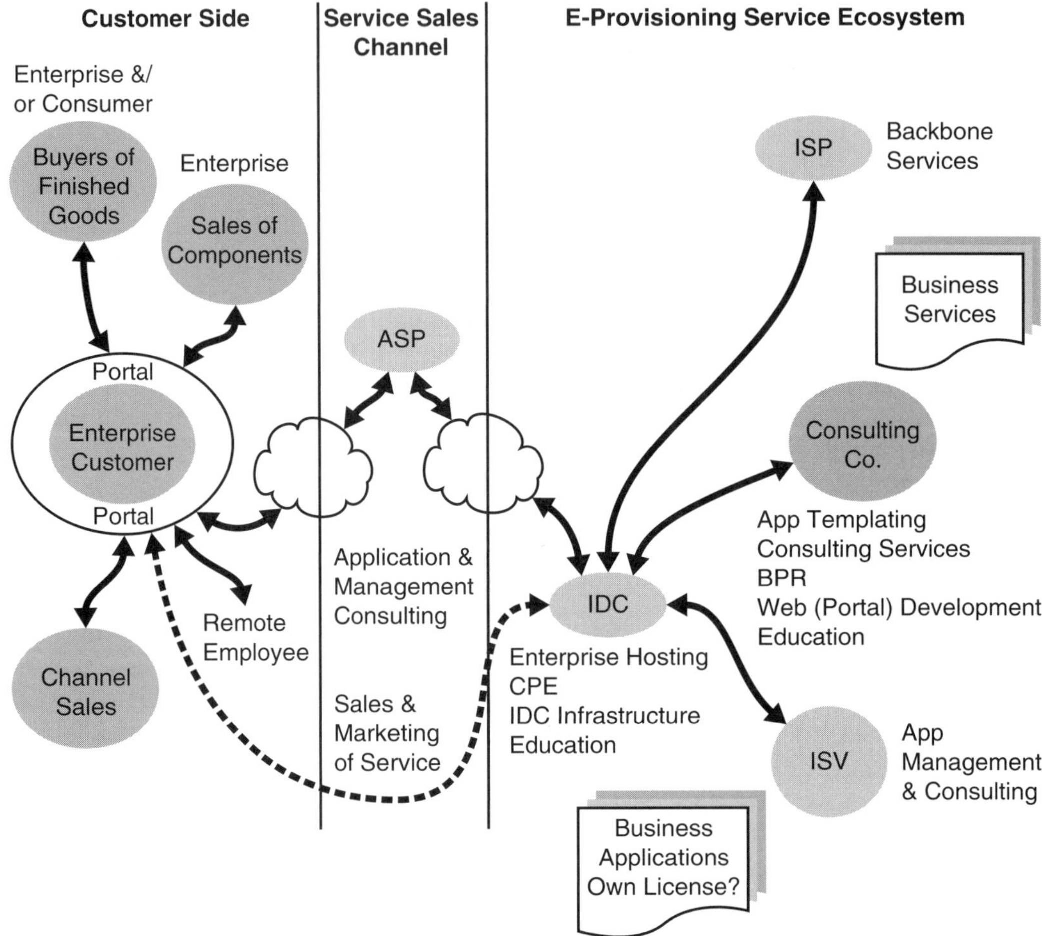

Figure 11-5 An example of e-provisioning.

It is easy to get trapped into trying to get the initial services right while the rest of the market passes by. At the end of the day, the service provider will succeed only by getting to the higher value services faster than its competitors.

For example, this service provider decided to outsource application management and other consulting services. It begins building these partnerships now, at the same time it is building expertise in the simpler service offerings in-house that will be used as building blocks for future, more complex, offerings. The service provider also begins analyzing vertical industries, deciding with which vertical industry leaders to align.

A service offering description is not a simple one-line document, as seen in Appendix D, but is a contract between the service provider and the customer, and should be treated as such. Normally, a service offering will include information about SLAs. This is one reason why it is good practice to have the offering and SLA reviewed by an attorney before release. SLAs are contracts between a service provider and its customer, guaranteeing certain levels of speed or response for functionality described in the service offering as seen in Appendix C.

11.5 Determining Focus Market Segmentation and Size

Focus market segmentation depends on the type of service offered, and customer needs assessed earlier in the process by the service provider and/or associations, organizations, and companies that specialize in market trends and expenditures (see Appendix H, "Helpful Associations, Organizations, and Publications"). This sort of information should be used as a supplement to any in-house analysis performed by the service provider and partners. The more information the better when trying to determine the best market segmentation for the defined service. For example: if a service offering is focused on stand-alone messaging, this market might be segmented into:

- Very small companies (fewer than 10 employees)
- Small companies (fewer than 100 employees)
- Medium companies (fewer than 1,000 employees)
- Large companies (fewer than 5,000 employees)
- Very large companies (more than 5,000 employees)

Once market segmentation is defined, the service provider must further determine its direct and indirect focus with market sizes assigned to each segment (see Figure 11-6). There may be segments it determines are out of focus. This decision is based partially on the service offering functionality, but also on identified core competencies and business focus, partnering strategy, and the service provider's financial strategies. Market size should be defined in three tiers: Total market size, addressable market size, and obtainable market size, generally for a specific year(s). This information is normally further defined by target region.

For example: The service provider in Figure 11-6 offers an email service that could be used by all the market segments identified, but it has infrastructure that supports wholesale operations, and can not profitably offer services to market segments below 1,000 employees. This service provider decides to focus its core competencies on large businesses and ASPs, using the ASPs as channels to the lower, less profitable market segments. This customer mix should be under continuous review by the service provider as a way to decrease unprofitable business and grow market share. Now the service provider needs to determine the market size to see if the business is viable. This service provider is headquartered in, and has facilities in, Germany with a direct sales force of 300 people, 200 of whom are located in Germany and 100 split between five different countries in Western Europe. The provider decides to focus its service first in Germany and then roll it out to the other five countries.

In parallel, the provider is interested in taking its services to other regions of the world and is actively pursuing a partnering strategy to jump-start this initiative. The provider looks to research available by International Data Corporation, Yankee Group, Gartner Group, and so

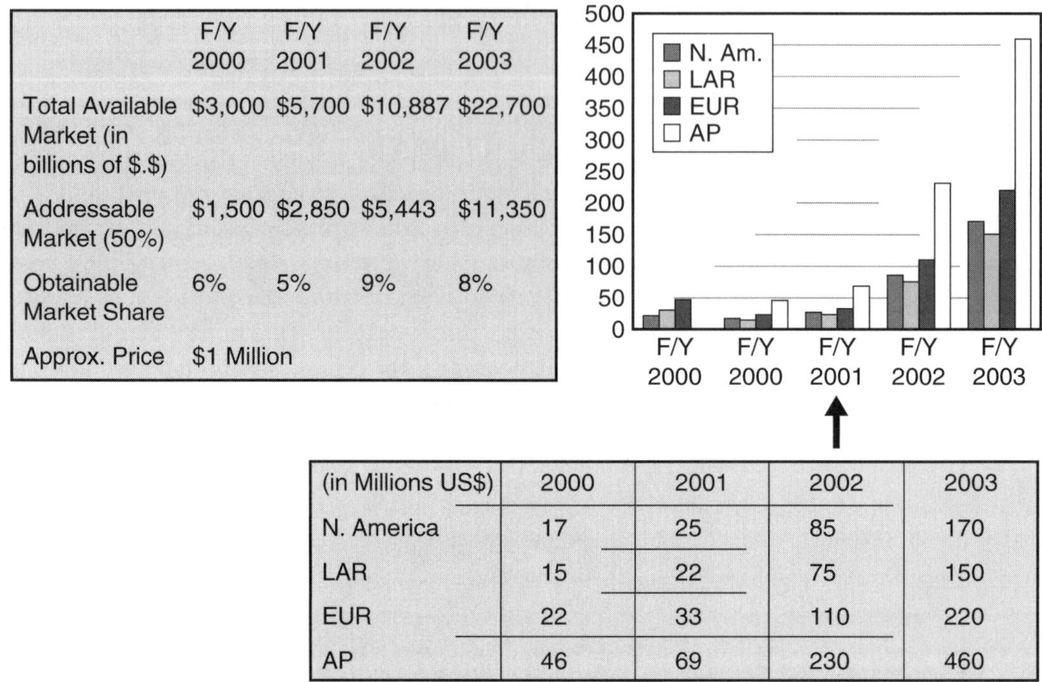

	F/Y 2000	F/Y 2001	F/Y 2002	F/Y 2003
Total Available Market (in billions of $.$)	$3,000	$5,700	$10,887	$22,700
Addressable Market (50%)	$1,500	$2,850	$5,443	$11,350
Obtainable Market Share	6%	5%	9%	8%
Approx. Price	$1 Million			

(in Millions US$)	2000	2001	2002	2003
N. America	17	25	85	170
LAR	15	22	75	150
EUR	22	33	110	220
AP	46	69	230	460

Figure 11-6 An example of market dynamics and opportunity.
Published courtesy of Hewlett-Packard Comapny.

forth and finds forecasts showing the growth of worldwide mailboxes from 1999 through 2004. It is further able to break this down by European region and by country within Europe. There are also statistics showing the propensity of enterprises to outsource this service. The worldwide numbers will give the service provider the total market available for its service. Taking information about the target countries, adjusted for the propensity for enterprises to outsource their mail systems, gives the service provider its addressable market. Now, the service provider needs to strategically decide how much of the addressable market it is realistically able to capture in year one and as far into the future as it intends to forecast.

Obtainable market size will be used in setting the size of the sales force, the sales quota, and marketing goals. Obtainable market statistics may be adjusted after market testing and the pilot phase. This is when the service provider sees in reality how well the sales force is able to sell the service, the length of a typical sales cycle, and the size of the average sale. Forecasting is an art. Market needs and technology changes so quickly that forecasting further than about 12 months is highly suspect. In this example the service provider also needs to determine if customers in different countries will agree to have their mail service delivered from, or hosted in, another country. This sort of information may be available only via special surveys, but it is extremely useful to know, as it affects the rest of the service offering strategy.

11.6 Services and Implementation Lifecycle

Services, like products, have a lifecycle (see Figure 11-7). A phased approach to service rollout is the best way to understand and fix problems in a way that will affect the fewest number of customers. A phased approach may seem like a luxury to many service providers, but it is a difficult and expensive process to reacquire lost customers and a phased implementation offers more control. Once the service is defined and the service description is market tested, it is best if the service provider does a pilot offering to test service delivery and whether the service will perform as promised. Pilot periods should last longer than one month to make sure billing processes are online and working. During this period there may only be one or two customers using the service. The service provider may want to convince customers to participate in the pilot by offering service at a lower price, or free, during the initial phase. Good examples of pilot customers are businesses owned by the same holding company as the service providers or its shareholders. A successful pilot is also a good time for public relations activities, to include publicity for pilot customers who suffered through the service provider learning processes. It is a time to communicate well and often with the sales force so they better understand what is available for sale and that it can be delivered successfully. It is also a time to get customer references and success stories written. In general, this is the time to get everything working and marketing collateral completed before the ramp-up stage.

In the ramp-up stage, the service offering is fully operational and is available to a segment of the total target market. In other words, the stage is bigger than a pilot offering, but smaller (fewer customers) than the mature, on-going operational phase. As in the pilot phase, there are no hard and fast rules for the length of this phase, only a suggestion that the service provider runs through a few billing cycles to confirm processes are in order. The pilot and ramp-up phases are also an excellent time to further research the service offering functionality and either update the current offering or add functionality to its next release.

Mature or on-going operations is the next phase. This is when the offering is fully operational, fully deployed, and ready to scale to high usage levels. At this stage competitors are coming into the market and the service provider needs to refine its delivery efficiency, maintaining as much margin as possible as the service moves toward a commodity stage. The service provider should already have information on service enhancement or subsequent service offerings and be communicating these next service offerings to the market in preparation for the commodity phase.

When the service becomes a commodity, there are many competitors offering the same service, and sales become price dependent. It is critical that the provider already has the next

Figure 11-7 Services and implementation lifecycle.

offering in place so margins don't erode any more than necessary. This is when the exit strategy and plan are used as a way to upgrade customers to the enhanced offering, or phase out customers who are not interested in the profitable service.

11.7 Services Strategy

Service providers are always looking for ways to keep the customer base loyal and increase market share, but they must do this by offering profitable services. The provider must always analyze its service profit levels. If not, it unknowingly becomes a philanthropic organization–something that was probably not part of the original business strategy.[1] When service offerings do not meet minimum profit targets, the service provider has several options. The first is differentiation. The service provider can enhance the offering and relaunch it, or change the functionality mix of other, profitable offerings, or "profit cows,"[2] as a way of getting new customers in the door or enhancing other service(s). For example, a service provider offered personal Web page (PWP) functionality that became a commodity service on its own, so the service provider decided to add this functionality to its e-commerce service offering. This means it might offer the PWP functionality bundled with the other offer for free, or at a greatly reduced rate, as part of a much higher margin e-commerce service. In reality, the total price of the e-commerce bundle covers the cost plus the required margin of the PWP functionality.

Besides differentiation, the service provider should develop a services strategy that creates high switching costs, but the barriers to switching must be subtle and sensitive, and, hopefully, invisible to the customer. It is best if the service provider not offer free services unless there is a strategic reason, like decreasing customer churn through higher switching costs. Free email service is a good example because once a consumer uses a service provider for email, switching costs can become high. Why? The average consumer does not know how to easily switch an email client to another provider. Also, because they have to tell everyone their new email address. This is part of the value of Hotmail, offered by service providers. It is typically, though not necessarily, installed from a CD that intrusively configures the PC. From the customer perspective, this is a no-tears method of obtaining Internet access. However, subsequent switching can be a nightmare for the noncomputer literate.

Whatever decision is made must fit in with the service provider's financial strategy and not alienate the target customer segment. Having established the prospective customer base, segmented by needs, it is necessary to set price, place, and promotion.

11.8 Pricing Strategy/Methodology

Unfortunately, many companies don't have much of a formula for pricing because they want to push into the market too fast and don't look at the fundamentals. Those that do it correctly look at pricing from two aspects—top down and bottom up.

For top down, the service provider looks at competitors in the market and unders... price of the services they offer. Service provider management also looks internationally, or outside their direct market, at players offering similar services, to understand their pricing strategy. When doing this, it is most important to compare apples to apples—like services with like services.

In the bottom up analysis, service-offering components are analyzed to understand the cost of each, to which an uplift is added. At this stage two things are extremely important: The service offering definition must be frozen and the company must understand its cost for each service component. An example of bottom up pricing can be found in Appendix E.

After the two approaches are complete, bottom up pricing is compared with the prices in the market (top down). If the market price is higher than the bottom up price, the service provider can raise the price or try to undercut the market depending on strategy. If, however, bottom up is higher than top down, it's time to make some decisions. Can the service provider communicate the extra value and educate the market so it is willing to pay the higher price? Does the service provider need to outsource service components from other vendors to decrease costs that can be passed on to the customer? Does the service provider want to buy some market share initially (not recommended)? During the decision process, the service provider should run cash flow projections to see if/when it will be profitable to offer these services to this number of customers for this price.

Pricing schemes are limited only to the imagination of the service provider. They range from up-front fees, to pricing per transaction, to offering free services that are paid for by the advertisers, to pay per use, to discounting—every combination of the above, everything in-between and many not mentioned. It is best to try to bundle service offerings, making it easier to price and administer the services. Customization becomes quite costly to the service provider. For example, typically an IDC would charge a one-time fee for set up, and then bundle functional components into offerings. The IDC wants to lock in resalable, standard bundles of services because it is cheaper to deliver and maintain. The IDC could charge an up-front fee plus the fee for bronze, silver or gold bundles. Incremental services are also offered for those customers needing more than what's in the bundles. Examples of these bundles and pricing are seen in Appendix E, "Pricing." Here incremental services are not customized services, but are reusable standardized services that don't happen to be part of the standard bundles.

Service providers want to avoid offering customized solutions; otherwise, their business becomes unprofitable because they need to support so many different offerings. That said, the service provider can offer services that look customized, but are actually made of predefined elements that can be delivered and operated profitably.

11.9 Determining Cash Flow

A final step in determining product, or service definition, is to find out if it is viable, that is, profitable, for the service provider to deliver and operate. Appendix F is an example of a simple cash flow forecasting model used by an IDC to determine profitability of its services. These models take the revenue projections gathered when determining the market size and pricing models and look at capital and operational expenses to understand the cash flow and net present value of the company's investments. This book will not dwell on the financial aspects of running a business or service provider, other than to offer general guidelines:

- Focus on a path to profitability
- Get as much market information as possible and cross-check the information received
- Do as much actual market testing as money and time allows
- Communicate as much as possible with investors and other interested parties. Understand what is important to them and make that part of the core mission of the business

These cash flow and financial models are normally used to run numerous scenarios and can be a tool when working out different pricing and capital investment strategies. A model, similar to the model discussed here, taking into account overall revenues and expenses, should be included in the financial section of the business plan as shown in Appendix B.

Experience shows that running a variety of scenarios through the models can help service providers work out more realistic plans to profitability. The cash flow review should also take into account market forecasts reflecting service commoditization as a way to plan service review cycles. The reliability of the models depends on the input—garbage in, garbage out (GIGO).

11.10 Placement and Promotion: The Communications Mix

The type of service dictates placement, promotion, and potential customer needs awareness. If customers are needs oblivious, then the messaging should focus on creating an awareness of need—education. A common tactic, in this context, is fear. Messaging makes the customer aware of his situation and the heretofore-unknown consequences. The messages are most effective if they are job threatening. For example, a provider offering data center services might focus on: service availability, service access, data security, and data loss. The messaging then has two parts: (1) create awareness of problem—"50 percent of unauthorized server access is undetected" (2) offer easy solution—"Service provider X guarantees closed access via its new service." This is sometimes known as the lifesaver strategy. The prospect is shown his/her vulnerabilities—thrown into the ocean of fear—and then the provider throws him/her a life raft by showing how these vulnerabilities can be avoided (for a fee, of course). This method is often used in advertising.

11.11 Value Proposition

After the needs assessment is complete, a value proposition is created for each service and each segment. Here is an example of the value propositions created by a service provider offering IDC services:

Service provider X's collocation facilities and network/environmental support allows customers to take advantage of its end-to-end 99.999 percent uptime guarantees, state-of-the-art data center construction, and fully Microsoft certified staff, enabling customers to keep their servers and other equipment functioning round-the-clock.

A value proposition should answer: Why does the customer need this service, and why should the customer use this service offering versus the competition's?

11.12 Marketing Communications

Marketing communications always need a target for the communication and clearly defined, measurable objectives. Examples of marketing communications objectives are:

- Provide information, reassurance, reminders, reasons for buying
- Change perceptions, attitudes
- Create desires, needs-awareness, linkages
- Educate. Turn the *needs-oblivious* into the *needs-aware*
- Generate sales leads (increase market penetration)

There are objectives for the service provider as a whole, as well as objectives for each service. Service objectives are created as part of market test, and should be grouped in a marketing communications program by focus. For example, there would be one program focused on the IDC's collocation service, and a different one for its dedicated hosting service. Within each program there might be specific subprograms with special messaging for specific customer segments: one program for channel ASPs and another for direct sales to large enterprises. Content and messaging are created around these objectives and then communicated to the market. Before general release, this content should be tested to see if the desired message is transmitted. Allowances should be made for regional and language specificity. How often is there an article in the paper about a product name relaunch because it meant something lewd in a foreign language. This is press coverage, but for all the wrong reasons.

The messaging is then put into marketing materials, called collateral, that normally take the form of data sheets, fliers, brochures, and so forth. Marketing messages should be kept short and clear.

To make objectives measurable, a metric is associated with each objective, such as the communications program for this service should generate x sales leads by y date.

11.12.1 Webcentricity

With the proliferation of the Internet in the marketplace, coupled with the need to be cost-effective and efficient in generating marketing communications programs, webcentricity becomes a viable, practical means of execution.

According to Irene Economou, HP marketing communications manager for the service provider industry, "You can really maximize your resources and execution if you approach delivering the content creation for your messaging through a Web-centric strategy that lends itself to a hierarchical approach of content presentation. For example, you may choose to define your product, solution, or service in a high-level summary on a Web site giving the 35,000-foot perspective. At this level, this will force you to be clear and concise in your description. Taking this the next step, key words in this summary can then be hot-linked to the next layer, or drill-down, of information.

This lends itself to branching out into multiple paths of information and delivery options, such as presentations, collateral pieces, partner references, success stories, competitive comparisons, and so forth. Each subsequent drill-down of information provides a higher degree of specificity or focal point. Documents can also be formatted to offer print-on-demand literature. Adding links that cross-reference topics or other content-appropriate information further provide breadth and depth of complementary data that supports the original source material."

11.12.2 Marketing Communications Venues

Marketing communications venues are many and depend on communication target audiences, budget, and timing. The following are sample communication channels:

- Advertising (business and trade publications, Web site, radio, TV, and so on)
- Media relations (press announcements, analyst briefings, executive tours)
- Web site and push email
- Direct mail
- Direct sales contact (salesperson, phone, Web site, email, post)
- Channels
- Tradeshows
- Launch events, announcements, and so forth
- Speaking engagements
- Trade association creation/sponsorship
- Other sponsorships
- Word of mouth

Marketing communication program objectives should be defined before strategies and tactics can be determined. This should take into account short-term goals, long-range plans, and associated budgets. In-house staffing versus agency outsourcing comes into play. Ideally, you will want to have an experienced marketing communications professional define the plan and manage your program. He or she can either staff internally or outsource for specific services (i.e., PR, advertising, collateral development). There are pros and cons to outsourcing all, or part of, these campaigns. On the pro side, good PR agencies specialize in these campaigns and have contacts and more knowledge than the service provider. On the con side, they may not understand the business, and education takes time and resources. PR agencies need to be carefully managed and measured against specific objectives, and their services can be quite expensive.

11.12.2.1 Looking More Closely at Each of the Venues

Advertising can lack focus and is expensive, with limited possibility to measure success—particularly if the target population is confined. Advertising may make sense as a way to communicate to the target market, especially to consumers, but think of it as an incremental sales tool for the sales force, not as the focus of the marketing strategy.

Media relations are important and offer some of the best opportunities for building awareness and credibility for your company activities. Even articles about service provider problems can be turned around into a positive story if you can not only define the problem, but recommend the solution. This is how you build credibility as a knowledge leader in your field, especially if you agree to be interviewed and quoted.

Placed articles and press releases are useful; often service providers use PR agencies with varying degrees of success (see comments on outsourcing earlier in this chapter). PR agencies are generally useful in setting up interviews and speaking engagements. When the PR plan is prepared, it should have input from the PR agency used, as well as channels involved with press activities. Make sure you also include a plan to brief key industry analysts that follow your service focus. Know the difference between the role of the press versus that of analysts; the press will want to know the news while the analysts will want to know the news' strategic implications and impact on the industry.

All service providers should have a Web site or portal of some sort, and it should be one of the prime venues for communication of services and corporate information. There are many companies specializing in push email marketing infrastructure that can help when developing the organization to push information to customers and prospects. As with any direct mail campaign, avoid spamming but target the information pushed. The provider walks a thin line with these campaigns risking the anger of customers and potential customers when they receive unsolicited and unwanted information. One way of mitigating the risk is by asking permission before adding the name to the distribution list. Keep the messages short, with a link to the main information located on your site. These programs are measurable through click-through statistics. It is an excellent way of keeping customer links updated.

Direct mail/email/fax is usually characterized by low response rate, but it is a less expensive option for a defined, finite prospective customer population.

- Make sure the mailing media reflects the brand image of the service provider.
- Make sure the message is clear and short. Which customers will read this? What should they do as a result of this information? Why?
- Make sure the service provider knows what happens if the customer does, or does not, do what is requested.

Now lets look at the direct sales force as a communications venue. A happy, trained, dedicated direct sales force is one of the best venues of marketing communication a service provider can have. It is motivated, controllable, measurable, and understands the business. The opposite is also true. If the sales force is unhappy, uneducated, and unmotivated, it can destroy a business by, among other things, starting a negative word-of-mouth campaign. A direct sales force is expensive and creates a high cost of sale, but is often necessary for large, big-ticket customer segments.

Creating and training the sales force are among the most important activities for any business. A parallel activity to marketing plan development is the creation of a sales plan to support the marketing plan that includes the sales process, sales resource identification, and execution plan. The plan includes resource qualification, retention, incentives, targeting, measurement, training and procedures (such as order and contract procedures).

The sales channel can represent a sizeable proportion of revenues, but managers should take time to recruit, manage, and incubate. Channels are difficult to control in terms of messaging, focus, and quality; although, certification programs can help. Channel strategy and planning is vital for any service provider as they decide on their services roadmap, outsourcing, operations, sales, marketing, and support. For the majority of service providers, channels will be involved in each of these areas. Channels can be an easy way of acquiring customers; the cost of sale is generally lower, but there must be a genuine value proposition for the channel (something in it for them). Options include:

- Commission
- Special volume discounts (allowing them to make margin)
- Comarketing (events, collateral, Web content); the service provider brand name can be leveraged here.
- Special certification programs

One somewhat surprising prospective channel could be competitor ISPs that might want to outsource some infrastructure and focus exclusively on front-office activities. A notable example of this is the U.K., where the largest consumer ISP offers Internet service to more than five million U.K. households. These households only know the brand of their ISP, yet the ISP outsources its data center to another service provider. The consumer ISP is wholly focused on leveraging brand and pushing portal functionality. Channels can take all forms and include partners like equipment vendors, system integrators, consulting companies, ISVs, and so on.

Tradeshows abound and are expensive. The service provider needs to research the tradeshow before investing, making sure there is a focus match. The tradeshow managers should agree to give information on attendee statistics for prior years to help the service provider make its decision. Check to see if speaking opportunities are included for participants or sponsors. Will the service provider receive lists of attendees afterward? Find out who else is participating in the show and where the booth will be placed. Are there adequate resources from the service provider to staff the booth? Will collateral and booth signage be available when needed? Is there a demo already created that can be included? Is the correct infrastructure available to run the demo?

Well-publicized launch events that include participation by target prospective customers and partners are essential. Timing is of utmost importance. Examples would be the opening of data center facilities to coincide with the end of a successful pilot period, especially if the timing is just before a competitor announces its service. The service provider can create an event to include a press conference in the morning when press can see the facilities and interview satisfied pilot customers. The afternoon would include a specific opening for important prospective customers with a tour of the facilities and a special drawing. Participants in this event include the pilot customers who talk with the prospects telling them how wonderful the services are. The afternoon leads into an exclusive evening event that includes TV or local celebrities. If the service provider hears about a competitor coming to market with a new service, it may try to get some sort of press release into the media first as a way to lessen the impact of the competitive announcement. Speaking engagements are also easy ways to get more exposure in an inexpensive way. If these engagements are positioned well, they can be excellent sources of publicity and media placement.

The service provider may want to consider being a founding member, or sponsor, of a trade association. This can be a vehicle for media exposure, as well as an excellent way to establish a platform for future lobbying efforts and for creating industry standards.

Other sponsorships can also heighten market awareness, but should be carefully targeted. Service providers can consider sponsoring nontrade associations, products, sporting events, and so forth. They should focus on things important to building brand awareness and trust, such as sponsoring university or educational Internet programs, and offering students jobs or training. A student who trains on a certain infrastructure is likely to use the same infrastructure, or services, when in the working world. This sort of program can be considered part of a long-term customer acquisition strategy.

Reference programs or word of mouth programs are often cited as one of the best vehicles to increase market share and show loyalty of the customer installed base. Prospects will often ask to speak with reference customers as part of their normal due diligence. One way to start building a reference program is by measuring and rewarding employees, especially sales people, when they sign up customers to participate. Elements of a reference program can include:

- Glossy collateral for distribution to prospects. These are normally called case studies or success stories
- Joint press releases
- Comarketing programs and funding
- Allowing *X* number of site visits per year for service provider prospective customers
- Special pricing or discounting
- Information on the service provider's and the referring company's Web sites
- Reminding employees to ask if a new customer would serve as a reference
- Offering excellent service so customers want to be references.

11.12.3 The Role of the Company Spokesperson

The role of the service provider spokesperson is especially important. Every employee in the company informally takes on this role. At any given time an employee may be talking about the company to a customer, friend, partner, or newspaper. All these are instances of public relations. The employee will be representing his/her employer, and the employer wants its employee to convey the best possible image about the provider's services. Internal communications is especially important so that employees are informed about services offered, their benefits, and the company's spin on any happenings that may be circulating in the market. These communications can be conveyed via email, circulars, newsletters, and so forth.

The service provider should have individuals, usually upper management, designated as official spokespeople. Many potential spokespeople may be concerned about conveying the wrong message to the press or analyst community. It is the responsibility of the service provider to train its spokespeople before letting them loose on the market. The good news is that many PR agencies offer this sort of training that usually includes presentations, role-playing, and video feedback.

11.13 Service Execution Components

To bring a service to market and support its lifecycle, several components should be considered (see Figure 11-8):

- A service owner within the service provider ("Program or Product Manager")
- A small number (maximum of three) of measurable service objectives
- A marketing (including marketing communications) and sales plan to achieve those objectives
- A way to test the plans (also getting support within the service provider for the plans)
- A resource plan to execute service operations and sales/marketing plans
- An organized way to execute the plans
- A strategy (or matrix) showing how the service provider will adjust its plans based on possible market and competition reactions to the new services
- An execution review cycle
- A service exit strategy

11.13.1 Owner

The outcome of a go-to-market strategy is critical for commercial success. Accordingly, the owner of the program needs to have real interest in a successful outcome. This is often achieved through incentives based on measurable objectives. In an organization the primary owner of the service's go-to-market strategy is usually someone in marketing who develops the service and service description. This individual may be called a program, or product manager and researches the market to understand needs, confirming these needs through testing and working closely with sales people and partners. This process is also a way of garnering further support for the new service through those selling it. To be successful, the program manager also requires support from other divisions in the company responsible for delivering and supporting the service after it's sold.

The owner may have additional fiscal responsibility, needing to prove the service offering makes financial sense based on current and expected revenues. Further, the owner is responsible for coordinating the cross-geography sales funnel and the sales, marketing, resourcing, and service exit strategies.

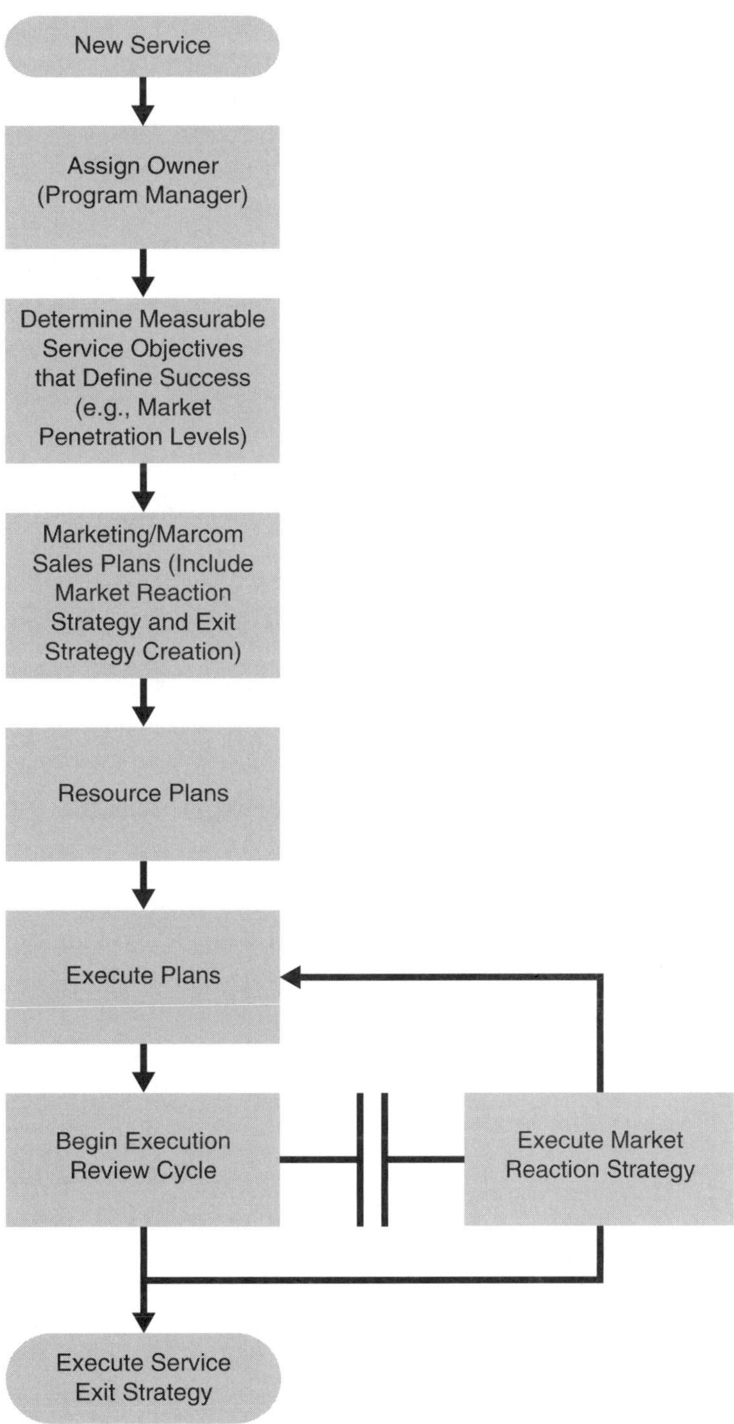

Figure 11-8
The execution flowchart.

11.13.2 Objectives

Marketing and sales objectives need to focus on rapidly building momentum for the new product/service. Objectives need to be measurable and split between short-term, tactical, quick-win objectives, and the longer term strategic objectives. Typical examples are "*x* signed contracts by date *y*" or "booked sales revenue of *x* by date *y*," and "increase market penetration from *a* to *b*."

These are examples of tactical objectives:

- Three pilot customers who agree to be references by March
- 10 Bronze customers, five Silver customers and two Gold customers by June
- Educate tier one target customers as measured by reaching year one quota numbers

Here are examples of strategic objectives:

- 200 customers in 12 months
- Increase market share to 40 percent by the second year the service is offered.

Objectives need to be decided and agreed to as soon as possible in the service lifecycle.

11.13.3 Marketing and Sales Planning

As mentioned earlier, at one level the prospective client is a business, but at another level the buyers are people within the business. These buyers will influence the sales outcome and it is important to understand their personal needs, interests, and goals when developing an execution plan.

11.13.3.1 Important Elements of a Marketing Plan

The marketing plan should include the following components:

- Marketing goals
- Service description and roadmap
- Target market description and size (worldwide market size, addressable market, market penetration for current and future years)
- Value proposition
- Competition
- Channel marketing plan
- SWOT analysis
- Marketing communications plan
- Market readiness
- Regional deployment readiness
- Service readiness levels (operational readiness)

11.13.3.2 Important Elements of a Marketing Communications Plan

A marketing communications plan shows how the company intends to communicate the value of its products and services to the market. The plan includes specific marketing programs, direct and indirect—how they are focused, the budget needed, timing, and so forth.

Elements of marketing communications programs include:

- A summary of the overall marketing communications strategy, targets, measurements, and vision
- Target segment(s) with each further defined into target companies, their needs, target people within those companies
- Message for each segment
- Collateral list for each segment
- Events, publications, sponsorships, campaigns, and other communications venues focused on the segment
- Details for how the message will be communicated via each venue
- How to educate the needs oblivious
- Market communications programs with channel partners and key customers
- Marketing communications budget and breakdown

All avenues of communication will need content and collateral to support the process. The communication method(s) should be carefully selected for each target segment and needs category. The marketing communication plan must take all aspects of communication into account. It can be made more effective, or focused, with the deployment of promotions and incentives. Possibilities include:

- Special price- or special-offer based discounts for beta customers; for example, buy Bronze, get Gold free for six months
- Special bonuses to each salesperson or channel closing one of the initial *x* beta customers.

Timing of communication is an important factor. For example, people are distracted in the run up to holiday periods. Also, keeping the service in the minds of target customers is extremely important and should be an ongoing process. This means planned communications should be part of the marketing communications plan; for example, monthly press releases for three months up to, and two months after, the launch of a new service offering.

11.13.3.3 Important Elements of a Sales Plan

The sales plan shows how the sales strategy will be executed. It should take into account direct and indirect sales channels, their focus markets, quota, compensation, and so forth. Specific elements of the sales plan should include:

- The sales strategy and target market penetration objectives
- The sales quotas for direct and indirect sales forces and how they will be measured

- How products and services information will be communicated to the field sales forces
- The funnel for direct and indirect channels, and how/when it will be updated
- How the service provider will focus its direct and indirect sales specifically, by region
- Named accounts to be the focus of the direct sales force including company names and information, their needs, targeted people in the companies, what they're using now, and so forth.
- An analysis of the sales force coverage and how the company will compensate for gaps in coverage
- How the sales forces (direct and indirect) will be trained
- Compensation planning
- Channel strategy and plan that will cover how the company will choose, focus, measure and compensate its channel partners
- If customers will become sales channels
- How the call center will be included in the sales plan and how the team members will be trained and compensated
- Coselling programs with channel partners and key customers
- What sales tools are available/will be developed
- Overall budget and breakdown detail by the above program descriptions.

Sales tools are many and varied, and it is a good idea to have a minimum list of items that are developed before or as a new service is pushed to market. A list of minimum sales tools and collateral could include:

- Sales guide: This would be an internal document giving details about the service, pricing, target customers, needs, how this fills their needs, what the competition offers, how to sell against the competition, short success stories that include why they bought this product/service, and how this service compares to competing services.
- Data sheet: An external document giving high-level information about the service, its features and functions, how it solves the customer's problems, and company contact information.
- Configuration guide: An internal document that gives post-sales technical resources information on configuring and provisioning the service. These documents usually include configuration checklists, contact numbers for verification, and process plans showing approximate timing for each item in the configuration process.
- Ordering guide: An internal document giving sales resources information on ordering the new service.
- Demonstrations: Customer demonstrations showing features and functions of the products and services.
- Case studies and reference account write-ups: External collateral giving customer testimonials about the service.

- White papers: Can be external or internal collateral pieces and are normally technical, but give more in-depth information about the services
- Return on investment studies: External collateral showing direct and indirect savings, or other returns on investment.

11.13.3.4 Sales Force Characteristics

Service providers used to look for sales representatives who had IT background and good interpersonal skills. Now there is a shift toward hiring sales people who have experience in IT, IP, and with certain vertical industries, the most popular of which are financial, communications, and manufacturing. Service providers are looking for sales people who have the aptitude to learn or expertise in consultative selling as a way to help prospective customers understand how to use offered services to get better business results. To obtain the best results, service providers need to be able to train their sales force to sell their services.

11.13.3.5 A Few Words About Training

xSPs should ensure that training for all staff is part of the plan from day one. Educate the decision makers early in the process so they make better decisions and then train the implementation and end-user staff to perform successfully in their jobs. Ideally a certification program should be developed to make sure the highly skilled are validated and rewarded, while dangerously unskilled workers are weeded out. Remember, the majority of system downtime is caused by mistakes made by untrained, or poorly trained people, *not* from hardware or software failures. This becomes especially important if the provider offers high availability or SLA guarantees.

xSPs may decide to resell training and associated services to their clients as a lucrative and high margin line of business. xSPs should consider the huge demand and growth for training services, especially online training. The types of training service providers need to consider for their staff include executive/business manager briefings, process management, software, middleware, development, networks, security, and performance.

Provision of an integrated and flexible training offering is key in today's world where learners of different styles and cultures expect to consume training in their desired mode that adapts to their learning preference and work dynamics. For example, shift workers may not be able to attend day classes. The key modes of delivery, for internal and external students, include traditional books and classroom environments, Web-based—with live Web shops, CD-ROM, and videos. Self-help training offered to end-users is another way to lower customer churn and reduce support calls.

11.13.4 Testing

At each step along the path of service introduction, market testing is important. While service offerings are developed, the service descriptions, marketing messaging, and pricing should be tested with prospective customers. Appendix H shows a sample test questionnaire used to test service descriptions and pricing. This is the time when intelligence is uncovered about prospective customer awareness, and how they respond to the service descriptions, marketing messages, and pricing.

Based on the testing interviews for a service provider in Asia Pacific, there were two distinct customer segments:

- The needs oblivious
- The partially needs-aware

Based on this, the service provider needs to create a marketing communications plan to educate its target customers, testing the messaging along the way.

Another important aspect of testing is the pilot phase. This is the opportunity for the service provider to stress test operations, pricing, and service descriptions, shaking out all aspects of the service processes before going operational.

11.13.5 Resourcing

Resourcing is the make/buy decision for plan execution. As part of this, the service provider needs to decide how much of the plan is to be executed in-house and how much is to be outsourced. Normally, the service provider would define its first-tier customer list and initially outsource the market analysis, testing of services/pricing, and PR/marketing communication plan development. Even so, the service provider needs to be involved in the process so it doesn't lose touch with its market.

11.13.5.1 Important Elements of a Resourcing Plan

A resourcing, or staffing, plan shows how the company plans to staff itself to realize the sales targets and growth goals detailed in the strategy and planning process. These plans should include an analysis of the company's current staffing, gaps, and hiring, training and deployment plans. Main elements of a resource plan include:

- Restatement of corporate strategy and goals
- Current staffing levels and resource focus
- Identified gaps and how these resources might need to be refocused to achieve corporate goals
- Plan to address gaps
- Outsourcing/partnering
- Hiring, training, and deployment plan for new hires
- Budget and breakdown by the above items

11.13.6 Execution

All marketing, sales, and resourcing plans go through some sort of approval process and will take time to implement. Well thought-out plans take this lag time into account. The owner is in charge of the orderly service introduction and its ongoing operation according to plan(s).

Plans need to be flexible enough to change as the market reacts (see the section "Reaction"). A periodic review should give a good indication of trouble spots as they occur.

11.13.7 Reaction

Monitoring market and competitor reaction is key during the service/product lifecycle. Competitors will react to the services and marketing employed, and the service provider must be ready to counterattack. As competitors react and come to market with new services, the service provider needs to analyze these actions in relation to its core business and P&L. The provider should decide ahead of time what parameters and boundaries are acceptable for any changes in pricing, functionality, and so forth.

For example: If competitor one decreases its prices for the same services and same service quality, the service provider needs to determine if it wants to do the same thing (not advisable), or offer more value-added services (better idea), and communicate the updated value proposition to the market. Notice that no mention was made of price—only value. If the sale is made on price, value is not understood and the service is a commodity.

11.13.8 Review

Constant review of the service marketing and sales results, as well as market needs/reaction, is required to determine success, or if changes are needed. Marketing, sales, and resourcing plans should be flexible and adjusted as market conditions change. The provider's success will, in part, be based on ensuring that each program/division has an owner responsible for its success that can be measured by quantifiable means.

11.13.9 Exit Strategy

No service offering lasts forever, and the owner needs to develop an exit strategy to address the time when the service offering no longer makes financial sense. A service provider may strategically want to continue offering some services even after profit margins are eroded, because:

- The functionality can be bundled with other service offerings that are still profitable
- The functionality creates a barrier to change for customers who use other, profitable services

Refer to "Service Strategy" earlier in this chapter for more information on this subject. The exit period is also a time to do a post-mortem review of the service program. The service provider can incorporate these learnings into future programs.

11.14 Summary

A go-to-market strategy includes information about:

- The overall company marketing goals
- The customer need, market drivers, and customer segmentation

- Customer needs awareness levels
- The service offering description
- Service pricing, placement and promotion

The strategy is executed via a series of plans, including:

- Sales
- Marketing/marketing communications
- Resourcing
- Partnering
- Operations

Service execution components include:

- An owner
- A small number (maximum of three) of measurable objectives
- Marketing, sales, resourcing, partnering, plans to achieve those objectives
- A way to test the plan
- The resources to execute the plan
- A method to execute the plan(s)
- A plan when the market and competition reacts to the services
- Ongoing execution review
- An exit strategy

11.15 Endnotes

1. Determining service offering profitability is covered under the "pricing" and "cash flow" sections.
2. "Profit Cow" is a bastardization of the Boston Growth Matrix "Cash Cow." Service providers are concerned about cash flow, as they often have very high cash constraints, they should be equally concerned about profit levels. Earlier market tolerance for continually unprofitable business is gone and service providers must show solid plans toward profitability.

11.16 xSP Strategy Checklist for Entering the Market

- ❑ What is the customer need?
  - ❑ How do they fill these needs today?
  - ❑ Who, specifically, in the company has these needs?
  - ❑ What does the customer's customer need?
- ❑ What service offering can fill these needs?
  - ❑ What is the services roadmap, and how can the service goals better focus today's offering?
- ❑ What is the market segmentation and target segment?
- ❑ What is the total market, addressable market, and obtainable market size?
- ❑ What part of the offering will be offered in-house? What is outsourced?
- ❑ What is the value proposition?
- ❑ Who is the competition?
  - ❑ Is a SWOT analysis complete?
- ❑ How will the service be priced?
- ❑ Have the service descriptions, pricing, and market messaging been tested?
- ❑ How will the service be promoted? Sold? Marketed?
- ❑ Are the marketing/marketing communications, sales, resource plans complete and agreed?
- ❑ Does the service make financial sense?
- ❑ Has the service owner been assigned?
- ❑ Are there measurable objectives for the marketing/marcom and sales plans?
- ❑ Are the execution review processes set up?
- ❑ Is there an exit strategy?

CHAPTER 12

Service Delivery and Provisioning

As the name suggests, delivering service is one of the primary functions of a service provider. Efficient service delivery, combined with high-quality customer care, will have a direct impact on customer perception and operational costs. Traditional telecommunications monopolies did not have to worry about customers' needs for new services or speed in service delivery—customers didn't have any choices. Today's highly competitive market means that end-user customers can dictate to operators the need to introduce new services quickly. This translates into minutes or hours versus days or weeks. Many new services are too complex for manual setup and delivery. Demanding, finicky customers combined with the available new technologies that can satisfy almost every customer whim result in a high-pressure environment in which new, high-quality services are expected quickly and accessibly. As more and more mission-critical processes are instrumented and Web enabled, increasing demands are placed on the Internet for speed and availability of these services/processes supported by a communications network. Let's explore what is needed to deliver and maintain service provider services.

12.1 State of Affairs

The existing service providers either evolved from the telecommunications business, were utilities operators, or were incorporated from inception to function as a service provider. Traditional telecommunications companies have large legacy systems, both in their infrastructure and their processes. Generally, companies starting out as service providers raced to market building IT infrastructure and processes to quickly meet their clients' growing demands. Getting new services to market quickly is vital for these types of organizations. Still, it is equally important to keep costs low and make sure the infrastructure and operational processes built are massively scalable, open, highly available, secure, and manageable.

While many operational functions are performed manually in the beginning, numerous organizations streamline these processes as the company matures. In the provisioning area, streamlining helps create economies of scale. How strikingly different this is from incumbent telecommunication companies that didn't need to get new services to market quickly, offer high-quality services, or be particularly careful about customer care. Why? They were monopolies. With deregulation, companies now need to offer new top-quality services within minutes or hours versus weeks/ months, and keep customers happy in highly competitive markets. In the telecommunications industry, deregulation usually refers to the process where the traditional monopoly telecommunications company, also known as a PTT, is broken up to allow competition. In the United States this was seen as part of the Telecommunications Act of 1996 and the AT&T split up.

New entrants to the market come from all sectors including ISVs, system integrators, and traditional brick-and-mortar business. These companies decide to become service providers because current revenue streams are being eroded as buying habits become pervasive and transaction costs decrease. Oftentimes these companies know they need to explore new channels to market, but don't know how to set up operational processes to support the service delivery needed to exploit new technologies. These businesses need to analyze where they are on the learning curve, both in understanding execution in their newly chosen businesses and in setting up internal processes to support them.

As we would expect from such a capital-intensive business, partnering will continue to be a key success factor for service providers, as they look for ways to maximize cash flow. All service providers should critically review their situation for forced operational inefficiencies as a result of relying on others for services infrastructure (IT and otherwise). The provider should review partners' operations to see if they have a good understanding of their internal processes.

To make matters worse, customers are demanding more and more self-service and self-provisioning, with service starting at the time of setup. Customer perception is that provisioning should be easy, so they should be able to do it themselves via the Web. Service providers like this idea because it requires fewer staff members; however, there must be an infrastructure, both technical and process, in place to support self-service and self-provisioning.

How can service providers manage customer perception to maintain customer loyalty and increase market share? They need to understand the status of their provisioning processes and infrastructure by asking:

- Are processes predominantly paper based?
- Are established processes nonstandard?
- Do processes involve a lot of people who are performing unnecessary steps?
- Are bottlenecks visible in purchasing, provisioning, billing, support, and customer care?

- Can bottlenecks (process points where service provisioning or delivery is delayed) be eased and processes optimized?
- Can processes be measured for efficiency?

To answer these questions, let's now turn to a definition and further explanation of service provisioning and service delivery.

12.2 What is Service Delivery and Service Provisioning

Service delivery refers to the service provider infrastructure and processes needed to deliver a service to either a consumer or enterprise. It includes all aspects of the fulfillment lifecycle:

- Purchase from order entry through testing
- Activation
- Maintenance from customer care (see Chapter 13, "Perception Is Reality,") to technical support and billing (see Chapter 14, "Billing")
- Selling, either cross selling other services or up-selling enhanced services
- Deactivating the customer

Service provisioning refers to the step in service delivery when configuration parameters are set up, the work force is assigned to install the CPE, network elements are configured, access is checked, and so forth. Lack of control over the delivery procedures will translate into lost revenue.

Process types generally can be grouped into operational and organizational. Operational processes are those directly related to the main business of the company. For service providers, these would be processes directly related to service creation, delivery, assurance, and usage. Service assurance is the system used to manage the processes and information required to make sure the promised services are running and available. Service usage is the system and processes used to understand how customers use the services offered. This information is important when managing and planning network resources, when creating, testing and marketing new and ongoing services, when billing on usage-based information, and in understanding if, and how, customers use the services available. Organizational processes support internal business processes like sales, marketing, finance, and customer care.

One of the biggest single operational investments in dollars, business importance, and manpower is a flexible automated provisioning system. Such a system can grow as business needs and support operations rapidly evolve, keeping up with the complex service delivery process and reducing the need for manual provisioning, which can take too long and contain errors. Manual processes do not allow quick service introduction and because there isn't one person or one department responsible for the entire process, service providers can't easily find or track information bottlenecks. This makes it difficult to work out how the process can best be optimized. An automated provisioning system gives service providers the ability to tell their customers if service is available, when it will be activated, how much it will cost, and what service levels can be guaranteed.

Service delivery and provisioning are, of course, important when deciding which services to offer and how they should be offered. They also affect customer loyalty, market share, and ongoing revenue streams, having a direct bearing on decreasing operational costs. Provisioning and delivery systems are expensive because they link so many different processes together (Figure 12-1), but these points should be a good start at creating a convincing business case for implementation. The business case should show direct and indirect savings, as well as increased revenues from the ability to offer:

- Fast, reliable service creation and service delivery
- Self provisioning
- Self tracking
- Minimized provisioning/delivery costs, especially on base line services
- Automated error handling

To do this, the service provider needs a strong foundation and process management that supports:

- Parallel processing
- Testing to perform conditional branches in the process
- Loops to perform rework
- Escalating work to other employees, departments, or applications
- Error control and exception handling
- Business level service design
- Metrics, feedback, and simulation
- Replicable infrastructure
- Adherence to SLAs
- Enabling technology for ASP process services

The core processes/information/products needed for service provider service delivery are:

- Sales and marketing processes
- Order handling
- Product catalog and product pricing
- Network inventory
- Activation software
- Installation
- Customer relationship management systems and databases
- Billing
- Process modeling tools
- Process management tools
- Flexible integration of applications

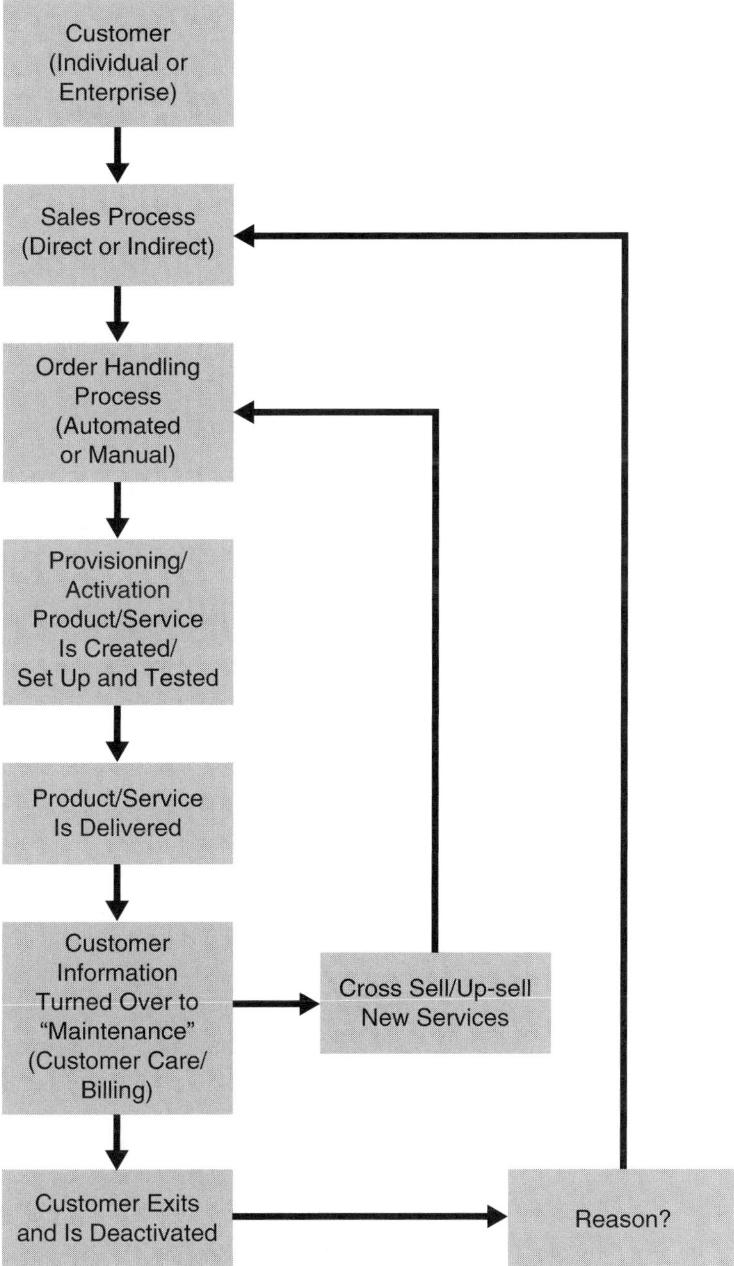

Figure 12-1 The operational processes for service delivery.

Sales and Marketing Processes Market research should provide information on customer needs and buying behavior from external and internal sources. As mentioned earlier, services must be easy to buy, offering a pleasant customer experience or the customer will leave before completing the transaction. During the selling process a customer negotiates and, hopefully, buys the service. Depending on the service provider, it is possible for the customer to place an order through the sales force, customer care, or, if automated, directly through the order management process. If customers themselves can configure the service, the process goes directly to service configuration.

Order Handling Order handling is the process that takes the request for service and starts the provisioning process.

Product catalogs A product catalog is a services database specifying all aspects of the services offered by the service provider. Information from this database is used both internally and externally. These catalogs give the ability to:

- Group several service elements into one service
- Introduce new services based on existing services or set up different levels of services
- Define and change product offerings as needed (personalized or customized services)
- Produce market forecasts
- Offer flexible pricing and price changes in real time
- Introduce special promotions and programs
- Record customer needs so they can be used later to generate new services

Network Inventory A network inventory is a database containing information about the network. It helps the service provider know what service options are available, which option is most reliable and within cost guidelines, understand service routing options, service guarantees, available carriers, and security levels, and which entities are to be provisioned. A network inventory is critical for service delivery, as it depends on having accurate information about the network. Manual records are less accurate and can directly impact the efficiency of the service delivery process.

Activation software Activation software provides a platform that controls the activation of a service by coordinating the configuration and activation of customer access and transmission technologies. It is especially useful when the service involves devices and systems from various vendors, or when the activation is dependent on services supplied by another operator. It monitors the service and reports faults, establishes the network connection for the service, reports events, and activates services across different network technologies, layers, and vendors' equipment. Activation software also provides interfaces for use by other systems, and combines the physical parts of the network in a logical wrapper service such that one logical service may contain many physical components.

Customer Relationship Management CRM controls all aspects of interaction with the customer. A CRM system can offer one view of the customer to the service provider. The advantage of these systems is that they can increase sales and create closer relationships between customer and service provider by:

- Extending buying hours
- Building a complete picture of the customer
- Providing marketing and sales information
- Directly targeting particular customer segments
- Offering flexibility in customer contact service levels
- Providing easy access to complete customer information

CRM is covered in more detail in Chapter 13.

Billing After the customer's service is set up, information must go to the billing system so the customer is billed for the new service; otherwise, this business is not revenue generating. Billing is covered in more detail in Chapter 14.

Process Modeling and Management Tools These tools help model and manage the service delivery processes to be implemented. They are usually graphical in nature and provide for the definition, reuse, control, and measurement of business processes across organizations. A business process defines which services are used, when they get called (the business rules), and which resources should carry out the service.

Integrating External Applications As the service delivery process becomes increasingly more automated, third-party applications will be integrated, both in-house and with delivery partners. There will need to be interfaces between the process, resources, and applications involved so processes can work efficiently across operations.

12.3 The Service Delivery Interface with the Logical Organization

In Chapter 10, "Organization," we discussed logical and physical organizational models for the service provider. Here we turn to the interface of these models with service delivery. The models are important when automating the service delivery process. Any automation must allow for both the end-to-end process flow and the interface flow.

In this chapter, we primarily focus on the service management layer of the TMN model (see Figure 12-2), as this layer is responsible for meeting the company's business goals and objectives. The layer manages the services that depend on the network infrastructure and forms a crucial link between the business and network management layers. As service providers face increasing competition in today's deregulated market, it is vital that the needs of the customer drive the business. This means the business management layers should dictate to the service, network, and element management layers, and not vice versa.

The TOM uses the layers of the TMN as its base, but divides the service management layer into two further sublayers: customer care and service development/operations (see Figure 12-3).

The boundary between these layers is significant, as it divides the customer facing customer care processes with the network facing service development and operations processes.

End-to-End
Management
Business
Management
Service
Management
Network
Management
Element
Management
Business Needs
Standards & Technology
Evolution

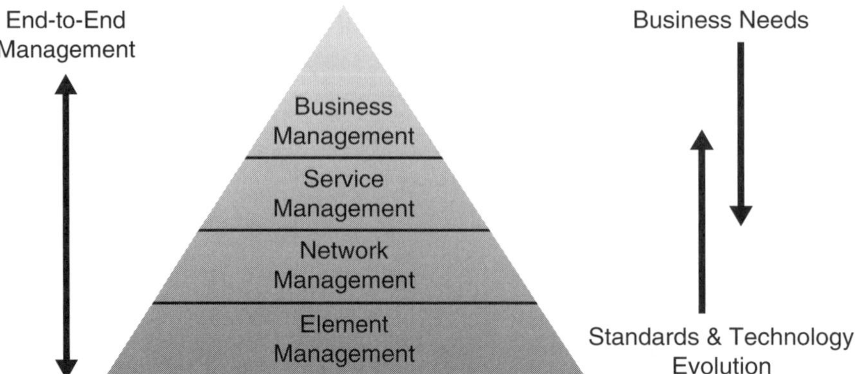

Figure 12-2 The telecommunications management network model.
©TM Forum's Telecom Operations Map.

Customer
Business
Management
Customer Interface Management Processes
Sales
Order
Handling
Problem
Handling
Customer
QoS
Management
Invoicing &
Collection
Customer Care Processes
Service
Management
Service
Planning &
Development
Service
Configuration
Service
Problem
Resolution
Service
Quality
Management
Rating &
Discounting
Service Development and Operations Processes
Network
Management
Network
Planning &
Development
Network
Provisioning
Network
Inventory
Management
Network
Maintenance
& Restoration
Network Data
Management
Network and Systems Management Processes
Information Systems Management Processes
Element
Management
Element Management Processes
Physical Network & Information Technology

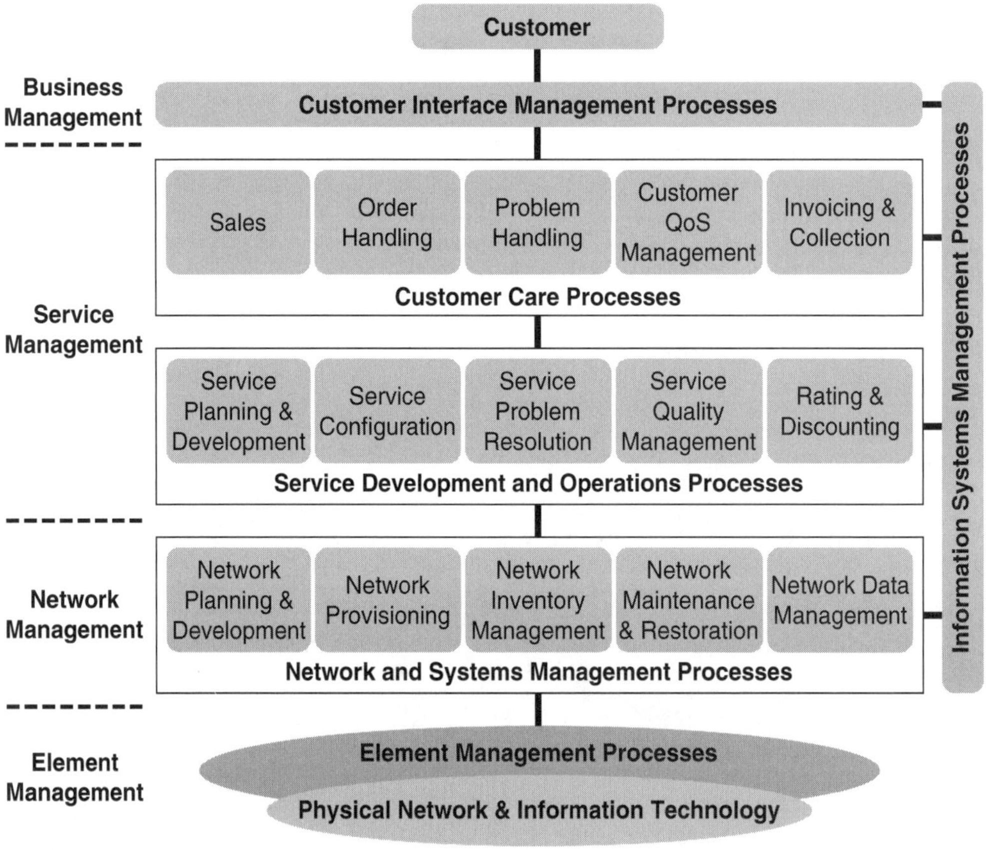

Figure 12-3 The Telecommunications operations map.
©TM Forum's Telecom Operations Map.

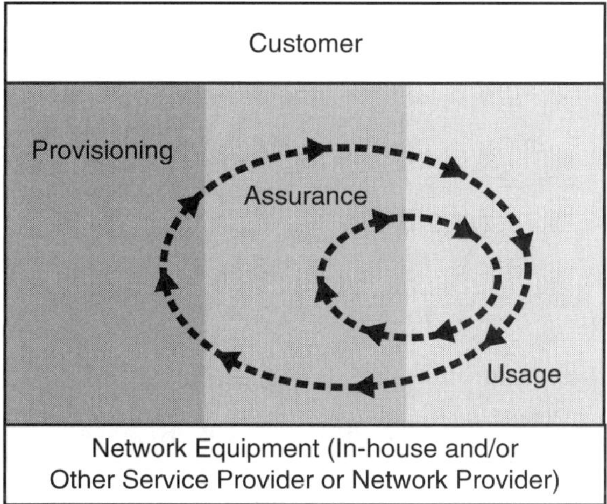

Figure 12-4 The PAU model.
Published courtesy of Hewlett-Packard Company.

The Provisioning Assurance Usage model (PAU) (see Figure 12-4) further breaks down the process flows to reflect how they relate to customer fulfillment, service assurance, and billing.

The two important flows here are:

1. The process flow from provisioning through service assurance to billing
2. The interface flow from the customer down to the network layer

These processes are fluid and may overlap across boundaries (see Figure 12-5).

12.4 Generic Service Delivery

Service delivery (see Figure 12-6) is made up of many complex tightly linked processes involving resources and technology. Typically, these processes are a mixture of systems and human elements with no single point of coordination. A change in one aspect will have a domino effect on the others. For example: automating order entry means the links to other aspects of the provisioning process need updating to reflect the automation.

Service delivery for a new service consists of four high-level provisioning areas:

- Sales/negotiation
- Orders capture/handling
- Service configuration
- Provisioning/activation

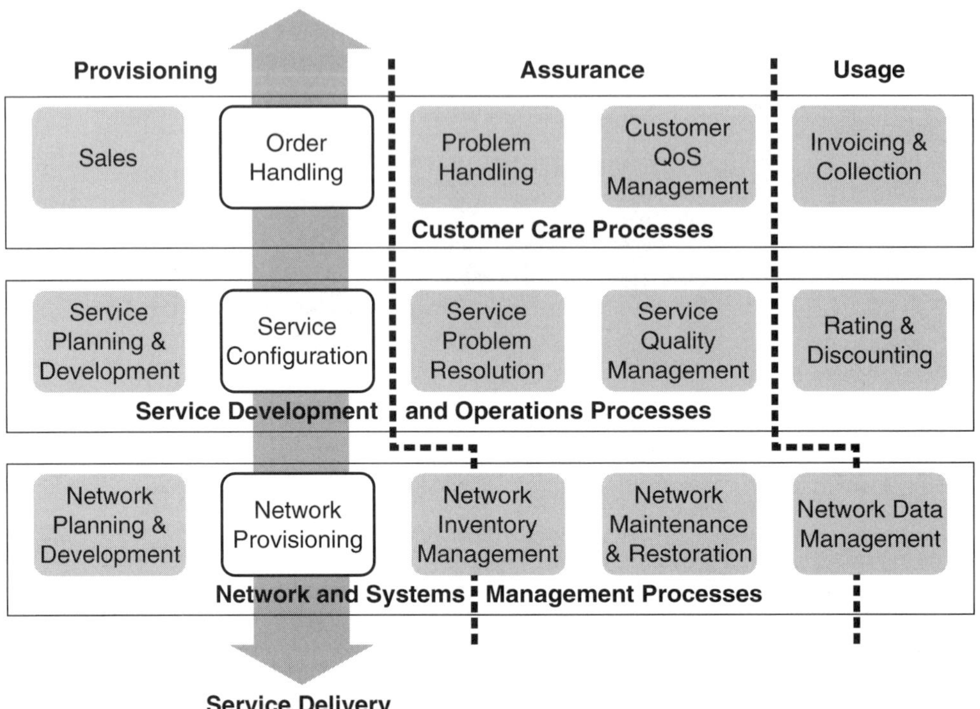

Figure 12-5 Mapping the TOM and PAU models.
©TM Forum's Telecom Operations Map.

The more preconfiguration, the more steps can be bypassed. Here preconfiguration means not only automation, but tuning the processes and equipment to support the business rules across organizations.

The following seven steps are generic processes for service delivery as illustrated in Figure 12-6:

1. Selling: The customer inquires, negotiates, and decides to buy a service. If the service can be self-provisioned, the customer can go directly to Step 4.
2. Order request: An order request is created and the sales staff verifies it is feasible to supply this service to the customer.
3. Service request: If the service is deemed feasible, a request for the service can be generated.
4. Provisioning request: The service is provisioned—configuration parameters are set up, work force is assigned to install the CPE, network elements are configured, access checks are performed.
5. Activation: The service is activated after Steps 1-4 are completed.
6. Test request: The service is tested to see if it is working and can be released to the customer.
7. Service delivery: Control passes to the service assurance and billing processes.

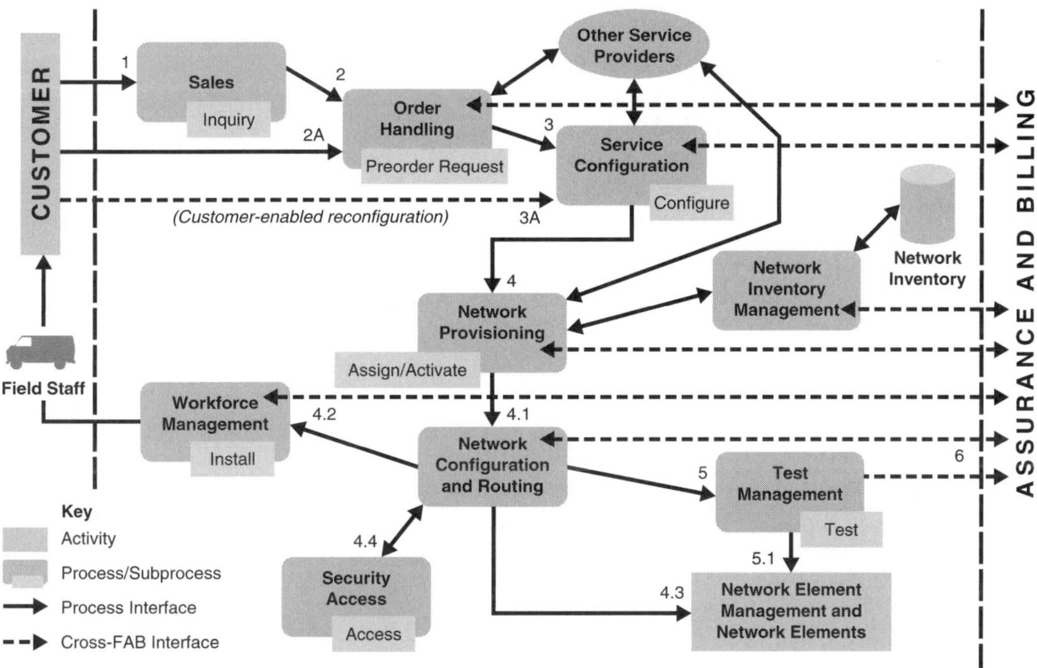

Figure 12-6 The generic service delivery processes.
©TM Forum's Telecom Operations Map.

12.5 Pitfalls of Service Delivery

There are two main pitfalls in the majority of today's service delivery:

- Manual service delivery processes
- Point-to-point service delivery processes that are not consistent across the organization

12.5.1 Manual Processes

Cost savings and error reduction are the two main drivers that force service delivery automation. Although other systems, such as billing, are often the first to become automated, the biggest cost savings are usually to be made when automating service delivery processes.

Manual service delivery processes (see Figure 12-7) are largely inefficient, costly, and error prone due to their complexity and large amount of human interaction. This leads to long, expensive service delivery lead times with numerous mistakes.

Defining and mapping the logical processes are the first steps in process automation. After processes are mapped, they must then be automated as much as possible.

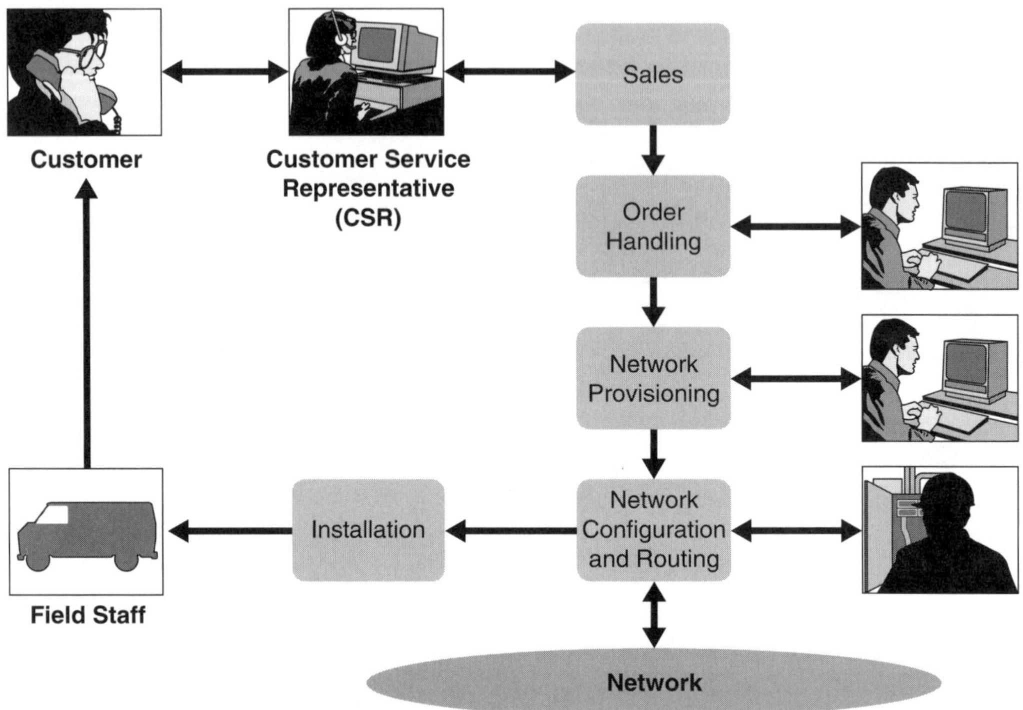

Figure 12-7 A manual service delivery process has many inefficiencies.
Published courtesy of Hewlett-Packard Company.

12.5.1.1 Point-to-Point

Often service delivery processes are embedded. Each department has its own process and IT system that interacts with other departments in the service delivery chain on a point-to-point basis (see Figure 12-8).

There is no visible end-to-end process allowing a seamless flow between departments and applications; therefore, identifying the process and changing it is difficult, if not impossible. As a result, there is inflexible, slow, and error-prone service delivery, making new services difficult to introduce. Normally these processes connect operations and systems like CRM, network management, order entry, billing, HR, finance, workforce management, and so forth. With no one owning the overall process it is difficult to control, track, monitor, and optimize interactions between these systems and operations. There can be no way to promise service delivery by a specific date and assure service levels because there is no, or poor, communication between departments.

What is needed is a way of effectively decoupling the process from the resources used to perform it. As shown in Figure 12-9, introducing a process management layer and integration bus can act as a common point between all resources during the entire process. The management layer is normally made up of the process as defined with the aid of graphical process modeling tools. The integration bus contains the physical connection and interaction among processes,

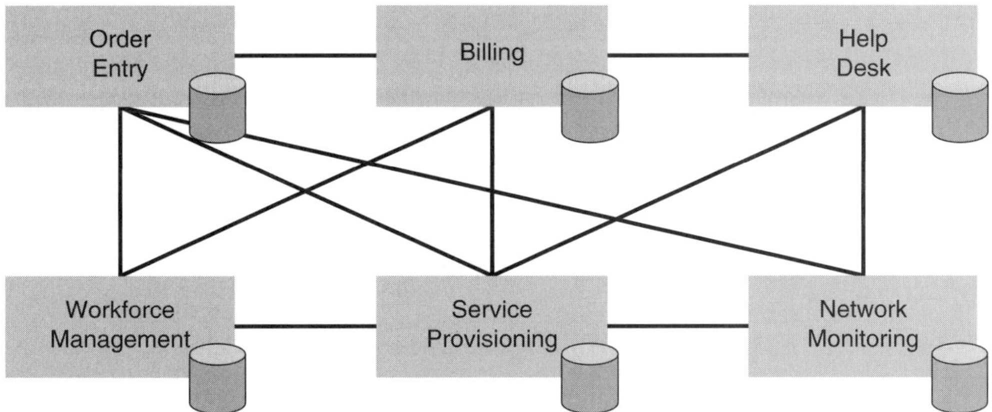

Figure 12-8 Service delivery processes are often embedded and touch on a point-to-point basis.
Published courtesy of Hewlett-Packard Company.

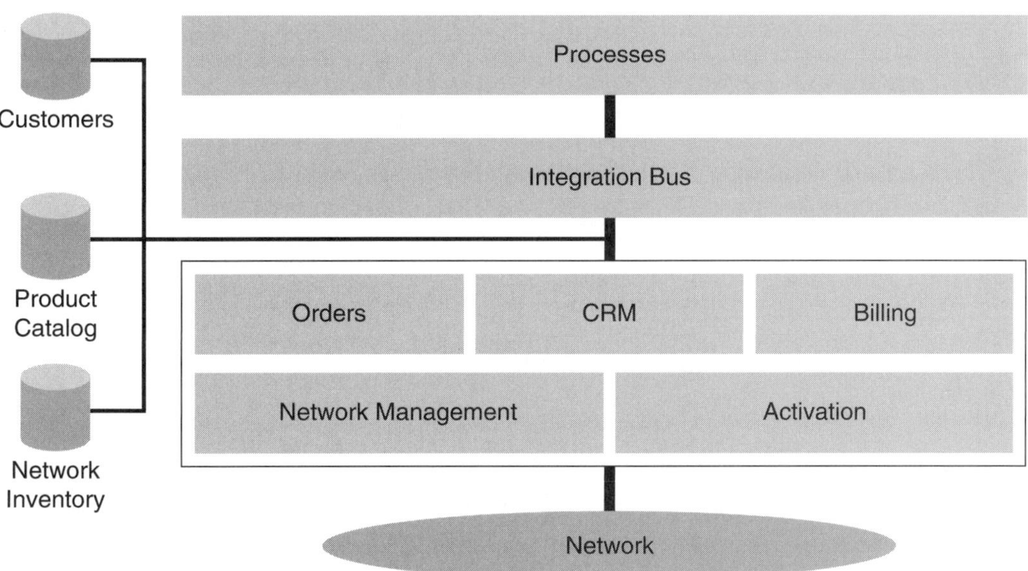

Figure 12-9 Process integration in service delivery.
Published courtesy of Hewlett-Packard Company.

resources, and applications so the service delivery process can work efficiently across departments. This is one way to reduce manual intervention and errors, while enabling reporting and analysis on process efficiency. The management layer and integration bus allow process flexibility and optimization. By enabling process optimization, service providers should see reductions in service delivery time, costs, and unpredictability. Key features and benefits of an automated service delivery system are shown in Table 12-1.

Table 12-1 Key features and benefits of an automated service delivery system

Key features	Benefits
Process and application integration-centric solution	Faster creation of new products and services with rapid roll-out across the infrastructure
Automation of complex delivery business processes	Reduces service delivery time to customer. Improves data synchronization
Internet and order management interfaces	Service self-provisioning; fewer errors
Reduced rekeying and manual intervention	Reduced manpower requirements
Comprehensive metrics and tracking capabilities	Measurable service and delivery SLAs
Fully extensible integration architecture	Maximize use of existing technologies, applications, and infrastructure (increased ROA). Decouples processes from resources/applications—increases flexibility and measurability.
Network equipment independent	Allows use of mixed network and switch vendors

Phase 1 implementation normally determines the end-to-end processes. Graphical tools are usually used to enable these designs. Other tools help apply and measure the defined processes. Phase 2 automates as many of the processes as possible.

12.6 Examples and Case Studies

Now let's look at examples of automated service delivery and how several businesses have benefitted.

12.6.1 ADSL Provisioning

12.6.1.1 Background

ADSL (asymmetric digital subscriber line) is an access service that enables the use of communication and information services. Its purpose is to allow subscribers (offices and home users) to send digital data over the local loop. Cost-effective technologies and regulatory changes are making ADSL more popular; but the traditional bottleneck was the last mile between the central office and the home or business. This last mile was developed using twisted pair copper wires that were fine for voice, but too slow to transmit high volumes of digital packets. With ADSL, data speeds are optimized so that more data is sent from the network to the customer than is sent from the customer to the network solving the bottleneck problem. This is ideal for home-based users and small businesses that are Internet users rather than Internet hosts.

Figure 12-10 shows a typical DSL network and how packets move through the network.

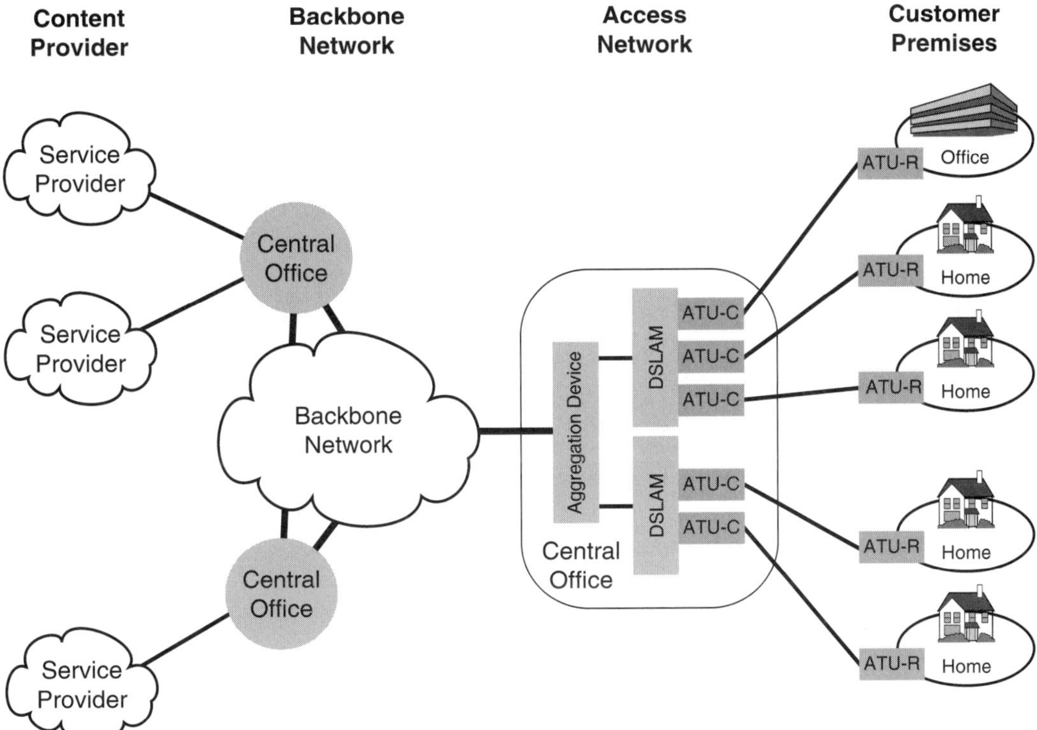

Figure 12-10 Components of a DSL network.
Published courtesy of Hewlett-Packard Company.

There are many reasons for providing DSL for high-speed remote access from a service provider's viewpoint. Here are some:

- High-speed access to the Internet over ordinary phone lines
- Supports real-time interactive multimedia and broadcast quality video
- Supports interoperability
- Supports high bit rates
- A single line can be used for both high-speed data access and conventional phone service
- Provides a secure communications channel
- Always connected (no dial-up needed)
- Proven technology
- Can carry both IP and ATM traffic
- Portal to NGN technologies

12.6.1.2 Provisioning Difficulties

ADSL is a perfect case for a service that needs increased efficiency in delivery processes:

- The delivery process is predominately paper based
- Providers have no control over delivery and can't confirm when installation will occur
- Providers don't know how much the installation will cost and can't confirm a bit rate guarantee over customer's line
- Providers can't confirm the type of service, the price, or a guaranteed performance to the customer before the order is placed
- The service takes too long to provision manually, with many inflexible, unscalable, point-to-point processes

DSL is difficult to provision because numerous devices from diverse manufacturers need configuration. Manual configuration can take a lot of time as each device may have a different interface. Manual configuration also means a higher possibility for human error and, in turn, a great amount of paperwork.

This is how typical providers offer DSL services:

1. The customer requests the service, either by phone or over the Web.
2. The customer and service provider determine if the service is available in that area.
3. The service provider determines if the service and customer premise equipment are available, calculates a final price and installation date, and confirms service levels.
4. The service provider installs and configures/provisions the equipment and tests it.
5. The customer database is updated and may be billed for the new service once the service is activated and tested.
6. The customer may request content services from this, or other, providers. The type of content may affect service levels.

Focusing on service qualification and provisioning (Steps 2-4), let's look at what changes when the delivery is automated. In Figure 12-11 we do not include the sales/marketing processes and assume that the CSR takes the order.

1. Sales: The customer either contacts customer service or looks directly at the product catalog to choose the service. If the customer goes direct, he/she would interface directly with the order processing system. The CSR and/or customer has direct access to the catalog showing all options for service.
2. Feasibility: The automated system can check front office feasibility real-time to check that the customer is in an area where DSL service is available.
3. Order processing: If the order is validated, it is automatically entered in the order system and the customer agrees to contract for the service.
4. Installation schedule: The workflow management system is used to choose a date and allocate an engineer to install the equipment at the customer's premises. The customer is notified of

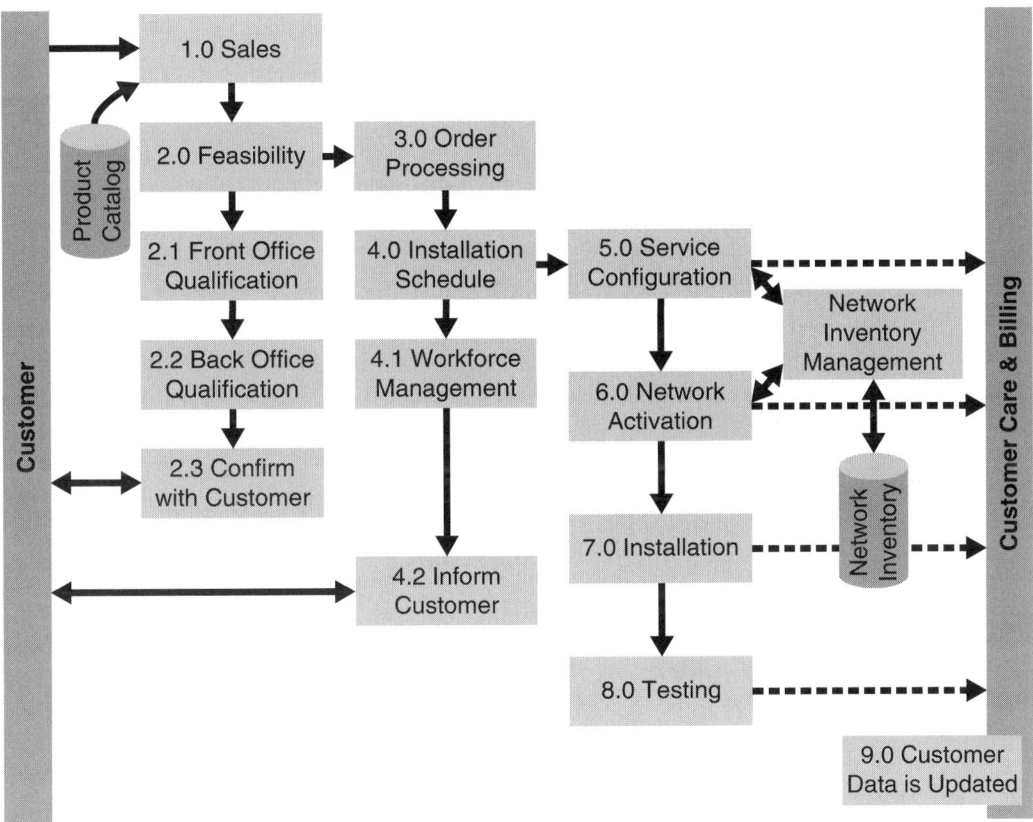

Figure 12-11 An example of an automated process.
Published courtesy of Hewlett-Packard Company.

the details either immediately during the call ordering the service or by email. Installation occurs subject to the customer's availability.

5. Service configuration: Various parameters are configured automatically:
   - Allocation of the local loop
   - Allocation of the DSLAM port
   - The ATM termination point
   - Allocation of a customer specific VPI/VCI to identify the connection to the ATM network
6. Network Activation: The network is now activated automatically and the network inventory system is updated.
7. Installation: The engineer installs the DSL modem at the customer's premises and configures it.
8. Testing: The new service is tested.
9. Customer data is updated: The customer care system and billing systems are automatically updated.

One example of automating a manual ADSL service is seen in Figure 12-12. The example shows Hewlett-Packard's process management tool and integration bus allowing the processes to be defined across the organization and optimized. Delivery of the service is shown in Figure 12-13.

In Phase 1 of the implementation, HP defined and mapped the cross-organizational processes used to provide the ADSL service. In Phase 2, HP automated as many process steps as possible. Three features were central to this implementation: application integration, predefined integration points, and process management—a combination of technologies often referred to as enterprise application integration (EAI). The advantage is that the provider can assign someone accountable for the process; the process can be measured, automated and optimized. Bottlenecks are spotted before they affect service delivery. Automating cross-functional business processes further means:

- Faster time-to-market for products and services
- Fewer errors in delivery
- Rapid product roll-out
- Reduced service delivery time to customer
- Support of self-provisioning
- Reduced manpower requirements
- Measurable service levels and service delivery
- Better return on assets (ROA)

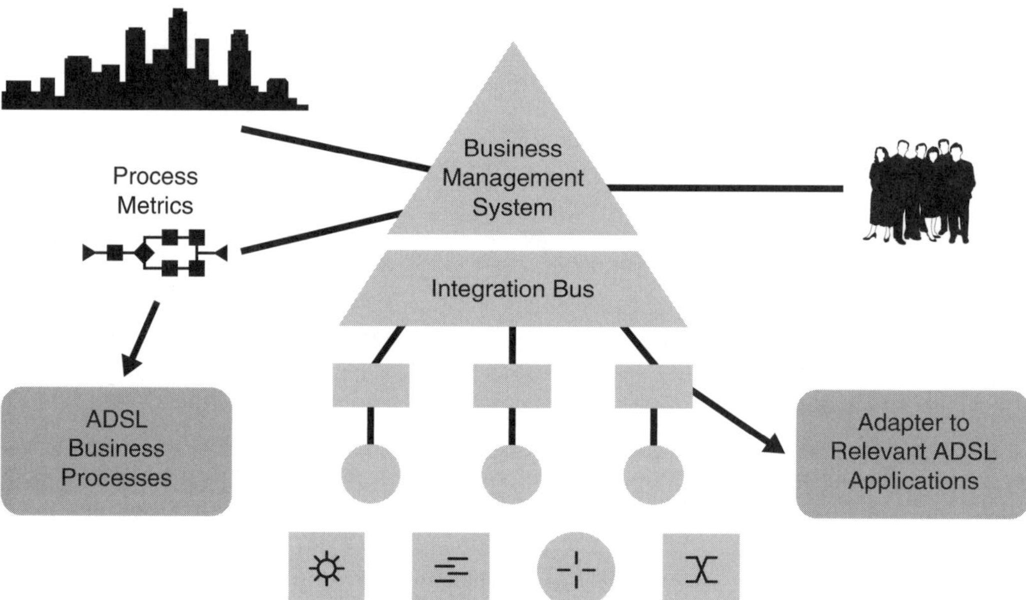

Figure 12-12 An example of ADSL automation.
Published courtesy of Hewlett-Packard Company.

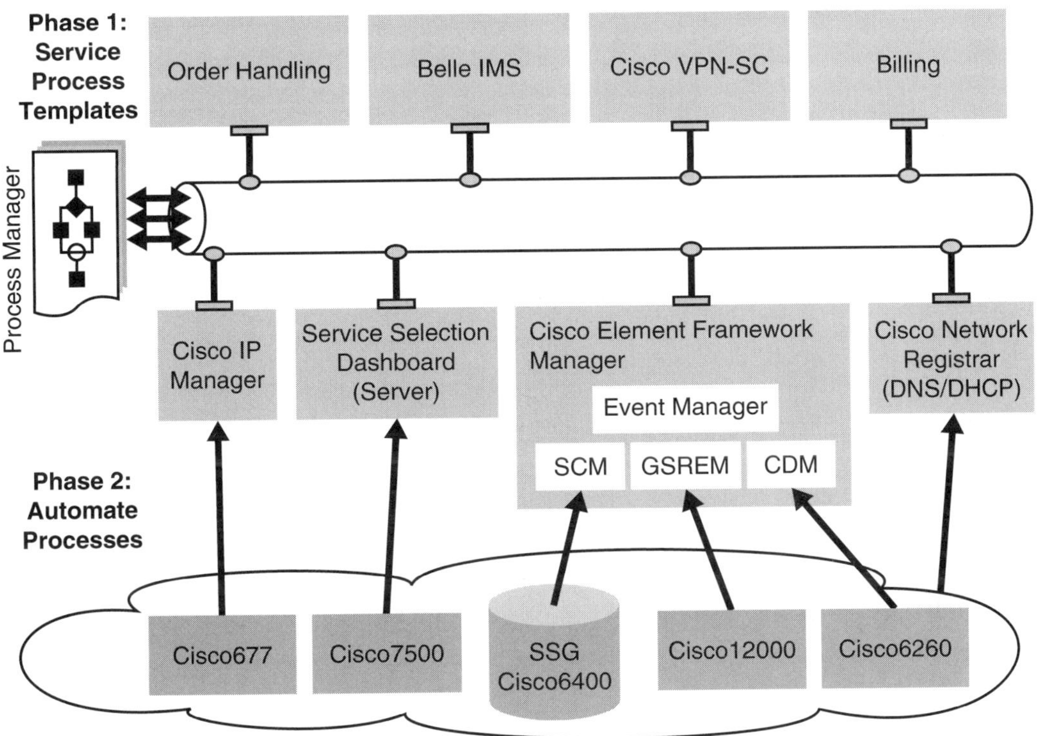

Figure 12-13 An example of ADSL service delivery.
Published courtesy of Hewlett-Packard Company.

12.7 Summary

Efficient service delivery is one of the differentiators in the service provider business and providers need to understand the service costs, timing, and delivery process. Service delivery and provisioning need to be synchronized, efficiently linking many parts of the organization. These processes should be removed from resources and applications so they can be optimized. Only by having a single view of sales, delivery, billing and customer care can service providers run the business efficiently and maintain the current customer base, increase market share, ensure offering high profit services, and keep operational costs under control.

12.8 Endnote

Parts of this chapter are taken from *HP Service Delivery: Service Delivery in the Communications Industry, A Primer*, a Hewlett-Packard white paper, v1.0, Elizabeth Ward, Hewlett-Packard Company, Palo Alto, CA, March 22, 2000, *www.ice.hp.com/cyc/af/00/101-0337.pdf.*

12.9 xSP Strategy Checklist for Service Provisioning and Service Delivery

The following is a checklist of items to consider when setting up provisioning and service delivery processes:

- ❑ What processes are needed to deliver the service?
  - ❑ Are end-to-end processes defined for service delivery?
  - ❑ Are they written down formally?
  - ❑ Has the staff been trained in them?
  - ❑ How is process status communicated between different fulfillment operations?
- ❑ Are processes predominantly paper based?
- ❑ Are the established processes nonstandard?
- ❑ Can service delivery times be guaranteed?
- ❑ Can speed or service levels be guaranteed?
- ❑ Can the service be delivered within the time requested by the market and faster than my competitors?
- ❑ If the end-to-end processes are defined, can steps in the processes be automated?
- ❑ Must the process be automated to offer the particular service?
- ❑ What are the competitors doing to deliver this service?
  - ❑ How are they coping with process inefficiencies?
- ❑ What timing for service delivery fulfillment is the market requiring?
- ❑ What service levels does the market require and why?
- ❑ Do processes involve a lot of people who are performing unnecessary steps?
- ❑ Are bottlenecks visible in purchasing, provisioning, billing and customer care?
- ❑ Can bottlenecks be eased and processes optimized before they affect service levels?
- ❑ Can processes be measured for efficiency?
- ❑ Is there one overall owner for the service delivery process?
- ❑ Must inefficient processes be used to interact with partners?
  - ❑ Are there ways to fix these inefficiencies? (Work with the partner or get a new partner?)
- ❑ Can processes be defined internally, or is outside help needed?
- ❑ What is the service delivery value chain? What processes are kept in-house and what can be outsourced to gain economies of scale and efficiencies?
- ❑ Have I tested the market to understand customer reactions to current service delivery?

CHAPTER 13

Perception Is Reality

Customer perception of a service provider is shaped by the provider's ability to respond to customer needs. The more responsive, the less likely a customer will switch. The less responsive, the more likely a customer will sound like a late-night comedian: "My service provider has amazing security, not even I can get in." "My service provider was down so often, I had it tested for clinical depression."

The interaction between provider and customer goes by many names, but the most commonly used in the industry are customer care and CRM. Companies providing better customer care and service have a better chance of staying in business.

Customer care is a generic term used in many industries to describe how businesses interact with, and serve, their customers—usually after the sale is complete. Customer care takes many forms, and one of its main components is the call center.

13.1 Call Centers

The call center, which goes by a myriad of other names, is a pivotal component to any customer care system. It is one of the main customer touch points that reflects the level and quality of service customers receive and will be the main input to the customer's perception of the provider. In general, the call center will deliver two distinct services, one focused on the support of customers, the other on sales and after-sales service. These core services are separate in terms of their purpose and, as such, will have different goals, measures, and cost models. When taken from the customer's point of view, he/she will undoubtedly use whatever communications method is easiest and the provider's IT systems must be integrated to avoid potentially unhappy customers. An example of this was illustrated in the Triara case study in Chapter 7, "Latin America – Triara," when customers called both Triara directly and their call center.

13.1.1 Call Center Staffing and General Considerations

The number of people staffing a call center can range from a few to many, depending on the number of customers and level of support needed. Staffing a call center depends on the efficiency of the operators and service levels required. Call centers can either be set up in-house or outsourced. When staffing in-house, service providers may, or may not, know information about call profiles and busy hours. If outsourcing makes more sense, expectations and reporting lines must be clearly defined from the start, preferably in writing. Outsourced call centers put a new link in the customer care chain, so customer control may become diluted. There is another down side: the company performing the outsourced business becomes the face the provider presents to the customer. Understanding how data, information, and communication will flow from/to the customer, through the outsource contractor, and to/from the provider is critical. Whether or not they are outsourced, pilot programs are highly recommended to make sure processes work smoothly before going operational. This is also a time when the service provider can understand better its call profiles and busy hours. When setting up a call center, or any customer care system, the service provider needs to develop operational processes, staffing, and IT infrastructure that will support its business needs today and into the future as the business builds and grows.

13.1.1.1 Staffing Levels

Staffing levels depend on parameters such as:

- Average call length
- Typical call type (sales versus technical)
- Average call wrap-up time
- Service levels required (time to pick up call)
- Busy periods (how many and how long)
- Whether or not there are services offering dedicated call center resources
- The length of the customer set-up/ education period

Statistically, customers will use the call center more when they are ramping up or starting a new service than during the maintenance or ongoing stages. Service providers should take this into account and offer customer training and on-site support to help the customer through these ramp-up periods. For service providers that want to keep call centers in-house and don't know information relating to the above bullets, their call center pilot phases will have staffing that changes real-time as the situation is clarified. Here are some suggestions:

- Start with three 10-hour shifts with one person acting as supervisor for each shift.
    - The shift overlap should correspond with anticipated busy hours.
- Assume one CSR per three enterprise customers
- Assume a technical call lasts about 30 minutes, a nontechnical call about 15 minutes
- Assume the call extends about 15 percent for call wrap-up (call documentation), so a 30-minute call needs another 5 minutes for wrap-up

- Add time for lunch, breaks, and other absences (illness, vacation). Typical utilization rates run 65-70 percent
- Assign a staff that works full-time shifts and three part-time shifts working nights, weekends, and to cover for holidays, illness, and other general absences
- The staff should have the skills to work on other projects during slow periods. Extra staff, perhaps pulled from other departments, should be available, real time, for busy hour surprises

The staffing assumptions (including an hour for lunch and two 15-minute breaks) should support about 14.5 technical calls or approximately 30 nontechnical calls per CSR per 10-hour shift. This is one example of many formulae on the market to work out call center staffing needs.

13.1.2 Outsourcing the Call Center

A service provider may want to outsource all, or part, of its call center because it might not be a core competency. Advantages of outsourcing include:

- Focus on core competencies: Even through the service provider still needs to have someone in charge of the call center function—managing the call center provider—the service provider spends its scarce personnel and cash resources on its focus business.
- Economize on capital investments: Instead of investing in expensive infrastructure and resources, service providers can outsource to call center specialists that already have the infrastructure and trained CSRs.
- Reduce operating expenses: By outsourcing the call center function, the service provider saves on overhead expenses associated with this area.

The main disadvantage of outsourcing this function is that one of the most important channels for sales and customer contact is no longer under the service provider's direct control. This means that quality control is of prime importance when considering outsourcing this function. There is also a high switching cost for the service provider if the outsourcing service doesn't work out. If this function is something the service provider is considering outsourcing, some things to consider are:

- Do the services offered and procedures support the service provider's business?
- Can the service provider leverage the outsource company's brand to increase its unique value proposition in the market and gain market share?
- Does the outsource company offer extra services that could enhance the service provider's market offering?
- Does the outsourcing service support the service provider's business goals and growth expectations, including a roadmap for future services and technologies?
- How will quality be measured and maintained?

- Does the contract have clauses that detail service levels (including fines if service levels are not met), processes, and termination for cause?
- Are there checkable references?

13.2 Other Ways to Manage Customer Perception

At Exodus Communications, customer care is kept in-house. They have a CRM system and a response center. Exodus offers customer self-help options that include opening their own trouble tickets. When an issue is escalated, it is reviewed in the Exodus "war room" until the issue is resolved. The customer is able to use remote-monitoring tools to review the status of the resolution of the trouble ticket.

Exodus expands its customer touch to include its executive management. All Exodus executives are directly responsible for big clients. They are required to have monthly one-on-one meetings with their customers to discuss what is going well and what's not.

13.3 Customer Relationship Management (CRM)

One popular trend in the market is CRM, an "automation and integration of horizontal business processes involving front-office customer touch points:

- Sales (contact management, product configuration)
- Marketing (campaign management, telemarketing
- Customer service (call center, field service)

via multiple, interconnected delivery channels. CRM application architecture must combine operational (transaction-oriented business process management) technologies and analytical (data mart-centered business performance management) technologies."[1]

Here are some other ways users define CRM:

- CRM is a philosophy centered on the customer facing functions of marketing, sales, customer service, and support.
- CRM combines customer interaction personnel, processes, and technologies to produce the best enterprise profits and highest customer satisfaction levels possible.
- CRM is part of the business strategy that helps identify and keep the most profitable customers, while keeping operational costs under control. It helps identify and clarify customer needs so transaction and interaction values can increase. It helps increase the overall value of the customer/company relationship.
- Use CRM to automate, and make the sales and marketing processes more efficient.
- CRM creates, and helps maintain, close ties to customers by tracking order histories, preferences, vendor performances, and post-sales support. It includes sales force automation, marketing automation, customer sales, and service applications. These systems were used to create closer and more efficient links for, and with, employees.

- The CRM system offers self-service options to both employees and customers. The system gives information relating to product(s), including price quotes, order tracking, self-serve product and service-related troubleshooting, and service call scheduling.

CRM is a business philosophy and is only successful for companies that truly mean or aspire to put the customer first. It is the system(s) integration employed by service providers, or companies, that provide(s) the information needed to best serve their customers. Some studies reveal that as few as 10 percent of service providers share customer information between departments. CRM ties together front and back office functions to give one total view of the customer, resulting in a true competitive advantage for the service provider. Ideally, functions tied together include all customer touch points, both Web and non-Web, in sales, marketing, customer care, and support. CRM systems integrate disparate call centers, the myriad direct and indirect channels, Web initiatives, and marketing and sales campaigns. By using CRM solutions, companies hope to improve their ability to understand, anticipate, and capitalize on customer opportunities—and gain marketing advantages over their competitors. As corporate Internet models continue to evolve, profitability and globalization carry on and seamless CRM becomes more significant. It is important to realize that a truly integrated CRM system comes at a cost. A CRM system is expensive in time and money to properly integrate, and much of the technology is still on the bleeding edge. Nevertheless, here are some trends that fuel the need for changes in the way enterprises relate to their customers:

- Fully integrated back office systems do not necessarily translate to a lasting competitive advantage. This efficiency needs to be linked to customer facing processes so customers are aware of how automation makes the enterprise serve them better.
- Product lifecycles are accelerating as a result of better communications, so vendors need to create reasons for their customers to stay and to create higher barriers to exit.
- The advent of the Internet makes it easy for customers to access a greater volume of information and to change vendors at the click of a mouse. Customers need to perceive value and rapport—feel like more than just another faceless customer over the Net or Internet to remain loyal. A CRM system can be one vehicle to create an infrastructure giving human qualities to an otherwise cold interface.

Service providers are trying to capitalize on technologies that can leverage voice, fax, email, and Web communication channels to create the best in customer management, personalization and one-to-one marketing. The importance of service delivery (Chapter 12, "Service Delivery and Provisioning") and customer relationship management is that, together, they are the most important enablers a service provider has to maintain customer loyalty, increase market share, pinpoint high margin services, and decrease operational costs.

13.3.1 CRM Components

Service providers produce business intelligence as part of their everyday operations and need to understand the best way to capture this to their advantage. This intelligence falls into two high-level categories: operational and analytical. Similar to intelligence agencies, information gathered as a result of everyday operations is useful and needs to be enhanced through analysis to pinpoint trends and understand how it affects the overall business.

13.3.1.1 Operational Intelligence[2]

The operational side of CRM systems looks at individual processes and includes customer facing applications integrated among the front, back, and mobile offices.

- Sales force automation, (SSA): lead/account management, contact management, quote management, marketing collateral, and forecasting. This term is now changing to sales automation because the functionality is greater than face-to-face sales forces.
- Enterprise marketing automation (EMA): pricing, product configuration information, ordering functions, and customer qualification.
- Customer service/support: all functions of the call center.
- Miscellaneous components: one-to-one personalization, billing, and e-services components.

13.3.1.2 Analytical Intelligence[3]

Analytical intelligence takes information gathered as a result of day-to-day operations, above, and analyzes it to understand overall business trends and performance, including sales and marketing, network performance, support, finance, and legal. This analysis normally uses some form of data warehousing.

Because CRM crosses many groups within the company, the service provider should create a common infrastructure umbrella that embraces the integration of the disparate systems under one owner, similar to that described in the section on service delivery in Chapter 12. Key areas of integration use multichannel customer contact as windows into sales, service automation, and business/customer intelligence.

There are many customer information systems floating through an organization. The vast majority are nothing more than relationships loosely coupled with niche marketing programs and with no cross company linkages.

13.3.1.3 Collaborative CRM[4]

As shown in Figure 13-1, META Group includes the idea of collaborative CRM that further aligns interactions between customers and enterprises via Web interfaces and Internet technologies. These new technologies are used to increase the value of the customer relationship and barriers to customer exit.

A CRM system attempts to link these disparate systems to give one view of information needed to run the business better. CRM systems further support one-to-one marketing and product customization based on customer profiling and rules' engines. To increase collaboration,

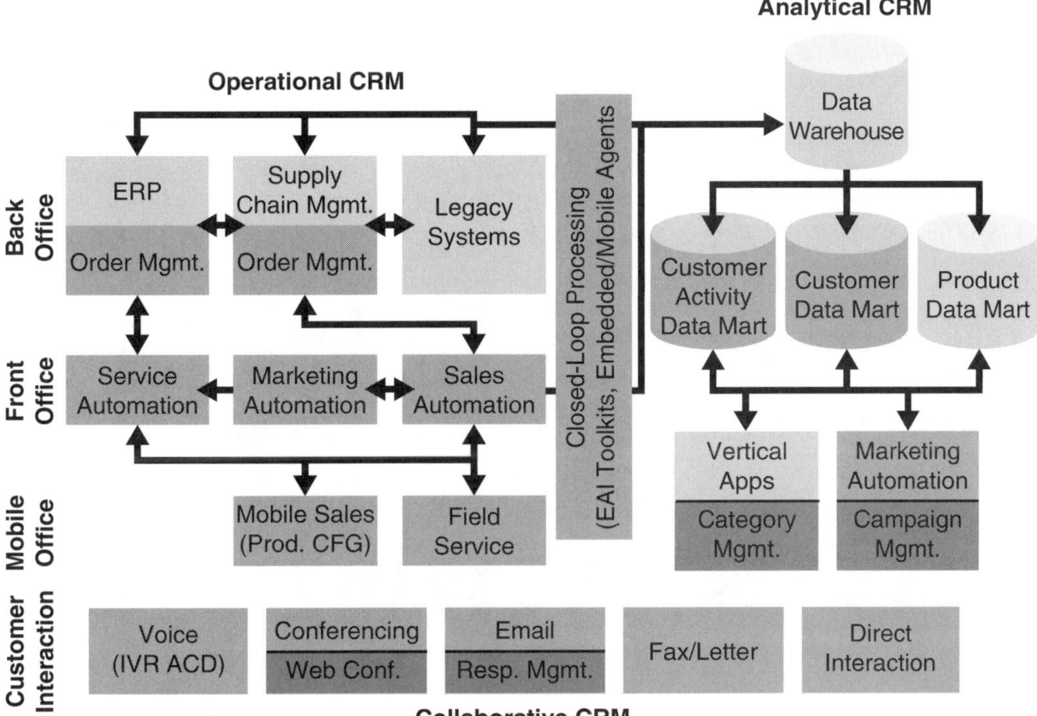

Figure 13-1 The CRM technology ecosystem.

Web transaction, and workflow, systems are integrated further, offering a seamless information flow about materials, financial information, and services (see Figure 13-2).

More specifically, CRM systems allow targeting prospects and acquiring new customers through data mining, campaign management, and lead distribution. These systems attempt to give service providers what they need to analyze information created over a long period of time and to create long-term relationship value for, and with, their customers. This sort of information, which could also include demographic analysis, can aid in overall marketing campaigns and overall corporate strategy, as well as with one-to-one marketing and proactive customer service. In the sales process, the systems enable a more efficient sales cycle using proposal generators, tools to help create configurations called configurators, knowledge management tools, contract managers, and forecasting aids. If a sales person has these tools available, he or she may be able to generate customer requested information faster and without having to call back. The tools enable selling processes to transfer seamlessly into purchasing transactions, done quickly, conveniently, and at the lowest cost. They should enable these processes to occur via any customer touch point, even over the Internet, and give one face to the customer. The systems help to ensure postsales service and support issues are handled by CSRs. Technology is available to sup-

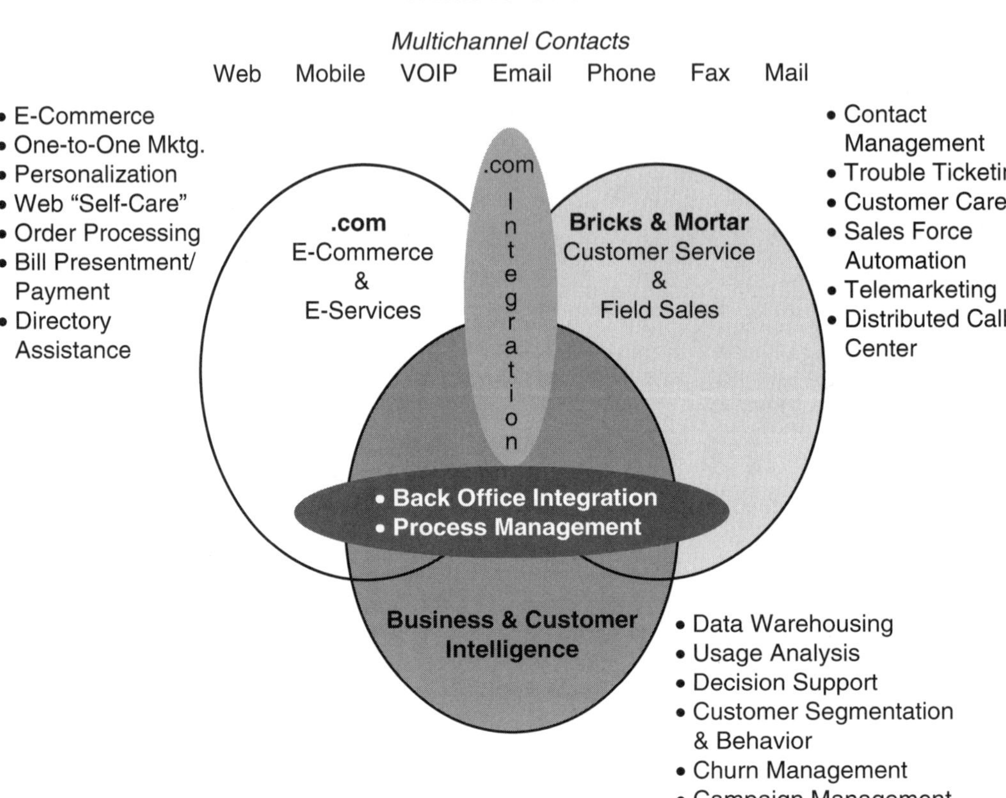

Figure 13-2 What is CRM?
Published courtesy of Hewlett-Packard Company.

port tiering of customers, allowing higher tier customers to get speedier service. Once a customer interacts with a CSR, or the self-help options, getting information should be faster and the quality of information should be better.

Today, most companies focus on one-to-one personalization as their CRM solution. In the near future, going beyond this narrow field will definitely give companies the edge over those who ignore the broader perspective.

13.4 How CRM Can Support New Services

Complex offerings that include brokered services and multichannel customer contact are becoming more important as ways to maintain profit margins. Multichannel customer contact includes Web collaboration, voice over IP contact centers, email management, email autoresponse, CTI, and intelligent network routing. Open integration is needed for new, Web-enabled applications and data. These systems can include technology to direct tiers of customers over the Web, or phone, requiring various levels of response times. This allows service providers to offer customers different classes of service charged at different rates (see Figure 13-3). Whatever system is used should enable a single view of the customer to make interaction more efficient.

CRM systems need to interact and get information from new services offered by the service provider including those from complex ecosystems that change on the fly. The concept of services brokering provides for the timely and reliable delivery of the broadest and most complete set of information relevant to a specific customer request, without jeopardizing the security or privacy of the information source. Brokering is achieved by enabling the real-time dynamic and seamless interaction of multiple external sources. These services will be provisioned by the service delivery systems described in Chapter 12 and focus on brokering requests between a central infrastructure called electronic service control point (ESCP) and the external parties involved in fulfilling the request.

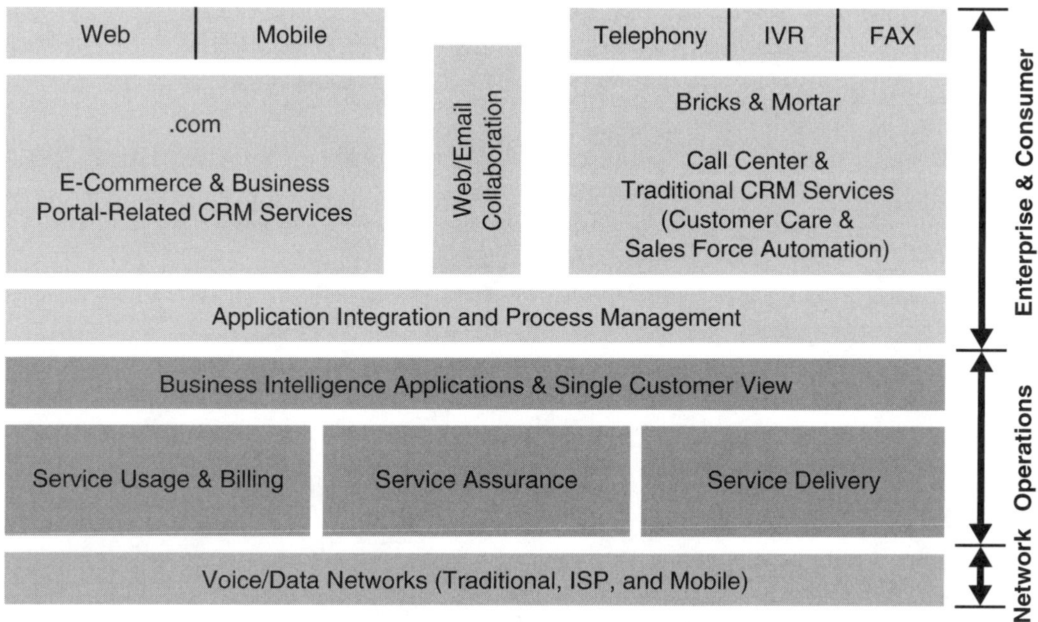

Figure 13-3 The CRM reference architecture for service providers.
Published courtesy of Hewlett-Packard Company.

Example A service provider offers employee relocation services to medium and large companies (see Figure 13-4). In this case an employee is relocated from Texas to Georgia. The service needs to get bids/information on:

- Selling the current Texas home
- Temporary housing, schools, health care, and public utility services in Georgia

- Moving household goods to Georgia
- Organizing trips to Georgia for the employee and family
- Buying a house in Georgia

The brokering infrastructure enables the service provider to present optimal options for relocation based on the employee/customer request and profile. This is achieved through the interaction between the provider ESCP and enterprise relationship management (ERM)[5] systems—service switching points that are ready to bid for the relocation business. Using ERM systems is preferred over portals as points of interaction with ESCP because the access and security mechanisms are better than are traditionally implemented in such environments and they need not be duplicated at the portal level. Alternatively, portals meeting these same requirements can be substituted for ERM systems without any problem. In this case, the ERM system acts as a service switching point through which the service interaction flows, and which triggers resolution requests to the ESCP.

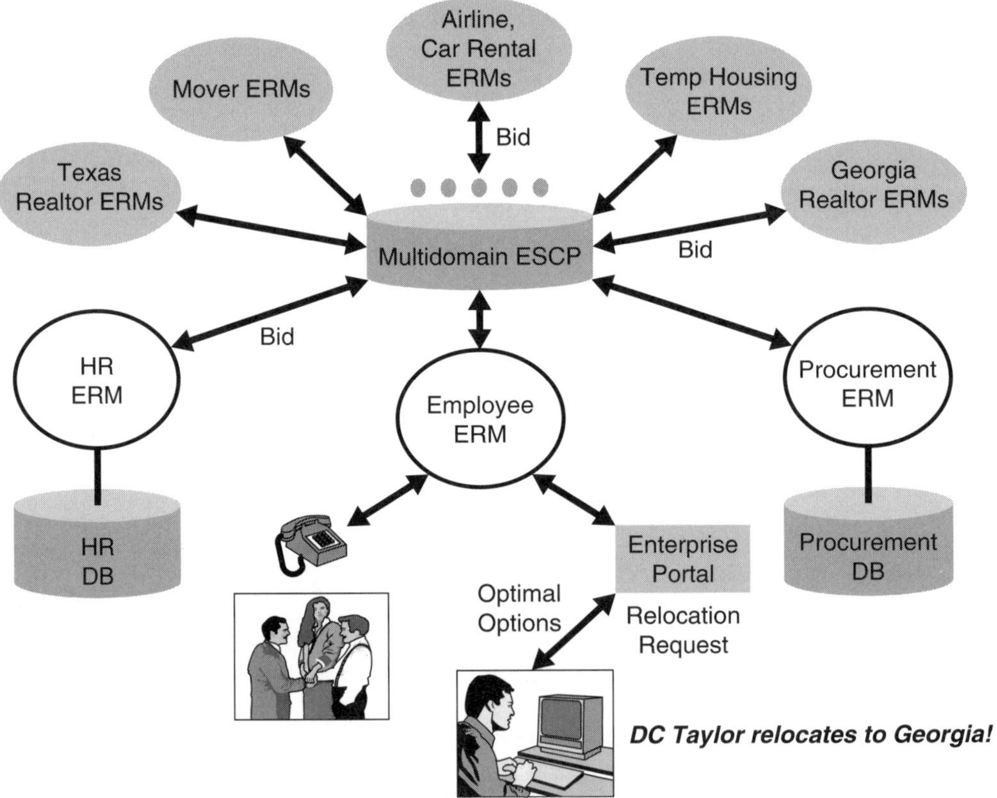

Figure 13-4 Example of service brokering for employee relocation.
Published courtesy of Hewlett-Packard Company.

13.5 An Example of a Phased CRM Implementation

This is an example of a phased CRM implementation. Phase 1 allows interaction between Web sites, the call center, and field sales/service. It integrates and routes all customer touch points including the Web, email, ACD, PBX, VRU, and telephone interactions. Tracking functions in this phase include the ability to track sales, contracts, customers, product development, inventory, and repair operations.

More specifically, Phase 1:

- Allows the collection and management of information for marketing campaigns and sales opportunities. This means sales and marketing representatives can share information enabling a more effective sales force.
- Integrates and automates service related inventory and onsite service calls.
- Manages and routes all incoming calls to customer support. CSRs can then log cases, set priorities, route cases, verify contracts, review case histories, manage configurations, and track case related costs.

Subsequent implementation phases increase functionality and provide a more complete integration with workflow, scripting, and reporting functions.

Service provider customer and order management is significantly more complex than order management in typical product companies such as consumer goods and equipment manufacturers. Table 13-1 identifies key differences:

Table 13-1 Differences in customer and order management between product companies and service providers

Item Description	Typical product company	Typical service provider
Product availability	Most products available everywhere. Some products not available in certain areas or for export to certain countries.	Most products specific to customer segment (consumer or business). Availability varies by location, sometimes down to street address.
Product features	Features are basic and often are identified by their own part number.	Features are complex with some features optional and others mandatory, many with parameters (number of rings before a call is forwarded).
Feature interactions	Typically a simple hierarchy of available features.	Features often interdependent or mutually exclusive. Features may be required or unavailable in certain areas.

Table 13-1 Differences in customer and order management between product companies and service providers (continued)

Pricing	Typically a cost to purchase, and potentially a recurring maintenance fee.	Order may have one-time charges, one-time charges spread across several months, usage-based features, and monthly recurring charges.
Order types	Typically a single order placed to obtain product.	Typically orders are required when service is connected, disconnected, or changed. Orders may be required if customer changes address.
Fulfillment time	Typically product is either available for shipping or on back order. Shipping time is predictable.	May involve multiple parties to fulfill order, each with its own timeline. Capacity may not be known by CSR at time service is ordered.
Revenue assurance issues	Typically product is paid for with a one-time fee; revenue is recognized immediately and customer is invoiced.	Most charges are monthly or usage-based; little or no revenue is recognized until service is activated and billing is notified.
Systems notified	Inventory must be depleted; customer record may be updated.	Ten to 20 systems typically notified, including facilities database, network activation system, and billing.
Regulatory requirements	Generally none.	Generally extensive, including rules of what a customer needs to be told when ordering service.
Interfaces to other companies	May be required when inventory is obtained externally, for example, in wholesale/retail scenarios.	Required in virtually all telecommunications orders, with around 15 possible transactions.

Figure 13-5 shows the components envisioned for the target architecture, and the integration points between the call center, CTI software, and CRM system required to achieve a seamless enterprise solution.

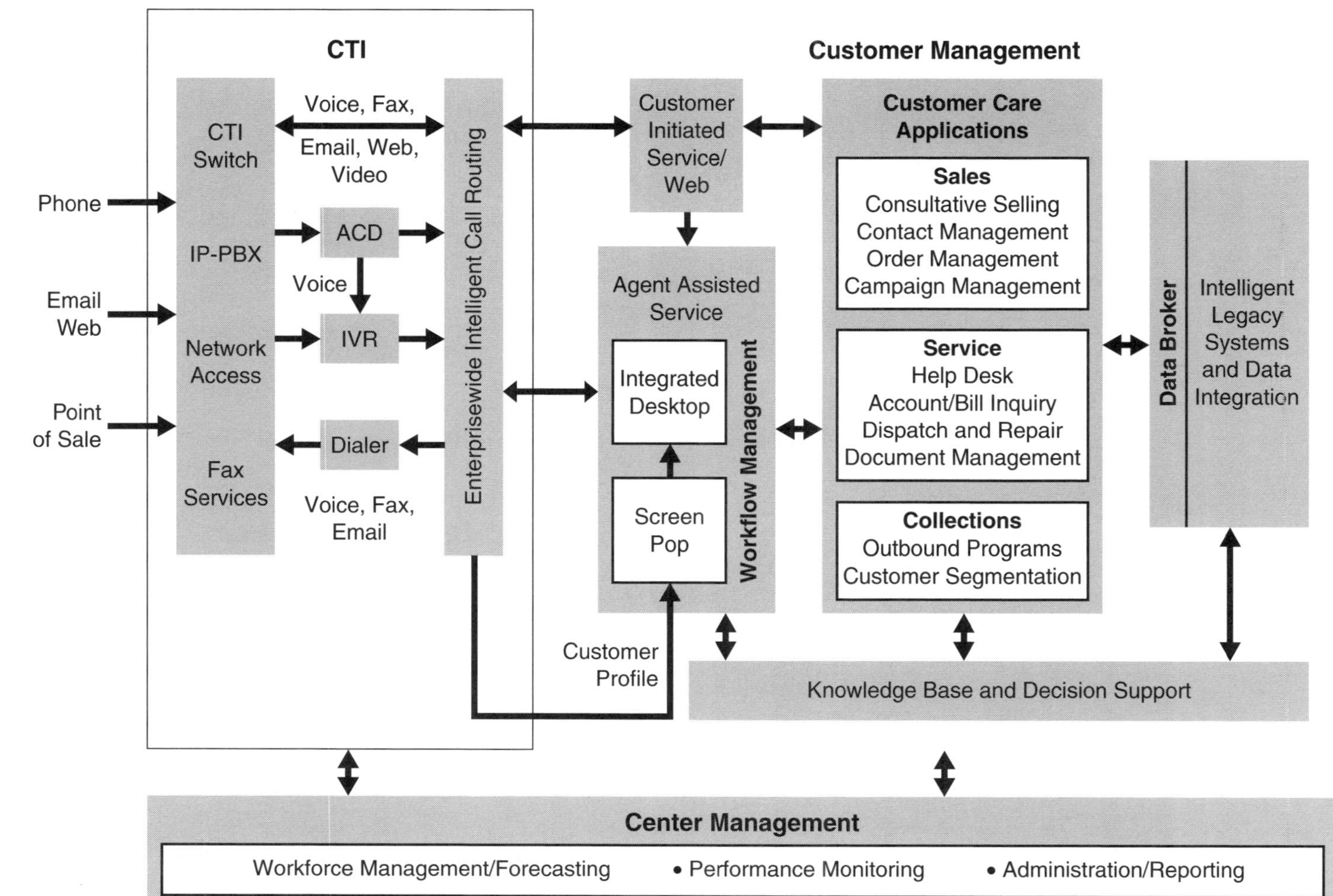

Figure 13-5 CRM architecture components.
Published courtesy of Hewlett-Packard Company.

There will be additional interfaces to other corporate systems developed in subsequent phases:

- Billing
- Process tool
- CTI
- Network software
- Document management
- Internet server
- Geographical information system (GIS)
- Data warehouse
- Credit checking agency (via the process tool)

Examples of process inputs and outputs between different functions can be found in Appendix I.

13.6 Summary

Customer care is one of the keys to managing market perception of the service provider. Call centers are one important aspect of customer care that focus on technical support and sales. They can be either outsourced or kept in-house, but running a call center is quite complex; it is not for amateurs. Customer relationship management is a new trend in the industry and these systems are more than just call centers. They are the glue that link information between operational areas of the service provider to give one view of the customer. Their operational management systems link day-to-day information while analytical management systems show trends and help management understand overall business performance. CRM systems will be used to support complex services as enabling agents to brokering functionalities. As such, they need to be designed to support touch points used today, with thought given to those used in the future.

13.7 Endnotes

1. "Application Delivery Strategies," META Group, March 16, 1999, pg. 1.
2. "Application Delivery Strategies," META Group, March 16, 1999, pgs. 2, 3.
3. IBID.
4. ERM encompasses the systems relating to customer/employee relationship management, back-end/back-office tools, and business intelligence across the enterprise.
5. IBID.

13.8 xSP Strategy Checklist for Customer Care

- ❑ How many customers per CSR?
- ❑ How many average calls per day?
- ❑ When are the busy hours and how long do they last?
- ❑ What is the average length per call for technical help? Nontechnical help?
- ❑ How many shifts will be available for the call center?
- ❑ Are there service levels that mandate call response within a certain length of time?
- ❑ Are there Web interfaces? VIR? Legacy systems that need to be integrated?
- ❑ Will there be dedicated CSRs for a particular customer?
- ❑ What sort of CSR training plan is offered for sales and/or technical CSRs?
- ❑ How will the call center scale to support the service provider ongoing business?
- ❑ How long will customers be in ramp-up mode for the service versus ongoing maintenance?
  - ❑ Is there an adequate customer education plan for the new services offered?
  - ❑ Does pricing take into account these two phases (ramp up and maintenance)?
  - ❑ Are there penalties if service levels are not met?
- ❑ Are processes set up to measure call center satisfaction and service levels?
  - ❑ Are call center procedures written and understood by all personnel?
  - ❑ Are processes set up to react if the call center doesn't meet service levels?
- ❑ Is call center outsourcing a consideration?
  - ❑ Can quality be guaranteed and measured?
    - ❑ Can the outsource company scale to meet the service provider needs?
    - ❑ What are the escalation procedures?
  - ❑ Can service levels be maintained and measured?
  - ❑ Can the service provider leverage the call center outsource brand?
  - ❑ Is the outsource company using the most up-to-date technologies including the ability to support Web and click to talk interfaces?
    - ❑ Does it have the technology roadmap and capital to support infrastructure enhancements as new technologies come to market to keep the service provider's call center at the forefront of customer care?
  - ❑ How is the service priced?
    - ❑ Are there volume discounts?
  - ❑ Are there clauses in the contract so the service provider can switch outsourcing companies if the call center is not meeting expectations?
    - ❑ Is there an exit, or transition, plan if the service provider needs to change outsourcing services?
    - ❑ Are there penalties if service levels are not met?

CHAPTER 14

Billing

Billing systems need to support three aspects of service provider operations: the services offered, customer satisfaction, and new revenue models that can change real-time. This means billing systems need to be closely linked to service delivery and customer relationship management systems. The system must be flexible and scalable to support new, more complex Internet services. It must also integrate with technologies used to deliver these new services to the market, meaning true convergent billing supporting a single customer view across a full range of services. Billing systems designed for processing voice call detail records (CDRs) may not be flexible enough to handle charging for data transfer or content purchases. Flexibility to modify pricing models is important since business models are so fluid. The billing system will have to support revenue sharing between ecosystem partners used to offer new, complex services. As the mobile and Internet worlds converge, billing systems will need to maintain carrier-grade reliability in the face of ever increasing usage volumes and real-time interactivity.

14.1 Trends Affecting Billing

Customer demand for enhanced and value-added services is forcing the first phases of convergence for fixed and mobile networks and circuit and IP networks. Convergence is seen in all services and technologies: wire line, data (IP, xDSL, ISDN, VPN), international/long distance, cellular/wireless, PABX/CentreX and cable, in multiple sites with numerous hierarchies. Convergence keeps changing as more and new networks come online. The information from these networks used to create services needs to be itemized on a single bill. Wireless access forces IP and mobile pricing integration and gives rise to more complex billing convergence issues. Service providers have an advantage with IP because of its lower unit costs when compared with traditional circuit infrastructure. This means those new to the market can take advantage of efficient transmission protocols, higher QoS, and new business models. IP networks improve network economies of scale because they allow for multiple products and services within one network, facilitate new delivery technologies, and allow entrants to have a virtual or physical presence. Since wireless access and data transfer services are growing exponentially, the billing infrastructure needs to support complex services that are based on these services. To make matters more complex, value-added services will be created on an as needed basis, changing constantly, and the billing system needs to cope with this. The customer must be identified before determining what billing functions are needed. In general, customers want Web-based self-provisioning, self-management, and QoS guarantees. They want the ability to personalize services, access their trouble tickets and service level reports, and pay for services on a per use basis. The customer needs correct information when ordering; the service needs to be delivered on time, using the correct billing parameters.

14.2 Main Billing Challenges

Despite a clear flow for information used in billing, there is still uncertainty about the best way to charge and bill for the new Internet environment. The main challenges facing service providers include:

- New billing architectures with new network elements
- Integration of new and legacy billing systems
- Integration with customer care, service delivery, and other operations needed for customer fulfillment
- New billing parameters
- Greater call detail record, or equivalent (xDR) volumes and complexity
- Billing for content and access
- Multiparty content billing
- Real-time billing
- Flexibility for new complex service configurations
- Multivendor/multitechnology collection
- Integration over a network that is not unified—unlike traditional circuit-switched environments.
- Supporting expected huge bandwidth and transaction volume growth.
- Supporting real-time aggregation
- Integrating with accounting data, wherever it's stored.
- Supporting many payment options: prepaid, regular, postpaid, hybrid
- Balancing speed and efficiency, for example: real-time billing needs versus processing high volumes in a cost effective way

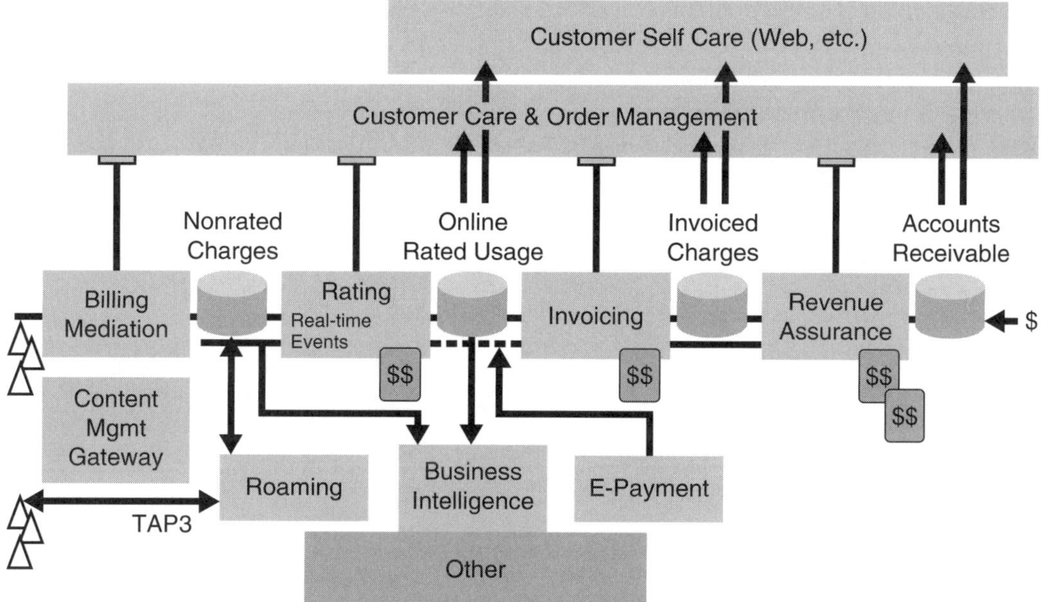

Figure 14-1 Sample billing architecture.
Printed with permission of Hewlett-Packard Company.

Most service providers offer a small number of flat-rate plans with bills calculated on the amount of accumulated access time. Service tiering capabilities are limited and most billing solutions available are proprietary and vendor specific. Limited data is available on traffic, performance, and service usage. There are no standard billing models—each service provider develops its own system (see Figure 14-1). There are no standard Internet billing records and this can be a real challenge with new high-volume services, like voice over IP (VoIP) emerging. In general, the billing system needs to support the greater demands from premium services, like real-time markets, spot rates, auctions, brokering, and so forth. How the provider bills for these services will affect the levels of functionality, and competitiveness, of the service provider.

14.3 Basic Data Pricing

The basis of pricing for data over an IP network differs from that of transferring data over circuit-switched networks. Customers may be charged for data transfer over circuit-switched networks whether or not any data is actually transferred. Data sent over a packet-switched network is sent more efficiently and TCP/IP enables pricing based on volume of data transferred. This means a user can be connected all the time and pay only when data is transferred. As transport costs go down, more providers are looking to charge based on value to the user, versus straight usage, to keep revenue margins. Services may be priced on a per-byte basis, that is, data volume, basis, type of service accessed, QoS required, time of day, location, and so forth. Some services may be free, or at low rates, as a way to draw customers in to use higher margin services. Providers will want to give incentives for customers to transfer data during off-peak hours and prices may reflect this strategy. Providers may have discounting schemes to promote multiyear contracts as a way of reducing churn. These parameters need to be registered in the rating engine.

14.3.1 Content Business Models

Providers may decide to price content according to the volume of data transferred, supplemented by monthly subscriptions. In this context the value of the content may not be proportional to the size transferred, meaning it does not promote the most efficient price/use performance of the network (network ROA). Pricing data transfer according to its value makes for better economies of scale and use efficiencies.

The service provider could bill its customers based directly on the content purchased from partners. In this case, the bill begins to look like a credit card statement and the provider can produce regular reports from the billing system showing how much is owed—purchase price less commission—to each content provider. The customer could purchase content by credit card directly from the provider. In this case, the provider would bill its content partners for a commission on purchases made. The provider could bill advertisers for sponsoring content, and pass on a share of the advertising revenue to its content partners. Only an event-based approach to billing can support the full range of possible content business models. The billing system will need to price a single event in different ways to different parties. Consider a tourist traveling to a new place in a rental car who downloads a map with directions to hotels, restaurants, and other places of interest. This single event may generate charges to the institutions advertising on the map, as well as the rental car company. The provider might invoice a fixed pay-per-use charge to the rental car firm, a percentage commission to the map provider, and charges to the advertised institutions based on the number of downloads per month.

14.4 Rating

Rating is the heart of the billing system and the place where personalized usage tariff plans manipulate customer usage data to determine the bill. In other words, pricing network services is the responsibility of the rating engine. Traditionally defined, the rating engine takes a transaction, as defined by a network detail record, and calculates the price based on a rate table, or predefined set of rules, established by product management. In a large part, the billing system determines the services offered, and how they are priced. To support new Internet services, rating systems must already know the customer identity; normally, legacy-billing systems introduce the customer identity after the rating process. Currency conversions also need to occur at this stage, versus legacy systems where conversion happens only after rating is complete. Major impacts of complex Internet services on rating include:

- Real-time operation: Account and tariff changes need to be applied real-time. This information also must be available real time to associated processes/functions like prepaid billing, electronic bill presentment, and the call center.
- Services and service bundles: Services are constantly updated and changed. Rating engines need efficient service and product management capabilities with enhanced performance and scalability.
- Pricing/discounting: As services become more complex, so does pricing. This complexity will push pricing and discounting functions into the rating phase.
- Rating for events: An increasing number of convergent events are occurring as a result of aggregation and correlation from several usage sources. As services become more complex, rating airtime evolves into rating by event.
- Customer identity: The advent of personalized pricing and discounting forces customer identity to be considered during the rating process.
- Management: Service provider emphasis on decreasing operational costs means services offered must be well managed. There is more pressure on the rating engine to rate usage information correctly and real time.
- Flexibility: Service provider emphasis on decreasing churn means the rating engine must be flexible enough to take inputs on the fly from many sources and output correct information.
- Taxation: Application of taxes may affect the base rate as the applicability of various tax laws to IP services is resolved.
- Cross service discounts: Product managers may wish to discount rates of one service based on another.
- Comparison rating: A competitive advantage in pricing can be illustrated by showing customers how much they save in comparison with competitor rates.
- Customer hierarchies: The pricing, or discounting, of a corporate sponsor may affect a customer's account.
- Incentive programs: Some percentage of a customer's charges may be paid to the value added resellers (VARs) or salesperson who acquired the account.
- Multiple currency: Multinational offerings, or offerings made to multinational corporations, may require rating in multiple currencies and/or performing automatic conversions.

Rating goes from obscurity to the spotlight within the billing system. Without a robust, flexible rating infrastructure, IP service providers cannot capitalize on IP protocol advancements to offer and bill for complex services.

14.4.1 How Rating Engines Work

The rater accepts network transactions from the usage collection subsystems, assigns a price, and provides the rated transaction to the billing database. From there, account balances are adjusted, and records are stored for later use by the invoicing, reporting, accounting and customer care systems. For prepaid services, the rater takes an account balance and determines exactly how much service a customer is entitled to. This is also called prerating. Based on this calculation, the provisioning system authorizes the network elements to provide exactly the amount of service corresponding to the customer's balance. Raters, and related interconnection subsystems, must be instrumented to keep up with the transactional load. If this does not happen, real-time posting and provisioning capabilities are compromised. It must also be fault tolerant since it is mission critical to the billing process. The rater and biller must record a complete audit history of rating and price change events since they are tightly coupled with financial subsystems in the company.

14.5 Rating System Parameters

Focus is shifting from network usage rating toward customer and service value-based billing. Future services may be priced on value to customers rather than the cost of delivery. Value is measured by service parameters, which are dependent on service characteristics. Examples of these characteristics are:

- Number of kilobytes (K)
- QoS
- Access point name
- Number of hits and/or interactions
- Mailbox size
- Storage size
- Start and end geographic points of the event
- Day and time of event start and end
- Classes of the event
- If the event is on-net or off-net

The price for each combination of characteristics can include: a charge rate based on a per-second, per-kilobyte charge, a fixed charge per event, or include minimum and maximum charge limits. Service detail records (SDRs) generated for events on an IP network have different attributes from circuit switched CDRs. The number of kilobytes transferred is a better measure of volume for a data download than the time taken. QoS is an important factor in pricing IP services. Bundling functions gives customers a view of the value offered in different packages. Limitations revolve around ability to provide inputs to the billing system.

14.6 Mediation

Mediation validates, filters, formats, and processes the collected service usage information into records for distribution to downstream applications such as rating, billing, fraud, and data warehousing. Mediation is the first point of convergence of the services in the whole billing process. Unlike circuit-switched networks, IP has no single network element to record all information necessary to price an event. Separate elements typically record engineering-level data regarding packets and routing rather than user-level data relating to the applications and services. The customer is known, as such, in the mediation layer via a unique customer identifier defined and related to specific customer service usage information. The mediation layer needs to be flexible, open, and easy to use to support the real-time requirements of new services. Mediation systems for complex Internet services need to collect usage data from the circuit, data packet, Short Message Services (SMS) signaling, and packet-switch networks.

For service content and value billing, usage information must be collected from the IP network and application systems including: authentication, authorization, and accounting systems. Billing information for some services, like SMS, can be collected directly from the different network elements involved in the service delivery path. Packet-data billing service usage records are much more complex than circuit-switched billing. IP data is not attached to a switch or generated in a single, identifiable, centralized place like a voice record. IP network elements provide different pieces of information and records must be captured from many different types of equipment, such as Web servers, radius servers, firewalls, routers, and gateways. A single element does not usually contain all the information about a transaction that would be required to create a record. IP mediation systems collect information from the application layer, as well as the IP networks. Included in application layer devices are all servers and systems used in delivering the services, such as email and Web servers, unified messaging platforms, and so forth, and IP network elements include routers and gatekeepers. Packet-switched mediation converts information from the charging gateway and IP mediation (see Figure 14-2) into data records that can be used by the billing system.

Pricing for data volumes could be accomplished as a single reading from the beginning to end of each session. This method only works for services based on straight time pricing. All other pricing will change frequently during a single session. A charging gateway may measure and consolidate information about changes in the network—when data is transferred or changes in service quality. Before these logs can be used for billing, they must be converted to event records by the mediation system. A record may be generated each time a user clicks on a request, a change in service quality is indicated, and so forth. For end-to-end QoS, event records generated by the IP mediation software on all the IP networks combine these logs. In order to bill for a service, the billing system must first recognize the service event, defined as a set of event attributes. Each time the service occurs it is recorded in an SDR.

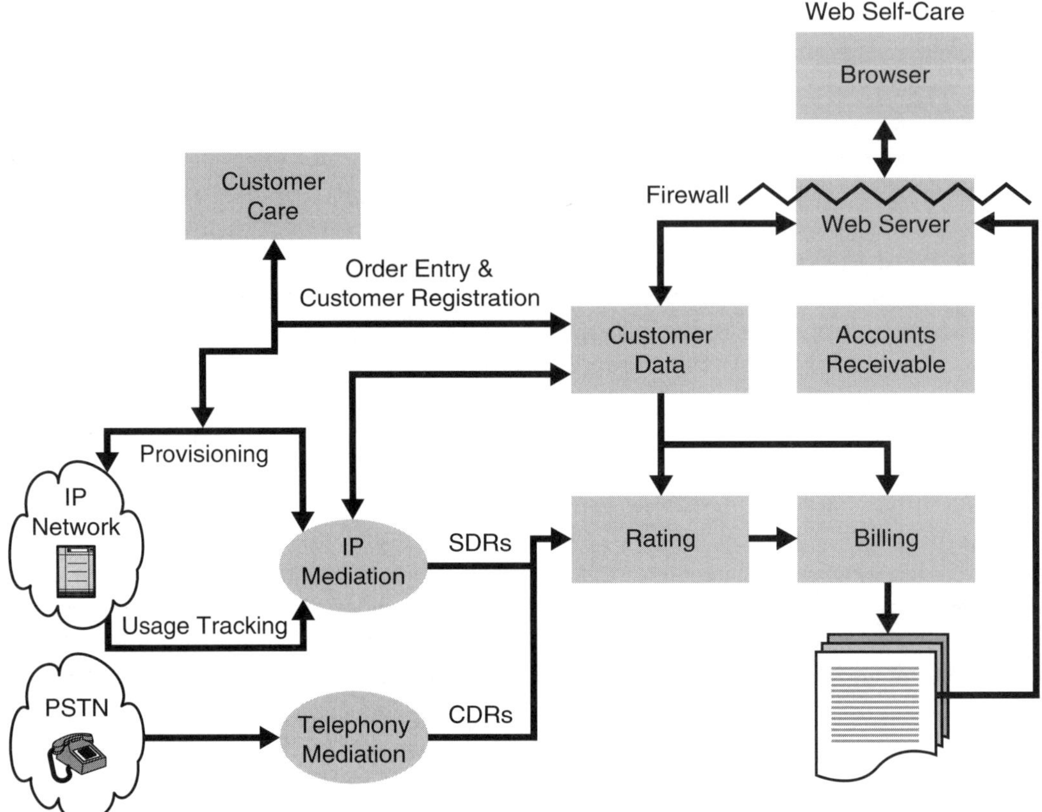

Figure 14-2 IP mediation.
Published courtesy of Hewlett-Packard Company.

Mediation complexity is greatly increased due to:

- Multiple applications
- Multiple equipment and application vendors
- Larger, faster networks with more devices
- Migration to broadband

Advanced IP mediation needs to operate in real time and be extremely scalable. It will abstract the complexity and heterogeneity of the underlying network elements and provide standard APIs to the OSS and BSS.

14.7 Invoicing

The invoicing operation includes all the remaining operations to prepare the final bill:

- Tax calculations
- Adjustments
- Currency conversion (if not done during rating)
- Global discount calculations (like total usage discounting)

Invoicing is still used in many countries, for both consumer and corporate segments, as one of the only legal means of getting paid. Normally the bill is sent on a monthly basis. Invoice operations will evolve to support the trends mentioned earlier in this chapter.

These operations face challenges in a number of areas. A convergent invoice will gather charges of all services used by the customer, ranging from voice through complex services. Billing cycle flexibility will increase allowing billing scheduling anytime convenient for the customer. Real-time invoicing will be required for paper and electronic bill presentation. A single bill gives customers a more complete view of services purchased, usage, and cost while reducing costs for the service provider. Invoicing is another tool for one-to-one marketing. Information about new products and services that fit the customer usage statistics can be included in the invoice.

Cross product discounting, or global discounting, are tools for use by the service provider to reduce churn. Levels of detail can be personalized per the customer's request and invoicing will have to support these requirements. For example, a high-level invoice can be sent to a corporate headquarters with detail for the particular departments. Some accounts can be managed in a prepaid and postpaid manner. Charges for use by children could be in the prepaid mode while other family services are postpaid, both presented on a single bill.

14.8 Electronic Bill Presentation—Turning Paper to Vapor

Most service providers consider Web-based bill presentation, payment, and customer self-care important requirements. These lower service provider costs of operation; many customers prefer these methods because they can access account details whenever convenient without having to wait for normal working hours, or waiting for CSR availability. It also gives customers a way to monitor service usage. Access may be by mobile device or computer, but screen size currently limits the use of mobile devices. Billing systems need a comprehensive set of APIs to support as many types of browser access as possible.

Advantages of electronic bill presentation to the biller include:

- Future cost savings
- New term competitive advantage and differentiation
- Barrier to exit; builds customer loyalty
- Increased customer contact; opportunity for branding and direct marketing
- Opportunity to add value to corporate customers

Advantages to the customer include:

- No initial investment required (other than a browser)
- Simplicity
- Convenience
- Geographic and device independent
- Control, flexibility, and speed
- Analysis of bills and spending patterns
- Ability to use alternative payment mechanisms
- Viable for all types of billing

Advantages to corporate customers:

- Offers analysis to gauge spending patterns
- Facilitates auditing and control
- Reduces bill processing costs
- Advantageous to geographically dispersed environment
- Not restricted to large businesses

14.9 Revenue Assurance

Revenue assurance is making sure that each and every chargeable event is accounted for within the system and is billed once, and once only, or written off. Failure to bill is usually due to errors in the tariff tables or other reference data (e.g., the product does not exist or the customer cannot be identified). This is called leakage. Failure to manage this can seriously upset accountants, auditors, regulators, and shareholders. Poor bill accuracy results in high levels of disputed bills, affecting revenues and cash flow. Revenue assurance becomes more challenging as parties used to enable complex services become more numerous and span several countries. There are no conventions defining how users of new services will be charged and how the contributing parties will be paid. For example, will customers be charged for bandwidth use, access, or time? How will contributing parties define the service value to the customers? Will the partners split the revenues equally? What will the interconnect partners see in their operations center when the call is set up?

14.9.1 Payment

Customers can pay bills in a variety of ways today, and options will only increase in the future. Service provider payment ecosystems will widen to include financial institutions. Service providers may decide partnering with these institutions gives them a strategic advantage as more and more customers automate payment. Automated payments could include automatic credit card debit, electronic payments like Web-based micropayment, and prepaid options such as e-wallet, automated clearinghouse (ACH), pay anyone capabilities, and calling cards. Supporting these and other payment options will complicate the revenue assurance operation. Extra pressure is put on the billing system since there are no accepted standards for the interfaces needed to support new payment options.

14.9.2 Credit Control

Billing systems control credit checks on potential customers before they are accepted for service. This capability might be used only when a new customer is set up, or may be accessed continually when offering services in prepaid modes. Conversely, external credit agencies and credit card companies may request credit verification information from the service provider billing system. Normally a credit limit is assigned to customers based on a calculated credit score derived from specified parameters. A credit limit action plan is normally defined per individual customer, or categories of customer. These action plans should be configurable and personalized.

14.9.3 Micropayment

Invoicing for small amounts of money is not always economically feasible. Secure micropayment methods and systems are needed for services payable by usage ticks. A tick could be a transaction, downloading a file, or pay-per-death game sequence. Micropayment methods improve revenue assurance since the service user can be identified through name and password sequences, then authorized (or not) to use the service. This market is currently underdeveloped, but has tremendous growth potential.

14.9.4 Service Roaming

With the continued growth of mobile services, seamless mobile roaming support is key. Billing for mobile Internet services needs to be an integral part of the billing function. From the beginning, mobile roaming was voice-only and billing was duration-based. Data usage is still billed based on duration. The readiness of the billing system's support of new data usage ratings/charging parameters is one of the bottlenecks for new charging principles. Innovative roaming agreements will be created to support next generation roaming. New backbones between next generation networks are required so the two networks can communicate. Despite the fact that next generation roaming allows users to access the Internet in several ways, many home operators will guard their customer information jealously and allow access to the Internet only via their home network. Billing systems need to support TAP3 formats to enable the return of roaming information to these home networks. Today, IP roaming seems relatively simple, but roaming mobile users will surely complicate the system.

14.9.5 Revenue Sharing and Settlement

Currently, the customer is normally owned by the company producing the bill. Further, the customer doesn't have direct arrangements with other partners involved in service fulfillment. The owning provider charges the subscriber and then pays other partners in the service production chain. As services increase in complexity, the user may want to interact with several content or service providers directly so the owning service provider needs to choose how it will be positioned and how much risk it will accept. In any event, all members making up the complex service must have some usage and customer data to assist in service delivery. New providers, acting as clearinghouses, may spring up to act as interfaces for customer usage data and rating information.

SLA penalties also put new strains on billing systems. The complexity of Internet services means tracking and correctly billing customers becomes more difficult. The fact that several players participate to produce a single service means that any SLA violation will be reflected down the value-chain. Providers are investigating SLA/QoS management on a service basis, but this is proving extremely complicated. Other solutions consist of calculating an average QoS on a regular time period basis and then applying the SLA violation calculation as needed.

14.9.6 Data Collection and Billing Mediation

As mentioned earlier, service usage information needs to be exchanged between partners. These data are coming from different sources and need to be identified, combined, and consolidated by the local mediation system before it is sent on to partners. Combining data records from different sources is an important way of identifying users. Services that are offered without downtime—always on—add a level of complexity because allowances must be made for partial usage records. For example, mobile device users that have changes in QoS and location will generate partial usage records that need to be linked. Call start and stop times need to be identified. This kind of data grows in direct relation to service complexity. Data sharing between partners is not clearly defined. Real-time data exchange and service provisioning for mobile devices are becoming a reality and need to be supported.

14.9.7 Interconnect Billing

In the telephony world, the interconnect billing system rates CDRs associated with national and international interconnect traffic. It produces usage statements that enable operators to invoice interconnect partners and verify demands for payment. The interconnect billing system interfaces with the mediation device, or a CDR collector, to collect charging information from the switches. The system receives the CDRs, checks for errors in formatting, and identifies the call type. The settlement management function rates the interconnect traffic. It can handle operator accounts and produce statements and reports. Statements are produced on summary, or detailed levels, using flexible billing periods, and are sent on to interconnect partners. Incoming statements are reviewed for accuracy. Many types of reports may be requested to review business results. Adjustments to final statements are made in cases of dispute. Cascade, as well as direct settlement, is supported. Further, interconnect billing systems interface with external systems to support almost any CDR format. This provides information such as: CDRs, traffic, charge, statement, and suspense data to provide information into external financial systems. Complex Internet services impact traditional interconnect billing systems because they will have to produce:

- Ratings for different billing dimensions, such as events, content, and QoS/SLA management
- Rating in real time or near real time
- Financial information to manage the profitability per service and per partner

- Several interfaces for data exchanges
- Improved performance
- Improved flexibility to easily adapt in real time to service changes

As more services and partners are added to the mix, much more usage data will enter the system for processing. Interconnect billing systems will need flexibility to support both service bundling and customer ad hoc requests.

14.9.8 Usage Management Trends

Usage management will need to contend with more applications with greater needs for usage data. Increasing volumes of usage data with shorter latency periods for data availability, increasingly complex services, and links with business rules put further pressure on usage management. Management systems are increasingly required to support a large number of different application areas enabling easy integration of best in class application components from multiple suppliers. There is a need to acquire and manage growing volumes of usage data from a increasing number of data sources. This means the need for correlating and aggregating data at multiple levels. There is a trend toward shorter latency in the availability of the usage data after the network event has occurred. There is a growing need for the ability to directly link the operational and configuration aspects of the management systems with the operator's business rules—in other words, the ability to dynamically change the available bandwidth on demand and bill for the actual usage.

These trends in the service provider market are putting pressure on the BSS to meet new functional requirements. The challenge for usage management systems is to improve from the present baseline. This means being able to:

- Handle greater requirements for usage data
- Support more sources and more destinations
- Have more involvement in the actual service delivery
- Support more variety in the data models and interface protocols
- Create a data record that describes the usage instance (Internet data record or IDR)

Strategic uses for usage data include:

- Cost reduction through enabling effective capacity planning
- Fraud detection and prevention
- The ability to identify and control costly resource utilization
- Revenue generation and churn reduction through QoS tiered subscriptions, off-peak usage subscription plans, promotional plans, resource utilization billing plans, usage profiling services, and enhanced customer services

14.10 Billing Requirements

Billing system requirements for complex services need to support a full range of mobile, data, and content services and will need to support:

- True multiservice, convergent billing
- Flexible, event-based pricing and discounting
- Multiparty content billing
- Rapid response to market changes
- Business billing
- High performance and scalability
- Online bill presentment and Internet self-care
- Real-time capabilities

The system must be auditable since it is tightly coupled with the financial systems.

Customers want a single bill to simplify understanding of the charges. Providers want convergent billing because it supports cross product discounting and a single customer view. Cross product discounting may include bundling products and offering special tariff plans with special discounts for multiple service use. Billing for all services on a single invoice reduces costs for the service provider. These kinds of offerings tend to lower customer churn. A truly convergent billing system provides a single data source on customer usage across a range of services, including usage, previous billing, payment history, disputes and adjustments, and credit limits. Automated debt escalation can be tailored based on customer's payment history across multiple services as a way to keep profitable customers. This is also a good source for targeted one-to-one marketing efforts.

Billing systems must be flexible enough to handle different types of event records for diverse services. These events must all be priced accordingly, which may include QoS, access point name (APN), content type, and other attributes. Billing is also a marketing tool and must support unique discounting, service packages, loyalty schemes, and messaging.

One service may include flow-through invoicing/payments to/from many partners. This means the billing system will not be able to assume a one-to-one mapping between an event and a line item on a customer's bill. It results in increased complexity in revenue assurance and in the processes for unloading disputed, or erroneous, events.

New technologies will generate a wide range of innovative products and services, many of which are not known when the billing system is implemented. Traditional billing systems have often been a bottleneck to the introduction of new products and services, requiring expensive and time-consuming software changes. Billing systems need to support event-based services where new products and services do not require software changes. Further, the billing system needs to support rapid tariff changes, and even fundamental changes in the pricing basis.

Billing needs to support business usage, meaning the ability to model corporate hierarchies to any breadth and depth, budget center reporting, and charge transfer/discounting between accounts in the hierarchy. Discounts may need to be based on individual product usage, packages, accounts, or the entire corporate hierarchy. Bundled minutes, or megabytes, may be shared between many users.

The volume of billable events is expected to increase exponentially as services become more complex. Many providers assume a tenfold increase in the number of events per product, per day compared to voice telephony. This volume level could easily outstrip the capabilities of today's billing systems.

The interactive nature of Internet applications has set new expectations for the wireless environment. Users expect immediate access to a high-quality connection that will give them an accurate usage statement reflecting their current usage status and outstanding charges via a wireless interface. As mentioned previously, real-time self-provisioning of services will be required. Changes made by the users are expected to be in force immediately upon the change. All of this requires implementation of real-time capabilities in the network, operational support, and billing infrastructures. For example, an automated credit-checking program must support notification of prepaid customers when their credit limits are running low. Instant electronic payment processing allows the customer to top off credit interactively. Provisioning systems must be automated (see Chapter 12) and closely interfaced to order entry and billing. Event records need to be generated and sent to the rating engine for pricing in subsecond time scales, also called hot-rating.

Common billing problems include incorrect accounts receivable information, incorrect rating and charges, incorrect invoice calculation, incomplete billing, incorrect messaging, nonbillable calls on the invoice, and incorrect invoices (what has been approved is not what is mailed).

14.10.1 Sample Billing System and Billing Process Measurements

Billing systems should be monitored for accuracy and customer satisfaction. Here are some sample billing system measurements:

- Invoice accuracy
- Invoice mail time
- Billing adjustments
- Dispute resolution
- Suspended usage
- Purged usage
- Aged usage billed
- Call processing times
- Payment application
- First service intervals
- Billed/carried ratio
- Customer churn
- Net revenue
- Revenue per employee days sales outstanding

14.10.2 Billing Outsourcing

Service providers may want to outsource their billing system. Guidelines for outsourcing are discussed in more detail in Chapter 10, but at a high level, advantages to keeping the system in-house revolve around control:

- Brand control
- Ability to link billing while focusing on one-to-one marketing efforts
- Flexibility on customer initiation and enrollment

Service providers may want to outsource the billing system due to the high costs of the system and its implementation and because billing is not something they want to build as a core competency.

Billing can be a service provider's competitive advantage by enabling the provider to quickly offer new services, supporting efficient provisioning and serving as an effective communication tool to the customer base.

14.11 Summary

Billing for IP services is significantly different from billing for circuit-switched telephony. Mediation is harder; bytes, bandwidth, and QoS provide a more appropriate basis for pricing than minutes. Billing systems need to take a high volume of usage information from many sources and rate them, real time, while applying universal discounting and settling charges, some of which are roaming, with diverse business partners. Customers expect self-provisioning and care with instantaneous results to their service. To keep up with these trends, billing systems need to be scalable, flexible, and robust with abilities to easily update tariff plans and rating logic. There also needs to be an ability to set up many APIs and protocols since industry standards are not defined in this highly fragmented area. Service providers are looking to billing as a source of new revenue through advertising, to cross sell/up sell services, and as a new wholesale service that can be offered to service providers that decide to outsource these functions.

14.12 xSP Strategy Checklist for Billing

- ❑ Identify customers and their billing needs
- ❑ Identify the services roadmap
- ❑ Does the billing system need to integrate with a legacy system?
- ❑ Does the billing system need to integrate with partners' systems?
- ❑ Are the billing measurements defined?
- ❑ Is the system scalable?
- ❑ Can the system handle tariff changes easily?
- ❑ Does it support hot rating? Hot invoicing?
- ❑ Can it handle pre- and postpayments?
- ❑ Will it offer combined service billing?
- ❑ Will it support electronic billing?
- ❑ Can the rating system support value-based billing?
- ❑ Can invoicing support cross region/country taxes? Currencies?
- ❑ Can it support/meet billing regulations in countries where it will be used?
- ❑ Does it support global discount calculations?
- ❑ Does it support electronic payment options? Micropayments? Service roaming? Revenue sharing?
- ❑ Does it have real-time capabilities?
- ❑ Can it monitor service usage?
- ❑ Can it support service provider marketing requirements?
- ❑ Is it auditable?
- ❑ Can additional hardware be added while the system is up and running?
- ❑ Does the billing vendor have relationships with the hardware vendor(s)? Do they work together on tuning and performance issues?
- ❑ What high-availability or failover options are there?
- ❑ Is there multiplatform support (NT, UNIX, and Linux)?
- ❑ For system management, what options are available? Does the vendor offer its own? How comprehensive is it? Is there integration with leading third-party suppliers?
- ❑ Does the application offer self-care, or integrate with third-party customer care packages?
- ❑ How are fraud detection and bad debt prevention handled?
- ❑ Can the system accommodate the introduction of new services—each with its own billing model?
- ❑ Does the billing system allow wholesalers to offer hosted infrastructure capabilities?
- ❑ Does the system support multiple companies, entities, and divisions allowing billing to roll up and be reported at any level of the hierarchy?
- ❑ Does the billing vendor have relationships with system integration partners? Which ones? Is the service provider able to choose a preferred system integrator or is the billing vendor providing all of the integration?

- ❑ What is the billing vendor's ratio of software license sales to services?
- ❑ Is there an upgrade path for the billing software?
- ❑ What ISV and technology partnerships exist?
- ❑ Who are the existing customers? What are their profiles? Are there any references?
- ❑ Is there support for convergent billing?
- ❑ Are APIs published?
- ❑ What is the support model?
- ❑ How quickly can the billing service be deployed and what effort is involved?

CHAPTER 15

Infrastructure

All service providers need access to some sort of IDC. They may not own the data center, but they always need a place to physically host servers, either for customers themselves, or for software used to provide final services offered by the provider. With this in mind, this chapter focuses on service provider infrastructure from the IDC point of view, lightly touching on interfaces with the OSS and BSS structures.

Service provider infrastructure needs to be scalable, flexible, dependable, supportable, secure, and manageable. These characteristics are needed throughout the delivery chain from service origination through ongoing maintenance and support and are usually measured by SLAs (see Appendix C, "Sample Service Level Agreement"). Service levels are often governed by the linkages between members of the delivery chain and are dependent on the chain's weakest link.

15.1 Logical Architecture

15.1.1 Requirements

To be successful, the service provider needs infrastructure that will support the business it is offering, which, in turn, needs to fill market needs—not the other way around. Figure 15-1 and information from Chapter 2, "Basic Operational Challenges," give an idea of an Internet services roadmap that needs to be supported.

An IDC needs to:

- Ensure mission-critical applications are available per service provider guarantees
- Ensure full and available capacity for any application demands at any time, anywhere as guaranteed by the service provider
- Support access for devices, resources, information bases, or services anywhere, any time

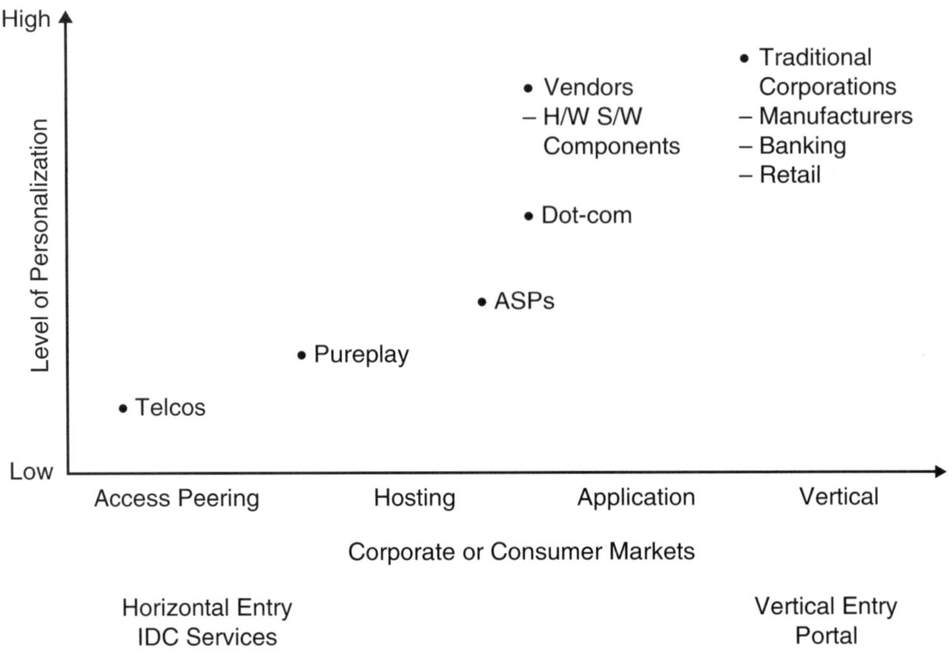

Figure 15-1 Positioning matrix.

- Provide absolute security for protection of data, information, systems, and privacy
- Offer total end-to-end management and control of all resources, delivering enhanced service levels in a cost effective manner

A service provider customer usually does not care what operating systems are offered, as long as the service is available as promised. This does not mean that the service provider needs to support everything. Far from it. The infrastructure needs to be something that the provider can operate efficiently so that services can be offered profitably and at a price point acceptable by the market. This leads the discussion into the second part of the chapter, namely, ongoing data center management after set up. Information contained in the IDC needs to be reliably backed up, stored, and restored. Procedures need to be established that ensure the IDC is professionally operated and maintained.

15.1.2 Logical View

An IDC infrastructure should realize a simple, layered architecture (see Figure 15-2). Applications running in the IDC plug into the infrastructure supporting service delivery, security, collaboration, and management. Services offered by the data center owner (internal services) and those offered by the data center's customers and partners (external services) should both operate as a plug-in into the infrastructure environment. This allows the IDC operator to protect the investment by changing

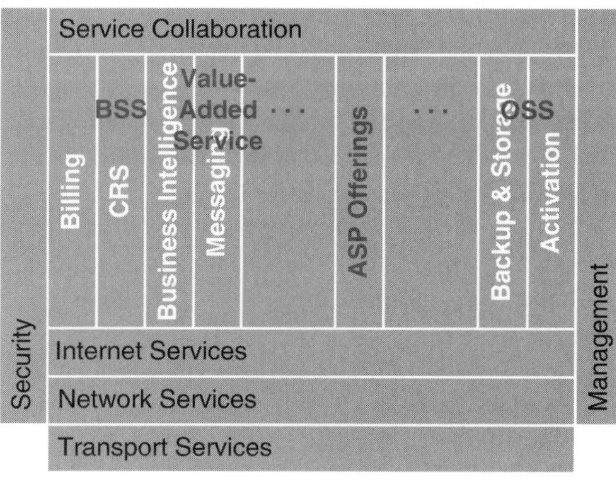

- The logical architecture is composed of a simple, layered infrastructure.
- The functionality used to operate the IDC and offered to the end-customer both run on the same infrastructure.
- Value-Added services plug into the “base” infrastructure.

Figure 15-2 Sample logical architecture.
Published courtesy of Hewlett-Packard Company.

and migrating the diversity, ownership, and business models associated with the services offered over the life of the data center. For deployments into environments where legacy systems exist, it offers an integration point, and provides the IDC owner with a nondisruptive way to migrate or transform these legacy services as the business evolves.

The layers of the architecture are transport, network, Internet service, service collaboration, management, security, and plug-ins. OSS and BSS systems in this framework can be viewed as resalable services.

15.1.2.1 Transport and Transport Services

This layer is the physical transport for service delivery to the IDC customer and its customers. It includes broadband data delivery technologies such as Synchronous Optical Network (SONET), Synchronous Digital Hierarchy (SDH), frame relay, ATM, and Public Switched Telephone Network (PSTN) for traditional voice delivery services.

15.1.2.2 Network and Network Services

This layer includes IP packet processing, including routing, bandwidth management, load balancing, IP address translation, and IP transformation. This would include VoIP gateways and VoIP gatekeepers.

15.1.2.3 Internet Services

This layer includes Internet facing services that process and support IP protocols operation. This includes HTTP servers, Internet protocol servers (ftp, news, chat, time, DNS), Java application servers, Mail servers (SMTP, IMAP, POP), and voice/video streaming servers.

15.1.2.4 Service Collaboration

This layer enables and facilitates the collaboration and interaction between services hosted in the IDC. It includes the OSS and BSS functions and software functions such as interservice messaging, message mediation, process engine/workflow, and service locator/brokering engines. Software processes supporting a service framework specification for real-time collaboration negotiation would also be found in this layer. These include:

- Management
  Provides network and service operations management facilities to ensure supervisory operation of the infrastructure and data center service delivery performance
- Network management
  Fault management, configuration, discovery, performance
- Service management
  Fault management, configuration, discovery, performance
- Security
  Provides user and system security and policy information to all layers in the architecture
- Network security
  Authentication, authorization, and activation (AAA)
- Plug-in collaboration security
  AAA, encryption
- Service plug-ins
  This layer contains the services of the IDC, including services that support the data center's business and facilitate the business operations of the hosted applications within the data center, as well as the hosted applications and services offered by the customers of the data center. Services include:
  - Business support systems
    Billing
    CLM (including order management)
    Business intelligence
  - Operations support systems (see Figure 15-3)
    Activation
    Backup & Storage management
- Other data center value-added services
  Messaging
  Unified communications
  Release field testing support
  Load testing support
  xSP hosted applications

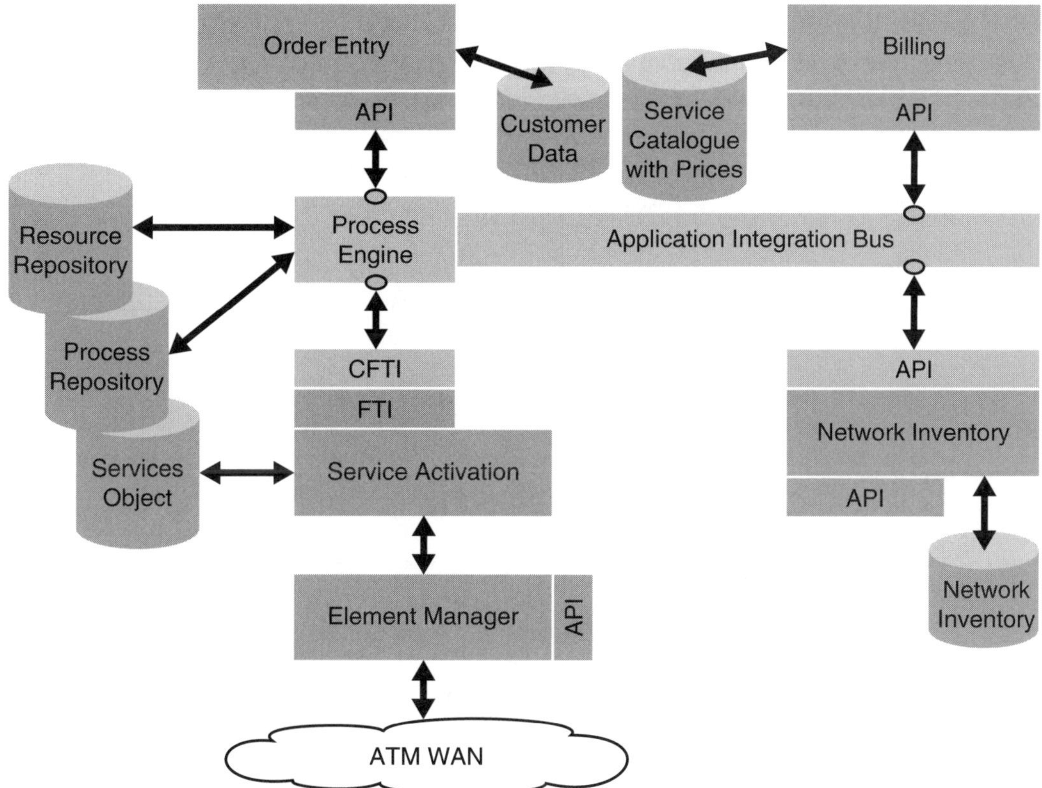

Figure 15-3 The IDC OSS.
Published courtesy of Hewlett-Packard Company.

15.2 Scalability

Service provider business is such that demands upon infrastructure are greater than in other industries. One of the greatest demands has to do with scalability. The infrastructure must seamlessly scale quickly to reflect user growth and volumes. Central to scalability are power, space, bandwidth, hardware/software, and the environmentals of the data center. A service provider can't expand unless these elements can scale accordingly. Service providers are afraid of the dark. They look for ways to ensure that sometimes-limited power is available as needed. Most data centers have redundant power feeds and massive generators. Service providers pay top dollar to ensure that diesel generators won't go dry. Data center owners try to get on utility companies' uninterruptible power supply lists, meaning the power would be cut only during the most dire situations.

15.3 Dependability

An IDC needs to be available at all times because it will be supporting mission-critical systems. Dependability extends beyond the equipment in the data center to the actual building and all elements between the service provider and the end-customer. End-to-end SLAs must take into account the weakest link in this chain and service levels will reflect this. The infrastructure must handle sudden volume peaks or spikes, as well as take into effect the unexpected, such as power outages, fires, construction accidents, and so forth. A good example is how service providers complied with their SLAs during California's utility crisis.

Service providers must also have the processes and procedures in place to make sure the services are dependable and available, as required. For example:

- IT user guides
- IT administration guides
- IT operational guides
- IT configuration guides
- Employee training plans
- Change/Approval processes
- Escalation processes (in case of disputes)
- Capacity management guides
- Service request processes
- Provisioning processes/guides
- Safety guides
- Security implementation guides
- Project office processes
- Billing process/accounts payable/accounts receivable guides
- Credit policies and checks
- Bill formats
- Customer care process/guides
- IT support process/guides
- Facilities support processes/guides
- HR policies/guidelines
- Codes of conduct
- Legal guidelines
- Administration guidelines
- Purchasing guidelines
- Audit guidelines

15.4 Supportability

Supportability goes hand-in-hand with dependability and manageability. Infrastructure needs to have patches and updates installed promptly and proactively. Resources need a training program so they are able to support updates to the service provider's infrastructure. Implementing patches and training may be something the service provider wants to outsource. Data center backups and recovery procedures need to be in place and tested.

15.5 Security

Security takes into effect physical and electronic security. Customers require guarantees that firewalls are solid and intrusion detection methods are reliable. Building and cage security must be total. For shared hosting, customer security is a special concern that needs to be addressed by the provider. How will shared hosting customers know that another company located on the same server isn't interfering with the data? Reports and auditing take effort, but are a must to prove a secure, safe environment to customers.

15.6 Manageability

Complete monitoring of a customer's service is of prime importance. Proactive notification of service outages is becoming a requirement of many customers because service outages affect revenues. Service providers manage their infrastructure by using hardware, software, and operations centers. Some service providers have network operation centers in each data center, some have one operation center that manages several data centers. Either way, the service provider needs one view of the network, and common processes, to proactively troubleshoot problems before they arise. These problems would include things like server usage levels and network usage levels.

15.7 Ongoing Care and Feeding

Building the service provider operation and entering the market is only one aspect of the business. More challenging is how to run the operation in a profitable manner. Two forces are at play here: limiting the offerings and filling the data center to ensure economies of scale. As seen in Chapter 11, "Entering the Market," service providers want to limit offerings so they can control inventory and build efficiencies in operations so they are not trying to support many diverse platforms. Chapter 11 discusses more about how these platforms can appear customized so customers think they are getting unique services, even though the bundles are simply repackaged service functionalities. More challenging for some service providers is how to keep IDCs filled or where to physically place the equipment they do have. Chapters 9, "Partners and Alliances," 11, "Entering the Market," 13, "Perception is Reality," and this chapter discuss how offering high-quality services, state-of-the art infrastructure, well-trained direct and indirect sales forces, marketing communications, and ensuring a good overall customer experience are the best ways to keep IDCs filled.

15.8 Case Study: Exodus Communications

15.8.1 Background

Exodus Communications began offering collocation services and is now one of the leading providers of complex Internet hosting for enterprises with mission-critical Internet operations. The company offers sophisticated systems and network management solutions, along with professional services, to provide optimal performance for customers' Internet infrastructures. Exodus manages its network infrastructure via a worldwide network of IDCs located in North America, Europe, and Asia Pacific. Additionally, Exodus offers several complementary services that can bring benefits to Internet operations, including:

- content distribution
- enhanced security
- storage management
- end-user performance monitoring
- Web site stress testing
- site capacity planning

Exodus provides its services to a mix of traditional enterprise companies and new Internet companies. In the first quarter of 1999, enterprise customers represented approximately 29 percent of Exodus's revenues. By the first quarter of 2001, enterprise customers accounted for 62 percent of revenues.

The Exodus network is one of the largest IP networks in the world. It reported a peak Internet exchange rate of 22.8 gigabits per second as of the first quarter of 2001. This privately managed network connects Exodus IDCs across four continents. Comprising the Exodus network is a global backbone, high-performance network architecture, and industry-leading public and private interconnect arrangements.

15.8.2 Scalability

Steve Kossa, western regional vice president of business operations for Exodus Communications, attributes four essential elements to scalability: power, backbone, hardware/software, and bandwidth.

The power infrastructure of an IDC is important for reliability. For example, during the recent California rolling power outages, it was vital that Exodus IDCs maintained power. Every Exodus IDC has redundant backup systems, comprised of uninterruptible power supply systems and diesel generators. Exodus keeps enough diesel fuel at each IDC location to power that site for 72 hours in the event of an extended power outage. In addition, fuel can be delivered within a few hours to any of the Exodus IDCs.

Exodus's backbone network connects all of its IDCs, using multiple high-speed OC-3, OC-12, and OC-48 lines, which virtually eliminate the risk of a single point of failure. Within each IDC, Exodus's LAN architecture scales to meet customers' increasing bandwidth requirements. This architecture enables Exodus to scale in anticipation of customer demand. The Exodus Internet node architecture employs very reliable and powerful routers, running at gigabit speeds.

15.8.3 Reliability

Peering is key for reliability because it allows Exodus to control connections with networks leased from other companies. Having a private network is important because Exodus can control the amount of excess capacity. For example, some service providers oversell their networks; in other words, they sell 150 to 200 percent of their capacity. Their theory is that users won't simultaneously require more than 100 percent of available bandwidth. Exodus's policy is to allow 30 percent capacity headroom, which provides added redundancy to ensure that customer service is not interrupted. Extensive physical security, such as housing customer equipment in secure cages, helps protect Exodus IDCs against forces of nature and man.

15.8.4 Supportability

Exodus's customized SLAs offer combined around-the-clock systems management and onsite personnel trained in the areas of networking, Internet, and systems management. The result is a physical and technical environment affording customers the reliability and flexibility necessary to outsource their mission-critical Internet operations. Exodus IDCs are custom designed and include raised floors, HVAC temperature control systems with separate cooling zones, and seismically braced racks. They offer smoke detection and fire suppression systems, motion sensors, and 24/7 secured access as well as video camera surveillance and security breach alarms. The systems are further supported via redundant subsystems, such as multiple fiber trunks and fully redundant power.

15.8.5 Security

New security vulnerabilities are discovered every day in software, hardware, protocols, and applications. While there are many security resources, such as CERT/CIAC alerts, vendor services, and USENET newsgroups, Exodus offers a world-class security practice that is comprised of more than 100 security specialists, many of whom are CISSP, GIAC, and/or GSEC certified, to protect e-businesses from the growing number of cyber crimes and cyber-terrorism attacks. Exodus security offerings, combined with unmatched security expertise, are focused on four core areas to address all levels of the customers' physical, network, and virtual environment: network and systems security, commerce security, security advisory services, and defense and response.

Specific services include an up-to-date targeted Security Alert Report, designed to help subscribers protect the integrity of their computing systems. Exodus professional services can design, test, and implement a comprehensive network security strategy for its clients. These services include:

- secure Web site design and configuration
- system and network penetration testing
- cyber attack management service that monitors customers' Web sites for suspicious activities
- 24/7 incident response management service
- security audits
- security training
- security planning
- VPN design and deployment
- site and operating systems hardening
- Health Insurance Portability and Accountability Act (HIPAA) compliance consulting

Exodus's managed firewall services include options whereby security experts work with customers to define their firewall security policies, and then customize, install, and manage the product chosen most appropriate to the customers' businesses. Exodus can set default policies and rules, install and perform ongoing support, and provide 24/7 ICMP monitoring and log files access via secure Web browser facilities.

Exodus also has a unique consulting service called the Cyber Attack Tiger Team (CATT). The purpose of the CATT service is to help customers prepare for and deal with computer hackers, crackers, industrial spies, and other types of attacks and infestations. Part of the charter of the group is to provide real-time incident response when a customer requires state-of-the-art computer forensics and defensive security measures by accomplished experts with world-class credentials. It takes a lot of effort and expertise to outfit such a unit, especially since it is available for hire at any time for customers who need immediate help.

15.8.6 Monitoring and Management

myExodus™ is a Web portal that enables customers to access a variety of operational management tools and applications provided by Exodus and its third-party application service provider (ASP) and managed service provider (MSP) partnersincluding monitoring and reporting, network and systems administration, customer support, and account management. The portal features timely information that companies can use to monitor and maintain system, network, and application uptime and performance as well as service quality, while minimizing the use of scarce internal resources. myExodus™ also enables Exodus to efficiently deliver news and updates pertaining to its customers' online business and to inform them about new products and services. myExodus™ also provides a view into Exodus's new Enterprise Systems Monitoring (ESM) service. Exodus ESM offers fully outsourced monitoring of key software infrastructure components, including custom applications, operating systems, and network devices. ESM assists customers in preventing outages and improving system performance by keeping them informed of key events and historical trends. ESM is part of Exodus's end-to-end monitoring and management solutions, which reduce the cost of monitoring for customers by allowing them to focus on their core business while maintaining performance and flexibility. The following is more in-depth information about how Exodus manages customer sites.

15.8.6.1 Managed Services Overview

Exodus provides a wide range of managed services and helps customers architect sites, integrate new technologies, and ensure high levels of performance and scalability. This range of managed services includes:

- Managed Hosting: Exodus's managed hosting service is a comprehensive, business-critical hosting solution for companies that want to completely outsource their Internet operations. The service uses pre-integrated, best-of-breed infrastructure components—based on Compaq/Windows or Sun/Solaris—and Exodus's proprietary technology. It delivers a complete outsourced solution, including space and connectivity, monitoring and management, technical expertise, security, scalability, and the support and performance required by mission-critical Web operations. Exodus's managed hosting service includes two integral components: Web application management and security.

  With Web application management, Exodus proactively manages a range of application platforms and databases—including the industry-leading Oracle 8i platform. This service includes proactive application monitoring, management, and full problem resolution. In addition, it encompasses ongoing support from technical experts, which allows a company's inhouse staff to focus on developing new application functionality, rather than spending time and resources to manage the applications.

  Exodus's work-class security practice helps protect customers from the growing number of cyber crimes. Many of these specialists are CISSP certified, and a number hail from the FBI, the U.S. Secret Service, the NSA, and other security organizations and companies.
- Storage: Web sites generate tremendous amounts of data, and analysts say that the demand for storage is increasing 75 percent to 100 percent per year. Exodus provides services such as backup and restore, disk on demand, and remote disaster recovery. To provide comprehensive storage solutions, Exodus works with companies such as EMC, Network Appliance, Sun Microsystems, Compaq, StorageWay, StorageNetworks, sanrise, and Scale Eight.
- Content Distribution: Exodus focuses on improving Web site performance at three key points in the data stream: the server, the network, and the edge. Content is moved closer to end users via the fastest and most cost-effective routes, which optimizes the user experience and allows companies to increase the intensity of their content and the global scale of their sites.

This broad range of services adds up to a complete managed hosting solution. Customers can rely on Exodus's expertise to run their critical Internet operations and have a single point of accountability for operating those systems. Exodus's range of managed services also result in increased flexibility. With a variety of options, outsourcing arrangements can be established on a turnkey basis or tailored to meet the individual company's specific needs, enabling a company to take advantage of as many or as few services as it requires.

15.9 Summary

Service provider infrastructure needs to be scalable, flexible, dependable, supportable, secure, and manageable. These characteristics are needed throughout the delivery chain from service origination through to the final customer. Usually they are measured by SLAs. Service levels are often governed by the linkages between members of the delivery chain and are dependent on the chain's weakest link. The architecture must support the service provider's business.

15.10 xSP Strategy Checklist for Infrastructure

- ❑ Does the IDC have sufficient power per square foot to support customers today?
- ❑ Is there a plan for future power scalability?
- ❑ Are there sufficient infrastructure, resources, plans, and procedures to support service level agreements?
- ❑ Are there plans in place for security of the premises, both building security and hardware and network security?
- ❑ Do the hardware, software, and platform configurations conform to scalability and security requirements?
- ❑ Does the bandwidth support surges in data center traffic?
- ❑ Is there a central management system for the data center?
- ❑ How are customers notified of system outages?
- ❑ Are there sufficient support contracts in place for vendors supplying the data center?
- ❑ Is the IDC supported in-house or outsourced? If outsourced, see checklist in Chapter 11 for outsourcing questions.
- ❑ How will patches, backups, and planned downtime be performed?
- ❑ Are there processes for keeping platforms and configurations limited?
- ❑ Are there technician training and retention plans?
- ❑ Are data center procedures and configurations maintained worldwide to keep economies of scale?
- ❑ Is the data center secure against acts of war and nature?
- ❑ Are there written data center operation procedures and guides? (See Chapter 11.)

CHAPTER 16

Afterword

Congratulations! By reading this book you have taken the first step toward understanding the many challenges of competing in the service provider market place. You have a high level understanding of the seven operational challenges: organization/operations, partners/alliances, sales/marketing, service delivery, customer care, billing, and infrastructure. In addition, you now have checklists and tools to successfully work through the challenges. Case studies from all over the world showed you how your peers are working through these highly volatile markets. You have a list of helpful organizations and periodicals to help you network and get more information in areas of particular interest. You are now at the cusp and ready to take the next steps toward increasing customer loyalty and market share, decreasing operational costs, and offering high margin services. It's a complex market, but one that ultimately will provide the future for all electronic transactions, both at home and at work. Good luck!

PART 4

Appendices

APPENDIX A

Definitions

ATM (Asynchronous Transfer Mode) One of the fastest network technologies available, it can transmit audio, video, and data up to 622 Mbps.

backbone Traditionally, the part of the communications network that carries the heaviest traffic.

back-office services Typically include human resources, financial management, CRM, ERP, and SFA functionality.

bandwidth A telecommunications company's line's capacity, measured in the amount of data it can transport in one second. Units of measurement include bits and bauds.

bottlenecks Process points where service provisioning or delivery experiences delays.

B2B Business-to-business (sometimes written B-to-B).

B2C Business-to-consumer (sometimes written B-to-C).

BSS Business support services. These services normally include customer care, billing and customer facing applications.

CDR Call detail records that contain call information collected by the switch.

collateral Marketing communication materials that contain key service benefits and marketing messages, such as data sheets, brochures, fliers, and so forth.

collocation A service offered by the service provider that houses servers owned by customers and offers direct connection to a network backbone.

convergence Typically the combination of voice and data services into one service. More and more wireless services are included in the mix.

CPE Customer premise equipment, such as handsets.

CRM Customer relationship management.

CSR Customer service representative.

customer mix Combination of customer segments or customer types.

dedicated hosting Hosting services usually used by large enterprises where each enterprise has one or more dedicated servers, owned by and located with a service provider.

deregulation (telecommunications industry) The breaking up of the traditional telecommunications monopoly (sometimes known as a PTT) to allow competition. In the United States, this was part of the Telecommunications Act of 1996 and the AT&T split.

dot-coms Pure Internet companies operating online businesses.

EAI Enterprise application integration.

e-commerce Typically includes advertising, shopping cart, and Web-based billing functionalities.

ECR initiative The efficient customer response is a European trade and industry body launched in 1994 to make the grocery sector more responsive to consumer demand and to eliminate unnecessary costs from the supply chain. ECR ensures that retailers and manufacturers work together to negotiate better deals that will ultimately benefit customers.

EPOS Electronic point of sale.

ERM Encompasses the systems relating to customer/employee relationship management, back-end/back-office tools, and business intelligence across the enterprise.

ERP Enterprise resource planning.

FAB Fulfillment-assurance-billing.

FSN Full-service network connection.

hurdle rate The minimum rate of return required to earn back the cost of invested capital. Also known as cost of capital.

HIPAA Health Insurance Portability and Accountability Act of 1996, a set of specific guidelines designed to protect patient records online and in print.

ICE Integrated collaborative environment solutions that include software that provides a framework for electronic collaboration, typically within an organization based on shared directory and messaging platforms. Core functionality includes email, group calendaring/scheduling, shared folders/databases, threaded discussions, and custom applications.

IDR Internet data record.

integration bus Contains the physical connection and interaction between processes, resources, and applications so the service delivery process can work efficiently across departments.

LAN Local Area Network typically links computers and peripheral devices over a short distance, such as within a house, building, or campus.

local loop The portion of the network between the home or office and the central office. Also called the last mile.

manual provisioning The manual set-up and delivery of a service provider service.

marketing The art of communicating the value of goods or services to a target market in a way that will convince potential buyers to make the purchase because the perceived value is worth the price.

Network Access Point (NAP) Customers lease space at one of four exchange points for the purpose of network interconnection and Internet peering. NAP provides a more robust connectivity option by its strategic geographic location. It facilitates connectivity between ISPs.

office automation services Typically includes email, groupware, and collaborative computing functionality.

OSS Operational support services are normally network facing processes like provisioning, activation, network element management, and so forth.

peering An arrangement among networks whereby the member networks agree to exchange traffic among all of the networks' computers. Peering takes place primarily between NAPs. Companies entering into private peering arrangements are those interconnecting networks independent of NAPs.

rating The rater takes a transaction, as defined by a network detail record, and calculates the price based on a rate table, or predefined set of rules, established by product management.

ROI The return on investment is the amount of earnings divided by the amount invested to generate the earnings.

SDR Service detail record.

service assurance The system(s) used to manage the processes and information required to make sure the promised services are running and available.

SFA Sales force automation.

SLAs Service level agreements. Contracts between a service provider and its customer, guaranteeing certain levels of speed or response for functionality described in the service offering.

service usage The system(s) and processes used to understand how customers use the services offered.

shared hosting Hosting services offered to enterprises on computers owned by and located in a service provider. Customers lease shared rack and server resources and typically pay for bandwidth on a per-megabyte basis; remote monitoring and management are typically included.

TCA Team collaborative application software provides an integrated set of Web-based tools for collaboration among team members from one or more organizations. Core functionality areas are shared workspaces for posting and exchanging files, tasks, and other project and team information.

ticks A unit of measure that could be used by secure micropayment or other types of billing systems.

total cost of ownership The overall expense associated with implementing a new project, service, or product.

TOM Telecom Operations Map developed by the TeleManagement Forum (TMF). It supersedes the Network Management Forum Service Management Business Process Model and the TM Forum Telecom Operations Map.

xSP Any company that offers services over an IP network. These services are usually charged on a per-transaction, per-unit, or per-service price. Examples of xSPs are ASP, ISP, CSP, MSP, or enterprises that want to offer these kinds of services internally.

APPENDIX B

Sample Business Plan

The sample business plan presented here can be used as a template. It contains sample language to give the reader an idea of the kind of information contained in various sections. This plan is a sample, only, and is not intended to suggest any exact wording or focus services, nor are the market numbers based on any actual data. There are places, noted in sentences in italics, where a company would insert specific information. A business plan is a living document and should be updated as the business changes. It is used to formally put forward ideas on what the business is, how it will be run, its plans for sales and marketing and their execution, resourcing plans, the company's value proposition, and financial projections. In short, it is the corporate bible used to do business and gain funding.

Business plans usually include these sections:

- Executive summary
- Business description (what services the company will offer)
- Overview of the market: Industry overview, needs of the market, total market size, addressable market, percentage of market the business expects to capture the first year(s)
- Corporate value proposition—why customers will come and stay
- Executive team
- Competitive analysis
- SWOT analysis
- Operations plan
- Marketing plan
- Sales plan
- Resourcing plan
- Financial plan

B.1 Sample Business Plan for Best Hosting Company

B.1.1 Executive Summary

Best Hosting was incorporated in 1996 in the state of Delaware and intends to provide business customers and content providers with an expert service partner to access and integrate their computer and communications resources into one unified network. Best Hosting will aggregate network protocols and information formats over a single network connection so that the end-user can realize the benefits of economies of scale, cost savings, and simplified administration. The company intends to capture 30 percent of its addressable market share during its first year of operation via acquisitions, direct and indirect sales, and unique services that will include: collocation, dedicated hosting, mission-critical business applications, and media on demand. It intends to keep costs controlled by automating processes and leveraging common infrastructure as much as possible. Break even is expected in the fifth year of the operation, taking into account the initial rise in churn after acquisitions and initial infrastructure investments. Initial capitalization is provided through private investments made by the board of directors and an initial public offering (IPO) of its stock.

B.1.2 Business Description

Best Hosting was formed to provide enterprise business customers and content providers with an expert service partner to access and integrate the computer and communications resources into one unified network. Many companies have a constantly evolving demand for faster and more robust performance from their information and communication systems and are faced with limited information systems budgets, multiple protocols, and noncompatible hosts that make communications difficult. In addition, new Internet-based technologies, such as e-commerce, multimedia streaming, and VPNs are forcing companies to rethink entire methodologies for networking and sharing information. Finally, finding and retaining highly qualified IT talent becomes a greater challenge for enterprise business customers as this resource pool is in greater demand.

Spurred by the sector's new legitimacy in the eyes of financial institutions and the availability of capital, acquisitions of national, regional and local service providers are accelerating significantly. Most national security providers lack the local presence to offer customized hands-on support and local service providers often lack the resources necessary to provide a full range of services at acceptable quality and competitive prices. For these reasons, many service providers:

- Have reached or surpassed their management capabilities
- Have been unable to attain critical mass sufficient to remain competitive in local markets
- Have been unable to access funds for capital improvements
- Face erosion of their customer base and revenue streams from alternative service providers offering new services or higher quality service.

Enterprise business customers need a trusted business partner that can ensure mission-critical applications are always available. The customers are looking to outsource as much IT infrastructure as possible to take these expenses off the balance sheet and to focus in-house IT talent on corporate priorities.

Best Hosting will create a full-service data communications company offering data center services that will support collocation, dedicated hosting, mission critical business applications administration, and media on demand to enterprise business customers.

B.1.3 Overview of the Market

B.1.3.1 Industry Overview

The Internet has become a global medium that enables millions of people to obtain and share information, communicate, and conduct business electronically. Its phenomenal growth since the early 1990s is driven by a number of factors, including:

- A large and growing installed base of personal computers
- An increase in Web-enabled and instrumented mission-critical applications
- Advances in the performance, speed, and the reduced cost of computers
- Improvements in infrastructure technologies
- Advances in mobile access technologies
- Access commoditization
- Increase user knowledge and trust to conduct business over the Internet

B.1.3.2 Needs of the Market

The enterprise business market needs business partners that will guarantee always-available services. Enterprises need a partner that will enhance their corporate added value through:

- Making sure outsourced IT infrastructure is always working and available
- Implementing new infrastructure and access services that will enhance services they can resell to their customers or make for a better end-customer experience
- Implementing new infrastructure and access services that will make enterprise employees happier
- Offering new services that will lower cost of operations and business

B.1.3.3 Total Market Size

Best Hosting will focus on the enterprise business customer in North America. An enterprise business customer is defined as having more than $1 billion in annual sales, more than 1,000 employees, and offices in the U.S. and Canada. XYZ Company defines this universe to contain one million companies in 2001. This market is expected to grow by *X* percent over the next five years and is reflected in the following tables:

Tables supporting the company's predictions would be inserted here.

B.1.3.4 Addressable Market

Best Hosting's target markets are Toronto, Quebec, Austin, Dallas, Houston, Los Angeles, Phoenix, San Diego, San Francisco, Salt Lake City, and St. Louis. XYZ Company defines this universe to contain 500,000 companies in 2001. This market is expected to grow by *X* percent over the next five years and is reflected in the following tables:

Tables supporting the company's predictions would be inserted here.

This reflects $*xxxx* million.

B.1.3.5 Market Capture Year One

Best Hosting's acquisition strategy means it will have a footprint in the target markets in the first year of service. The core acquisition targets have a total of three million customers and current revenues are forecast at $6 million for the first 12 months of Best Hosting operation.

B.1.4 Corporate Value Proposition

Best Hosting will offer the most up-to-date services and infrastructure in its focus regional markets. It will guarantee 99.9 percent service availability with remote management tools. The call center guarantees call pick up within 30 seconds and follow-up within four hours. Shared hosting setup is guaranteed complete within six hours next business day after contract signing and dedicated within one business day.

B.1.5 Competitive Analysis

The market for providing service is extremely competitive and highly fragmented. Best Hosting expects to compete with the following types of service providers:

- National commercial Internet access providers, like *(names of competitors here)*
- Regional and local ISPs, like *(names of competitors here)*
- Cable operators, like *(names here)*
- National long-distance carriers, like *(names here)*
- Regional Bell operators and CLECs, like *(names here)*
- Enterprises that become service providers
- ISVs and hardware vendors
- Nonprofit and education service providers
- Unknown segments

B.1.6 SWOT Analysis

An individual SWOT analysis should reflect each of the competitor categories listed previously. This is a sample:

B.1.6.1 Regional/Local ISPs

Strengths The majority of this sector is undercapitalized. Best Hosting's capitalization plan ensures it will have capital influx through the first three years of operation. This sector service quality varies widely. Best Hosting will ensure service quality through a unified backbone and operational infrastructure. Services are not uniformly offered in the target markets. Best Hosting will leverage its infrastructure to offer services uniformly throughout its target markets.

Weaknesses Successful regional and local ISPs have close relationships with their customer base and relationship management becomes more complex after acquisition. There are large operational challenges in integrating the disparate operational processes and systems of the acquired companies. There may be a turnover in employees when companies are acquired. Best Hosting is employing various employee retention programs to manage these situations.

Opportunities Best Hosting has the opportunity to build a regional infrastructure that will unify cross-regional companies and offer consistent, high quality services.

Threats Government regulation, unknown competitors, unsuccessful IPO.

B.1.7 Operations Plan

B.1.7.1 Overall Strategy

Best Hosting's strategy is to acquire existing ISPs and to provide Internet access and related services to enterprise business customers located in metropolitan areas in the United States. The target markets in this region are underserved by national online service providers and present a significant initial market entry opportunity. Target markets are Austin, Dallas, Houston, Los Angeles, Phoenix, San Diego, San Francisco, Salt Lake City, and St. Louis. These metropolitan areas provide a large user base with a high percentage of data telecommunications products and services early adopters.

Following the initial round of ISP acquisitions, Best Hosting expects to create additional stockholder value by expanding an internal base of new services and new clients, while continuing to acquire ISPs. The objective is to increase return on assets and economies of scale by increasing subscriber density at each point of presence (POP), meaning a decrease in the cost of network operations, customer support, back office functions, and operational/management overhead. The company intends to meet the service and content requirements of Internet users while benefiting from the economies of scale enjoyed by national ISPs.

Best Hosting will operate on the leading edge of technology trends and evolving industry standards. It will use emerging technology to develop technical expertise and continually create a broad array of new services to meet ongoing demands of subscribers. The company intends to develop network-independent high margin services that will support market expansion beyond what is typically available to regional and local service providers. The services strategy is divided into three broad categories:

- Collocation/dedicated hosting
- Mission-critical business application administration
- Media-on-demand services

B.1.7.2 Acquisition Strategy

The initial round of acquisitions will focus on ISPs that have at least 40 percent of their markets with annual churn lower than 25 percent. The strategy contains the following key elements:

- Acquire a core group of ISPs simultaneously with funds raised through the initial public offering
- Consolidate their operations and network-related services to one base of operations
- Use these acquisitions to deploy a national, broadband access and backbone infrastructure

In conjunction with these elements, Best Hosting plans to develop strategic alliances with ecosystem partners needed to offer the high margin services demanded by the focus customer segments.

(When you're developing your own strategies, you'll want to include as many details as possible.)

B.1.7.3 Services Strategy

Best Hosting will focus on three broad categories of service:

- Collocation/dedicated hosting
- Mission-critical business application administration
- Media-on-demand services

Media-on-demand services Best Hosting will offer customer driven media-on-demand services supported by broadband and application service management technologies. The service-on-demand model will allow customers to actively choose their application and service delivery. Best Hosting infrastructure will include cable modem, DSL, wireless, and Windows Driver Model (WDM) access technologies allowing customers to manage their QoS requirements within a prescribed set of boundaries, meaning customers can decide what service they want and when they want it. Initial services include video-on-demand, video conferencing, and distance learning.

This is where you could insert your service descriptions. For more information on this see Appendix D, "Service Descriptions."

Collocation/dedicated hosting (The example of media-on-demand services is the kind of content that would be used for each category of service.)

Mission-critical business application administration (The example of media-on-demand services is the type of content that would be used for each category of service.)

B.1.7.4 Sales and Marketing Plan

Best Hosting will review the current sales plans of the acquired companies and maintain and leverage as much of the 600 local direct sales resources as possible. These resources will be retrained to sell the new services. The sales force will be enlarged to include indirect channels such as vendors, ISVs, consultants, and retail outlets. These channels will be focused as follows:

This is where you could insert a listing of all the channels and their focus customers.

The company will review the current marketing and marketing communication plans of the acquired companies and leverage these as much as possible. Best Hosting will participate in the following public relations campaigns, events, and activities:

Insert your listing and explanation of the PR activities here.

B.1.7.5 Executive Management

This section includes information about Best Hosting's executive officers.

Name Age Position Compensation

The biographies of the executive officers would be inserted here.

Executive decisions at Best Hosting will be made by committees to include:

- Compensation committee: This committee is responsible for…
- Nominating committee: This committee is responsible for…
- Audit committee: This committee is responsible for…
- Technology committee: This committee does is responsible for…

Board of Directors and Compensation The board of directors includes industry leaders who will aid in promoting business growth. They include:

Name Organization

A list of the members of the board and their compensation would be inserted here.

B.1.7.6 Resourcing Plan

Based on the operational and business plan, Best Hosting will use the following organization and resourcing for start-up and ongoing operations:

You could insert a listing of the company's staffing here.

B.1.8 Financial Plan

Best Hosting has three main elements to its finance plan:

- Initial capitalization by the executive committee
- Financing and partnerships with key ecosystem partners like hardware vendors, application vendors, consulting partners, and so forth.

- IPO planned for *(date)*

Explain each of the elements as fully as possible.

Expected Costs and Expenses Expected costs and expenses fall into the following general categories:

- Transaction expenses associated with ISP acquisitions
- Access
- Costs of revenues
- Operations
- Costs of sales and marketing
- General and administrative
- Amortization
- Depreciation

Each of the elements should be explained as fully as possible.

Expected Revenues and Profits Revenues are expected to fluctuate depending on a variety of factors, including capital costs incurred with the introduction of new products and services. Best Hosting plans to minimize these capital costs through the vendor financing and partnering programs described previously. Factors affecting revenues include:

- Pricing and services mix
- Subscriber churn
- Competitor reaction to services
- Market demand for services
- Acquisition costs
- (Performance of general telecommunications services

Each item should be explained as fully as possible. You can also include the pricing information here. For more information on that, see Appendix E, "Pricing."

Financial Projections (You can include the information in your financial projections here [see Appendix F, "Sample Cash Flow"]).

APPENDIX C

Sample Service Level Agreement

SLAs are contracts between the service provider and service purchaser that detail the levels of service the purchaser can expect and remedies to be provided if service levels are not met. Because SLAs are contracts, they should be reviewed by attorneys representing both sides before being offered and signed. The SLA in this example should *not* be used without review by an attorney and no warranties are expressed or implied. This is only a sample.

C.1 Service Level Agreement

During the Term, subject to the terms of the Agreement, compliance by Customer with its obligations under the Agreement, and the dependencies listed in Table C-1, (Company) will meet the following Service Levels and will provide the following credits when it fails to meet those Service Levels:

Table C-1 Summary of service levels.

Service	SLA	Metric	Standard	(Service Name)*	Business Critical*
Applications Management	Application Availability	Application Uptime	99%	99.7%	99.99%
	Issue Response Time	Level 1 Response	30 min/30 min	20 min/20 min	10 min/10 min
		Level 2 Response	2 hrs/2 hrs	90 min/90 min	1 hour/1 hour
		Level 3 Response	4 hrs/Next Business Day	4 hrs/Next Business Day	4 hrs/Next Business Day

Table C-1 Summary of service levels. (*continued*)

Service	SLA	Metric	Standard	(Service Name)*	Business Critical*
	Escalation Help Desk	Level 1 Escalation	2 hrs/4 hrs	2 hrs/4 hrs	2 hrs/4 hrs
		Level 2 Escalation	4 hrs/ 8 hrs	4 hrs/8 hrs	4 hrs/8 hrs
		Level 3 Escalation	1 bs day/ 2 bs days	1 bs day/ 2 bs days	1 bs day/ 2 bs days
	Customer Satisfaction	Quarterly Survey	Satisfied	Satisfied	Satisfied
Application Hosting					
Performance Mgmt.	Network Availability Overseas	Packet Loss Latency	<1% <75 msec 250 ms	<1% <75 msec 250 ms	<1% <75 msec 250 ms
	Server Availability	CPU Utilization	<70%	<70%	<70%
	Storage Availability	Storage Utilization	<90%	<90%	<90%
	Disaster Recovery	RTO	QuickShip 168 hours	72 hours Tape	<4 hours
		Recovery Point	Last available data	Last available data Cold Server	<4 hours 2 min – 4 hours ~500 miles Sterling, VA production
Security Mgmt.	Breach isolation	Time to Isolate	<30 mins.	<30 mins.	<30 mins.

* Requires the implementation and maintenance of the system according to the (COMPANY) SLA Architecture Standards.

C.1.1 Application Availability

Service Level—(COMPANY)'s goal is that the Managed Software will be available for the percentage of scheduled uptime for the level of service purchased by Customer. (See Table C-2 for more details.)

Standard	(Enhanced)	Business Critical
99%	99.7%	99.99%

Measurement—the application uptime for the period plus *excusable application downtime* for the period divided by the scheduled application uptime for the period.

Measurement Period—Monthly

Performance Credit—The performance credit for this Service Level metric, when it is in violation, will be calculated as follows: Service Level goal minus actual Service Level for the period multiplied by the Base Fees for the month.

C.1.2 Issue Response Time

Service Level—(COMPANY)'s goal is that initial responses to Severity 1, 2, and 3 issues properly submitted to the (COMPANY) Help desk regarding covered problems with the Managed Software will occur within the following times applicable to the Service Level purchased by Customer:

Table C-2 Service level for managed software.

		Initial Response Time	
Severity	**Purchased Service Level**	**(COMPANY) Business Hours**	**Off-Hours**
Level 1	(COMPANY) Standard	30 min	30 min
	(COMPANY) (Enhanced)	20 min	20 min
	(COMPANY) Business Critical	10 min	10 min
Level 2	(COMPANY) Standard	2 hrs	120 min
	(COMPANY) (Enhanced)	90 min	90 min
	(COMPANY) Business Critical	1 hr	60 min
Level 3	(COMPANY) Standard	6 hrs	Next Business Day
	(COMPANY) (Enhanced)	4 hrs	Next Business Day
	(COMPANY) Business Critical	4 hrs	Next Business Day

Measurement—The sum of each case multiplied by the allowed response time for the case divided by the sum of each case multiplied by the actual response time for the case.

Measurement Period—Monthly.

Performance Credit Calculation—The performance credit for this Service Level metric, when it is in violation, will be 2.5 percent of the applicable month's Base Fees.

C.2 Definitions

Severity Level 1—Production system is completely unavailable or is inoperable, or is affected such that critical business processes are completely unavailable or inoperable.

Severity Level 2—Production system is available, but critical business processes and multiple users are substantially adversely impacted, or the test or development system is completely unavailable or inoperable, or is affected such that critical business processes are completely unavailable or inoperable.

Severity Level 3—Production system is available, but a single user or non-critical business processes are substantially adversely impacted, or the test or development system functions, but multiple users are substantially impacted.

C.2.1 Escalation for all Service Level Options

Service Level—(COMPANY)'s goal is that unresolved Severity 1, 2, and 3 issues properly submitted to the (COMPANY) Help desk regarding covered problems with the Managed Software, will be escalated by (COMPANY) by email to the following contacts within the times shown in Table C-3:

Table C-3 Email response times.

Severity	Notification Within	Customer Notification	(COMPANY) Notification
Level 1	2 hours	Project Manager	Customer Relationship Manager
	4 hours	VP CIO	(COMPANY) Executive
Level 2	4 (COMPANY) business hours	Project Manager	Customer Relationship Manager
	8 (COMPANY) business hours	VP CIO	(COMPANY) Executive
Level 3	1 (COMPANY) Business Day	Project Manager	Customer Relationship Manager
	2 (COMPANY) Business Days	VP CIO	(COMPANY) Executive

Measurement—Sum of each case multiplied by the allowed response time for the case divided by the sum of each case multiplied by the actual response time for the case.

Measurement Period—Monthly.

Performance Credit Calculation—The performance credit for this Service Level metric, when it is in violation, will be 2.5 percent of the applicable month's Base Fees.

C.2.2 Performance Management

Performance management can be measured in terms of packet loss, latency, server CPU utilization, storage availability, disaster recovery, recovery time objectives, recovery point, security management, and customer satisfaction.

Packet Loss

Service Level—COMPANY's goal is that there will be less than one percent packet loss for data transmitted over communications systems provided by (COMPANY).

Measurement—Actual Packets sent minus Actual Packets received divided by Actual Packets sent.

Measurement Period—Monthly.

Performance Credit—The performance credit for this Service Level metric, when it is in violation, will be 2.5 percent of the applicable month's Base Fees.

Latency

Service Level—(COMPANY)'s goal is that the elapsed time for a packet sent from a (COMPANY) router to a router at Customer's location, within the United States on communications systems provided by (COMPANY), will be less than 70 msecs.

Measurement—Average of sampling during the month according to (COMPANY) procedures.

Measurement Period—Monthly.

Performance Credit—The performance credit for this Service Level metric, when it is in violation, will be 2.5 percent of the applicable month's Base Fees.

Server CPU Utilization

Service Level—(COMPANY)'s goal is that CPU utilization will typically run below 70 percent capacity.

Measurement—Average of sampling of 5-minute snapshots of all running processes during the month according to (COMPANY) procedures.

Measurement Period—Monthly.

Performance Credit—The performance credit for this Service Level metric, when it is in violation, will be 2.5 percent of the applicable month's Base Fees.

Storage Availability

Service Level—(COMPANY)'s goal is that available storage allocated to Customer will be more than 90 percent full.

Measurement—Average of sampling during the month according to (COMPANY) procedures to measure actual disk storage filled divided by actual disk storage allocated to Customer.

Measurement Period—Monthly.

Performance Credit—The performance credit for this Service Level metric, when it is in violation, will be 2.5 percent of the applicable month's Base Fees.

Disaster Recovery

Definition—Disaster means a Force Majeure Event as defined in the Agreement or any other occurrence that results in the destruction or damage of the Server(s) upon which the Managed Software is installed such that the Managed Software is not available to Customer.

Destruction or Damage—If such destruction or damage is not due to the negligence or misconduct of (COMPANY) or its subcontractors, Customer will be charged for replacement Server(s).

Recovery Time Objective (RTO)

Service Level—COMPANY)'s goal is that the time elapsed between the time a Disaster causes the Managed Software to be unavailable and the time the Managed Software is available following the Disaster will not exceed the following time period applicable to the Service Level purchased by Customer (see Table C-4):

Table C-4 Managed software availability after a disaster.

Service Level	RTO
Standard	168 hours
(Enhanced)	72 hours
Business Critical	24 hours

Measurement—The actual time elapsed between the unavailability of the Managed Software due to a Disaster and the availability of the Managed Software following the Disaster.

Measurement Period—Monthly.

Performance Credit—The performance credit for this Service Level metric, for any month in which (COMPANY) is in violation, will be 2.5 percent of the applicable month's Base Fees.

Exclusion–Any failure to meet the RTO Service Level following a Disaster because the telecommunications, third-party services, or any equipment at Customer's site are damaged or impacted and that damage or impact causes the unavailability of the Managed Software.

Recovery Point

Service Level—(COMPANY)'s goal is that the data recovered in the event of a Disaster will include the data in the Managed Software at least as recent as the following time period prior to the Disaster applicable to the Service Level purchased by Customer (see Table C-5):

Table C-5 Recovery point.

Service Level	Recovery Point
Standard	The last available data
(Enhanced)	The last available data
Business Critical	24 hours

Measurement—The actual recovery point for data in the Managed Software in any Disaster.

Measurement Period—Monthly.

Performance Credit—The performance credit for this Service Level metric, for any month in which (COMPANY) is in violation, will be 2.5 percent of the applicable month's Base Fees.

Exclusion—Any failure to meet the Recovery Point Service Level following a Disaster because telecommunications, third-party services, or any equipment at Customer's site are damaged or impacted and that damage or impact causes the unavailability of the Managed Software.

Security Management

Service Level—(COMPANY)'s goal is that it will determine the point of breach within 30 minutes of detecting the breach.

Measurement—The sum of the time each case took from breach detection to breach determination divided by the total number of cases multiplied by 30 minutes should equal one or less.

Measurement Period—Monthly.

Performance Credit—The performance credit for this Service Level metric, when it is in violation, will be 2.5 percent of the applicable month's Base Fees.

Customer Satisfaction

Measurement—Completion by Customer's users of the quarterly satisfaction survey that will be provided by (COMPANY).

Measurement Period—Quarterly.

Service Level—The average of all responses will rate Customer as at least satisfied with (COMPANY) Services for each quarterly satisfaction survey. This Service Level metric will not be measured in any quarter where less than 60 percent of Customer users surveyed provide adequate responses to (COMPANY) within two weeks of delivery of the survey by (COMPANY).

Service Level Grace Range—The actual customer satisfaction ratio may, in any one period but not for two consecutive periods, drop to dissatisfied without (COMPANY) incurring a performance credit for the period.

Performance Credit Calculation—The performance credit for this Service Level metric, when it is in violation, will be calculated as 2.5 percent of the Base Fees for the month in which the survey is delivered.

C.3 General Terms

Initial response will be a phone call or pager response placed to the number provided by Customer if Customer telephoned (COMPANY), or if Customer contacted (COMPANY) by email or fax, initial response will be either a phone call or an email response. Escalation will be by email. Customer is responsible for providing current contact information to the (COMPANY) Help desk including email, phone and fax numbers for all contacts and escalation points.

(COMPANY) (Service Name) and Business Critical Service Levels require the implementation and maintenance of the system according to the current (COMPANY) SLA Architecture Standards.

Achievement of the Application Availability Service Level is dependent upon proper configuration of Customer's system, compliance by Customer with its obligations under Schedule *X*, and the availability of the underlying relevant application and infrastructure components receiving or delivering information to and from the Managed Software at levels equal to or greater than the Application Availability Service Level.

Service Levels only apply to Customer's "production" environment—the system it uses to manage its actual business processes, as compared to test, development, training, backup, and similar environments. Service Levels apply beginning with the second full calendar month after Base Services begin. Except as agreed to by the parties, Service Levels do not apply for the month during which any update, upgrade, revision, patch listed in Schedule B as "optional," or any enhancement, is introduced to Customer's production environment, and the month following such introduction, except for the following: Application Patches and Legal Changes described in Schedule B as being provided by (COMPANY). If Customer insists upon an update, upgrade, revision, patch or enhancement that (COMPANY) advises against in writing, problems arising from such action will be excluded from Service Level compliance.

Issues that are the result of, or solutions which are dependent upon, available uninstalled application patches that have not been installed by the choice of Customer, or third-party products and interfaces not part of the Managed Software, will not count in the overall calculation of the applicable Service Level performance.

Customer will maintain appropriate maintenance agreements with, and will provide all assistance requested by (COMPANY) to obtain timely services from, Customer's third-party service providers providing support of Customer's relevant applications and infrastructure components. (COMPANY) will maintain appropriate maintenance agreements with third-party service providers providing support of (COMPANY) applications and infrastructure components necessary for provision by (COMPANY) of the Base Services. For purposes of all time calculations, downtime due to Disasters, defects in third-party software, hardware or systems, or downtime based on waiting for issue resolution by all outside third-party providers, will be excused downtime.

Customer Managed Software users, IT personnel and other technical or management personnel and the connectivity requested by (COMPANY) will be available as required by (COMPANY) to assist (COMPANY) in addressing issues hereunder.

The Customer Project Executive will perform his/her responsibilities in a timely manner, such as coordinating Customer resources, prioritizing work and providing information and assistance required by (COMPANY), and ensuring that Customer commits full-time resources to assist in resolution of Severity 1, 2, and 3 issues.

The total credits provided by (COMPANY) in any month will not exceed 20 percent of the Base Fees.

Credits will be offset against Base Fees for the following month and noted in the invoice for that month.

APPENDIX D

Service Descriptions

Service descriptions should be more than just one liners. They should include substantive descriptions showing what is offered, service levels, and the service provider's added value. They should be included in the business plan, as well as used in customer collateral. Service descriptions should also be reviewed by attorneys before being sent to the market because they become part of the SLA and the wording must be exact. This appendix is an example of a service description used in a business plan. It is for informational purposes only and should not be used without review by an attorney.

D.1 Collocation Services

D.1.1 Overview

(COMPANY) collocation services provide business customers with Internet-based computer-hosting services. These services are offered within a (COMPANY) managed data center infrastructure without the capital or uncontrolled operational expense of having to invest in, build, and operate their own IDC facilities or source expensive, high-capacity telecommunications equipment.

Customers lease secure space for their servers and other equipment in (COMPANY)'s IDC facilities allowing them to take advantage of the millions of dollars that (COMPANY) has invested in a state-of-the-art IDC. (COMPANY) collocation facilities and network/environmental support also allow customers to take advantage of (COMPANY)'s physical facilities, infrastructure, and staff, further enabling (COMPANY) customers to keep their servers and other equipment functioning around-the-clock.

(COMPANY)'s high-speed, reliable, bandwidth-rich network eliminates the need for customers to establish and maintain their own leased-line connections to local service providers or POPs that can result in significant cost savings.

Experienced (COMPANY) staff provide 24/7 monitoring and support and customers can have full access to their equipment 24/7. (COMPANY) can add bandwidth, rack space, and server capacity to meet the needs of growing customers. The customer has complete control of the server's technical environment. All server administration is performed by the customer through remote administrator privileges.

D.1.2 Services Offered

Overall functionality (see Figure D-1) depends on the collocation service chosen. (COMPANY) offers three levels of service: Bronze (see Figure D-2), Silver (see Figure D-3), and Gold (see Figure D-4). Each tier offers increasing levels of service, from the standard Bronze to the highest Gold.

D.1.2.1 Bronze

Bronze service gives customers the basics needed for collocation in the areas of cabinets, security, power, network, content, and availability.

Secured cabinet option: Customers place their equipment in shared, locking cabinets with nine high-strength aluminium shelves.

Secure remote application administration: The ability to manage the addition, modification, and deletion of OS resources and administer applications through secure remote access administration facilities.

Uninterrupted power supply: Power supply to customer equipment is guaranteed through UPS facilities. This guarantee ensures that, should power go off for more than one minute, backup power will be available for the next three hours for all customers in the (COMPANY) data center.

Network connectivity: Reliable, (as defined by the [COMPANY] service level for the service class), high-quality connections through leased line from 64K up to 128K, 256K, 512K, dedicated T1 or dedicated T3, or dial-up connections. The service includes redundant circuits and backup lines to keep the customer's applications running in the event of a circuit outage. 64k bandwidth guarantee is included in the basic price. Average monthly usage above 64k will be billed at tiered rates (see pricing) if customer selects a higher bandwidth.

Server purchase option: In the event that customers need higher ongoing capacity than is currently available in their configuration, (COMPANY) offers servers for purchase. (See pricing for details.)

Content switching service: (COMPANY) offers collocation service customers with the performance enhancement option of content switching for either local or global servers. These content switches offer load balancing across sites and hot content replication in real time to dynamically scale the Web performance.

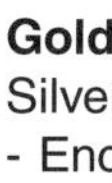

Gold:
Silver plus Bronze and:
- Enclosed cage facility option
- Guaranteed infrastructure availability: 99.99 percent
- Problem Resolution: dedicated call center resources, fastest problem resolution, free hotline support

Silver:
Bronze plus
- Dedicated secure cabinet
- Guaranteed infrastructure availability: 99.9 percent
- Faster problem resolution

Bronze:
- Shared secure cabinet
- Secure remote app administration
- UPS
- Internet access
    - Customer to IDC = (Dial-up)
    - IDC to Customer = 64K
- Server purchase option
- Content switching service
- Guaranteed infrastructure availability: 99.5 percent
- Shared call center resources—Standard "guaranteed response times" by severity level
- Network performance: <1% packet loss, <75 msecs
- "Guaranteed" physical security
- Reporting/Billing: monthly availability, network usage, security infringements, Help desk statistics

Figure D-1 Functionality available with the three levels of service.
Published courtesy of Hewlett-Packard Company.

Guaranteed Infrastructure Availability

(COMPANY)'s Bronze level collocation service is guaranteed to deliver at least 99.5 percent availability at the IDC infrastructure level, which includes all networks and hardware configurations inside the (COMPANY) IDC. It also includes the IDC environmental support services. It does not include any system management.

Measurement: Availability is measured by taking the actual service uptime for the month plus any agreed scheduled server downtime and time for troubleshooting and recovery divided by the scheduled service uptime for the month.

Bronze:
- Shared secure cabinet
- Secure remote app administration
- UPS
- Internet access
    - Customer to IDC = (Dial-up)
    - IDC to Customer = 64K
- Server purchase option
- Content switching
- Guaranteed infrastructure availability: 99.5 percent
- Shared call center resources—Standard "guaranteed response times" by severity level
- Network performance: <1% packet loss, <75 msecs
- "Guaranteed" physical security
- Reporting/Billing: monthly availability, network usage, security infringements, Help desk statistics

Figure D-2 The Bronze Service Functionality.
Published courtesy of Hewlett-Packard Company.

Credit calculation: If availability targets are not achieved as measured over an entire month, the customer receives a credit sum on the next monthly bill equivalent to the total loss of service for the period (number plus duration of outages). For example, the service is down three times during the month, once for 5 minutes, once for 10 minutes, once for 15 minutes. The customer receives a credit for a total of 30 minutes of free service.

Problem Resolution

(COMPANY) will provide a shared call center resource for reporting problems with (COMPANY) service.

Measurement: The Help desk will respond to customer issues based on a problem severity classification system. Three severity levels are:

- Severity Level 1—Production system is completely unavailable, inoperable, or is affected such that critical business processes are unavailable or inoperable.
- Severity Level 2—Production system is available, but critical business processes and multiple users are substantially impacted, the test and development system is unavailable or inoperable, or the system is affected such that critical business processes are completely unavailable or inoperable.
- Severity Level 3—Production system is available, but single user or noncritical business processes are substantially impacted, or the test and development system functions, but multiple users are substantially impacted.

Table D-1 shows the Help desk's response times for Bronze service level issues.

Table D-1 Bronze service level response times.

	Initial Response Time	
Severity	**(COMPANY) business Hours**	**Off-Hours**
Level 1	30 mins	1 hour
Level 2	2 hours	200 mins
Level 3	6 hours	next business day

Escalation Procedures

(COMPANY)'s goal at the Bronze service level is that unresolved Severity 1, 2, and 3 infrastructure issues properly submitted to the (COMPANY) Help desk, will be escalated by (COMPANY) to the contacts in Table D-2 by email:

Table D-2 Bronze escalation procedures.

Severity	Notification Within	Customer Notification	(COMPANY) Notification
Level 1	2 hours	Project Manager	Customer Relationship Manager
	4 hours	VP CIO	(COMPANY) Executive
Level 2	4 (COMPANY) business hours	Project Manager	Customer Relationship Manager
	8 (COMPANY) business hours	VP CIO	(COMPANY) Executive
Level 3	1 (COMPANY) business day	Project Manager	Customer Relationship Manager
	2 (COMPANY) business days	VP CIO	(COMPANY) Executive

Credit calculation: Problems not responded to within these periods will be subject to a 2.5 percent credit of the monthly base fees posted to the next customer statement.

Network Performance

(COMPANY) manages network performance against two metrics: network packet loss and network latency.

Packet loss measurement: (COMPANY) will monitor the network such that it guarantees there will be less than one percent packet loss for at least 97 percent of the time in a month for data transmitted over communications systems provided by (COMPANY) inside its IDC. Packet loss will be monitored monthly and measured by averaging hourly packet loss percentage measurement from (COMPANY) designated network management platform for each month. (COMPANY) will send the customer a monthly statistics report detailing the results.

Latency measurement: (COMPANY) will monitor the elapsed time for one trip network delay measured every hour with minimum packet payload between the (COMPANY) designated management station and the (COMPANY) Internet router within the same data center under normal situations. The network delay will be less than 75 ms for at least 97 percent of the time in a month. (COMPANY) will send customer a monthly statistics report detailing the results.

Security

(COMPANY) will provide secure facilities and will guarantee physical infrastructure security for all its collocation services

Security measurement: (COMPANY) is only responsible for monitoring security of its own infrastructure. Should a security breach occur and be reported by the customer to (COMPANY), (COMPANY) will make every effort to determine the point of breach within 60 minutes. The target of security measurement is measured by taking the sum of time each case takes from breach determined (i.e., the time when a security breach was known to occur by [COMPANY]), and the time such a breach is reported to the customer, excluding the time of subsequent investigation and rectification divided by the total number of cases and further divided by 60 minutes on a monthly basis. Should this calculation be greater than one, then a service credit will apply. (COMPANY) will not be liable or responsible for any security problems as a result of OS or application loopholes because of customer-supplied software. (COMPANY) will send customers a monthly statistics report detailing the results.

Reporting and Billing

A monthly bill will be provided with a full services breakdown, if required. In addition reports can be provided with the following information:

- Monthly availability
- Network usage statistics
- Security infringements
- Help desk statistics

D.1.2.2 Silver

Services in (COMPANY)'s Silver category include all of those offered in Bronze, plus:

- Dedicated secure cabinet Customers place their equipment in dedicated, locking cabinets with nine high-strength aluminium shelves.
- Guaranteed infrastructure availability (COMPANY)'s Silver level collocation service is guaranteed to deliver at least 99.9 percent availability at the IDC Infrastructure level.

The credit calculation remains the same as Bronze level.

Problem Resolution: (COMPANY) will provide a shared call center resource to answer any reported problems with (COMPANY) service.

Silver:
Bronze plus
- Dedicated secure cabinet
- Guaranteed infrastructure availability: 99.9 percent
- Faster problem resolution

Figure D-3 Functionality available under the Silver option.
Published courtesy of Hewlett-Packard Company.

Measurement: Issues at the Silver service level will be responded to in the manner shown in Table D-3.

Table D-3 Silver service level response time.

	Initial Response Time	
Severity	**(COMPANY) business Hours**	**Off-Hours**
Level 1	20 mins	40 mins
Level 2	90 mins	2 hours
Level 3	4 hours	next business day

Escalation Procedures

(COMPANY)'s goal at the Silver collocation service level is that unresolved Severity 1, 2, and 3 infrastructure issues properly submitted to the (COMPANY) Help desk, will be escalated by (COMPANY) to the contacts by email shown in Table D-4.

Table D-4 Silver service level email response times.

Severity	Notification Within	Customer Notification	(COMPANY) Notification
Level 1	2 hours	Project Manager	Customer Relationship Manager
	4 hours	VP CIO	(COMPANY) Executive
Level 2	4 (COMPANY) business hours	Project Manager	Customer Relationship Manager
	8 (COMPANY) business hours	VP CIO	(COMPANY) Executive
Level 3	1 (COMPANY) business day	Project Manager	Customer Relationship Manager
	2 (COMPANY) business days	VP CIO	(COMPANY) Executive

Credit calculation: Problems not responded to within these periods will be subject to a 2.5 percent credit of the monthly base fees shown as a credit on the next monthly statement.

Security

(COMPANY) will provide secure facilities and will guarantee physical infrastructure security for all its collocation services.

Security measurement: (COMPANY) is only responsible for monitoring security of its owned infrastructure. Should a security breach occur and be reported by the customer to (COMPANY), (COMPANY) will make every effort to determine the point of breach within 45 minutes. The target of security measurement is measured by taking the sum of time each case takes from breach determined, i.e., the time when a security breach was known to occur by (COMPANY), and the time such a breach is reported to the customer, excluding the time of subsequent investigation and rectification divided by the total number of cases and further divided by 45 minutes on a monthly basis. Should this calculation be greater than one, then a service credit will apply. (COMPANY) will not be liable or responsible for any security problems as a result of OS or application loopholes because of customer supplied software. (COMPANY) will send customers a monthly statistics report detailing monthly results.

D.1.2.3 Gold

Services in (COMPANY)'s Gold category include all of those offered in Bronze and Silver, plus:

- Enclosed cage facility option
    - Customers position their equipment in dedicated, locking cages with steel mesh walls and high-strength aluminium racks.
- Guaranteed infrastructure availability to 99.9 percent

The credit calculation remains the same as Bronze level service.

Problem Resolution: (COMPANY) will provide a premium problem resolution service with dedicated call center resources and free hotline support to answer any reported problems.

Gold:
Silver plus Bronze and:
- Enclosed cage facility option
- Guaranteed infrastructure availability to 99.99 percent
- Problem resolution: Dedicated call center resources, fastest problem resolution, free hotline support

Figure D-4 Functionality available with the Gold service option.
Published courtesy of Hewlett-Packard Company.

Measurement: Table D-5 illustrates the response level for Gold customers.

Table D-5 Gold service level measurement.

	Initial Response Time	
Severity	**(COMPANY) business Hours**	**Off-Hours**
Level 1	10 mins	20 mins
Level 2	1 hour	90 mins
Level 3	4 hours	next business day

Escalation Procedures

(COMPANY)'s goal at the Gold collocation service level is that unresolved Severity 1, 2, and 3 infrastructure issues properly submitted to the (COMPANY) Help desk will be escalated by (COMPANY) to the contacts in Table D-6 by email:

Table D-6 Gold service level unresolved severity issue resolution.

Severity	Notification Within	Customer Notification	(COMPANY) Notification
Level 1	2 hours	Project Manager	Customer Relationship Manager
	4 hours	VP CIO	(COMPANY) Executive
Level 2	4 (COMPANY) business hours	Project Manager	Customer Relationship Manager
	8 (COMPANY) business hours	VP CIO	(COMPANY) Executive
Level 3	1 (COMPANY) business day	Project Manager	Customer Relationship Manager
	2 (COMPANY) business days	VP CIO	(COMPANY) Executive

Credit calculation: Problems not responded to within these periods will be subject to a 2.5 percent credit of the monthly base fees posted as a credit on the next monthly statement.

Security

(COMPANY) will provide secure facilities and will guarantee physical infrastructure security for all its collocation services.

Security measurement: (COMPANY) is only responsible for monitoring security of its owned infrastructure. Should a security breach occur and be reported by the customer to (COMPANY), (COMPANY) will make every effort to determine the point of breach within 45 minutes. The target of security measurement is measured by taking the sum of time each case takes from breach determined, i.e., the time when a security breach was known to occur by (COM-

PANY), and the time such a breach is reported to the customer, excluding the time of subsequent investigation and rectification divided by the total number of cases and further divided by 45 minutes on a monthly basis. Should this calculation be greater than one, a service credit will apply. (COMPANY) will not be liable or responsible for any security problems as a result of OS or application loopholes because of customer supplied software. (COMPANY) will send customers a monthly statistics report detailing monthly results.

D.2 Limitations

None other than those cited previously.

D.3 Service Level Agreements

Table D-7 is a service level summary for the three collocation services on offer by (COMPANY).

Table D-7 Service level summary for the three collocation services on offer.

Service	SLA	Metric	Bronze	Silver	Gold
					Dedicated hot line number
Collocation	Infrastructure Availability	Infrastructure Availability	99.5%	99.9%	99.99%
	Issue Response Time	Level 1 Response	30 mins/60 mins	20 mins/ 40 mins	10 mins/20 mins
		Level 2 Response	2 hrs/200 mins	90 mins/ 120 mins	1 hour/90 mins
		Level 3 Response	6 hrs/next business day	4 hrs/next business day	4 hrs/next business day
	Escalation Help Desk	Level 1 Escalation	2 hrs/4 hrs	2 hrs/4 hrs	2 hrs/4 hrs
		Level 2 Escalation	4 hrs/ 8 hrs	4 hrs/8 hrs	4 hrs/8 hrs
		Level 3 Escalation	1 bus day/ 2 bus days	1 bus day/ 2 bus days	1 bus day/ 2 bus days
Network Mgmt.	Network Performance	Packet Loss Latency	<1% <75 msec	<1% <75 msec	<1% <75 msec
Security Mgmt.	Breach isolation	Time to Isolate	<60 mins	<45 mins	<30 mins

APPENDIX E

Pricing

The pricing model contained in this appendix takes into account several levels of detail. At its most detailed, it takes into account costs for all elements that make up the service to be offered on a cost-plus basis (uplifts for general and administrative (G&A) expenses and a margin). The highest-level view is suitable for customer collateral. This pricing is based on the service description from Appendix D.

E.1 Pricing Level 1: Most Detailed

Spreadsheet E-1 is the most detailed view of bottom-up pricing. It indicates the cost associated with each functionality offered in the service bundles plus an uplift, illustrating how the service provider determines its bottom up pricing.

E.2 Pricing Level 2: Intermediate Level

Level 2 pricing is an intermediate step between base pricing (Level 1) and the pricing used in a customer brochure (Level 3). Pricing Level 2 takes Pricing Level 1 individual functionality prices and groups them in the different bundles that are offered to customers.

E.3 Pricing Level 3: Suitable for Customer Collateral

Pricing Level 3 further streamlines the pricing information into a format that is suitable for customer brochures.

Cage Facilities		Price/rack	Customers/Rack	G&A Overhead	Margin	Price/Customer
	Shared	$91.17	2	$5.47	1.1	$56.16
	Dedicated	$227.93	1	$27.35	1.1	$280.81
	Enclosed Cage	$1,641.00	1	$196.92	1.1	$2,021.71

Content Switching Service	Device Costs	Floor Space	No. of Customers	G&A Overhead	Margin	Price
	28.823	$0.10	200	$17.31	1.1	$177.67

Hardware Leasing	Service level	Hardware Costs/Month	Sys Admin/Month	G&A Overhead	Margin	Price
	Bronze	$1,322.43	$2,666.67	$158.69	1.1	$4,562.57
	Silver	$2,102.67	$8,000.00	$252.32	1.1	$11,390.49
	Gold	$45,559.27	$8,000.00	$5,467.11	1.1	$64,929.02

IDC Floor Space			G&A Overhead	Margin	Total
	ft2	$6,666.67	$7,466.67	1.1	$8,213.33

Customer Care		Personnel Costs	No. of Customers/ Six Person Team	Infra Costs	G&A Overhead	Margin	Price
	Dedicated	$32,500.00	1	$3,333.33	$4,300.00	1.1	$39,416.67
	Shared	$1,625.00	20	$166.67	$215.00	1.1	$335.04

Backup/Restore Services	Service level	Personnel	No. of Minutes	Device Costs/ Month	Floor Space/ No. of Customers	No. of Customers/ Device	G&A Overhead	Margin	Price
	Bronze	$0.69	3	$11,850.50	$0.004	160	$9.14	1.1	$93.82
	Silver	$0.69	6	$11,850.50	$0.004	160	$9.39	1.1	$96.39
	Gold	$0.69	15	$11,850.50	$0.004	160	$10.14	1.1	$104.09

Storage	Service level	Price/Device/Month/MB	No. of MB	G&A Overhead	Margin	Total
	Bronze	0.056666667	100		1.1	0
	Silver	0.056666667	200		1.1	0
	Gold	0.056666667	300	2.04	1.1	020.944

Access		Price	G&A Overhead	Margin	Total
	64	$228.67	$27.44	1.1	$281.71
	128	$513.33	$61.60	1.1	$632.43
	256	$1,026.67	$123.30	1.1	$1,264.85
	512	$2,053.33	$246.40	1.1	$2,529.71
	Dedicated T1	$7,066.67	$848.00	1.1	$8,706.13
	Dedicated T3	$9,466.67	$1,136.00	1.1	$11,662.93

Set-up Fees		Personnel Costs/ 5 Day Week	No. of Weeks	Price in NT$	G&A Overhead	Margin	Price
	Inventory/Infrastructure Availability/Allocation, Staging/Network Readiness/Testing/ Deployment/Provisioning/ Activation	$1,666.67	2.00	$3,333.33	$400.00	$1.10	$4,106.67

Spreadsheet E-1

Collocation		Includes:	
Set-Up Fees:	1-Time Fee		**1-Time Set-Up Fees**
		Inventory/Infrastructure Availability/Allocation, Staging/Network Readiness/Testing/Deployment/ Provisioning/Activation	$4,106.67
			Price/$/Month
Bronze			
	Access	64	$281.72
	Rack	Shared Secured Cabinet	$56.16
	Content Switching Services		$177.67
	Hotline Support	Shared	$335.04
Total Bronze			$850.59
Silver			
	Access	64	$281.72
	Rack	Dedicated Secured Cabinet	$280.81
	Content Switching Services	Per Customer	$177.67
	Hotline Support	Shared	$335.04
Total Silver			$1,075.24
Gold			
	Access	64	$281.72
	Content Switching Services		$177.67
	Rack	Enclosed Cage Facilities	$2,021.71
	Hotline Support	Dedicated	$39,416.67
Total Gold			$41,897.77
Incremental			
	Access	64	$281.72
		128	$632.43
		256	$1,264.85
		512	$2,529.71
		Dedicated T1	$8,706.13
		Dedicated T3	$11,662.93
	Storage	Per 100 MB	$0.00
	Cage Facilities	Shared Secured Cabinet	$56.16
		Dedicated Secured Cabinet	$280.81
		Enclosed Cage	$2,021.71
	Content Switching Services		$177.67
	Hardware Leasing	Bronze	$4,562.57
		Silver	$11,390.49
		Gold	$64,929.02
	Space/Square Foot	ft2	$8,213.33
	Customer Care	Dedicated	$39,416.67
		Shared	$335.04
	Backup/Restore Services	Weekly	$93.82
		Twice a Week	$96.39
		Daily	$104.09

Spreadsheet E-2

Collocation		Includes:	Price/$/Month
Set-Up Fees:	1-Time Fee	Inventory/Infrastructure Availability/Allocation, Staging/Network Readiness/Testing/Deployment/ Provisioning/Activation	**1-Time Set-Up Fees** $4,106.67
			Monthly Charges
Bronze	Access	64	
	Rack	Shared Secured Cabinet	
	Content Switching Services		
	Hotline Support	Shared	
Total Bronze			$850.59
Silver	Access	64	
	Rack	Dedicated Secured Cabinet	
	Content Switching Services	Per Customer	
	Hotline Support	Shared	
Total Silver			$1,075.24
Gold	Access	64	
	Content Switching Services		
	Rack	Enclosed Cage Facilities	
	Hotline Support	Dedicated	
Total Gold			$41,897.77
Incremental	**Access**	64 128 256 512 Dedicated T1 Dedicated T3	Upon Request
	Storage	Per 100 MB	
	Cage Facilities	Shared Secured Cabinet Dedicated Secured Cabinet Enclosed Cage	
	Content Switching Services		
	Hardware Leasing	Bronze Silver Gold	
	Space/Square Foot	ft2	
	Customer Care	Dedicated Shared	
	Backup/Restore Services	Weekly Twice a Week Daily	
Discounts	**Dedicated Hosting**		
	3 Year Contract	15%	
	2 Year Contract	10%	
	1 Year Contract	5%	

Spreadsheet E-3

Sample Cash Flow

This Appendix includes a sample cash flow model that a service provider can use for business and services planning. The service provider should do cash flow modeling to understand if the revenue from the service supports the proposed business. This particular model measures net present value, but companies might be interested in measuring financial success differently. There are many other options like Economic Value Added (EVA), ROA, ROI, and so forth. Also included is a sample list of assumptions. Each cash flow will have assumptions due to modeling projections.

F.1 Examples of Assumptions

1. Assuming revenues of service type-collocation, Web hosting, and so on and when they start during the year
2. Assuming how many customers are in which services. For example, 100 customers year one, 50 percent collocation/50 percent dedicated hosting; assuming three-fifths bronze, one-fifth silver, and one-fifth gold
3. Hurdle rate
4. Tax rate
5. Depreciation over three years for hardware equipment and software
6. Revenue/expense ratio assumptions
7. Assumptions for implementation hires
8. Base revenue growth/year
9. Support cost assumptions (amount and how long)
10. Any financing assumptions: if leasing scenario, cost of solution is based on XX leasing model. Include details of the leasing model in the assumptions, for example: 36-month lease, interest at x percent, and so forth

11. A statement about if the model reflects total cost of ownership, or not. If not, what does the model include
12. Type of currency
13. Any other assumptions that relate to the information involved in the model

Spreadsheet F-1 is an example of a cash flow model used by several service providers throughout the world. It includes information about projected revenues, NPV, IRR, income statement and cash flow impacts, graphical representations, and service revenue summaries.

(a)

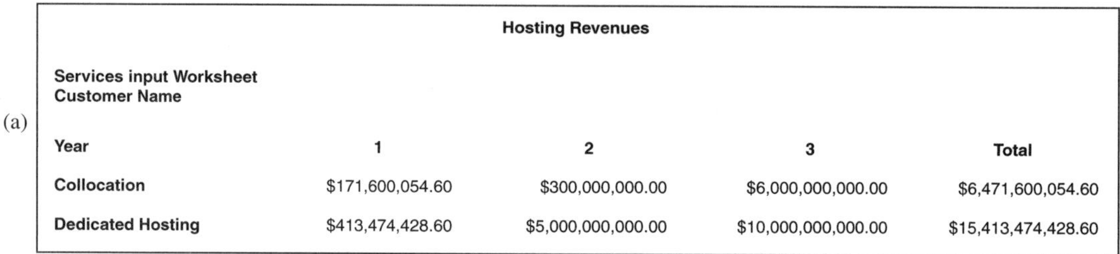

Hosting Revenues

Services input Worksheet
Customer Name

Year	1	2	3	Total
Collocation	$171,600,054.60	$300,000,000.00	$6,000,000,000.00	$6,471,600,054.60
Dedicated Hosting	$413,474,428.60	$5,000,000,000.00	$10,000,000,000.00	$15,413,474,428.60

(b)

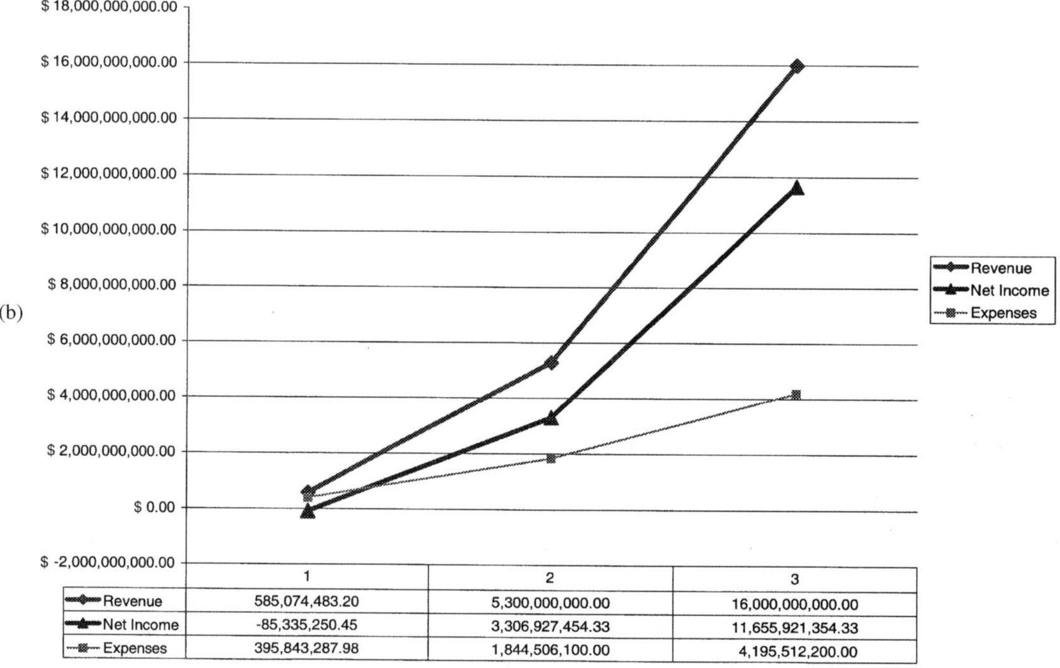

	1	2	3
Revenue	585,074,483.20	5,300,000,000.00	16,000,000,000.00
Net Income	-85,335,250.45	3,306,927,454.33	11,655,921,354.33
Expenses	395,843,287.98	1,844,506,100.00	4,195,512,200.00

Spreadsheet F-1

Reprinted courtesy of Manchester International and Hewlett-Packard Company ©1998.

(c)

Discounted Cash Flow Analysis

Discounted Cash Flow

Name of Company

		1	2	3	Total
Income Statement Items					
Revenue		$585,074,483.20	$5,300,000,000.00	$16,000,000,000.00	$21,885,074,483.20
Costs of Goods Sold		$148,566,445.67	$148,566,445.67	$148,566,445.67	$445,699,337.00
Expenses		$395,843,287.98	$1,844,506,100.00	$4,195,512,200.00	$6,435,861,587.98
Interest Expense on Capital Equip. and Land		$126,000,000.00	$112,900,000.00	$99,600,000.00	
Pretax Income		-$85,335,250.45	$3,306,927,454.33	$11,655,921,354.33	$14,877,513,558.22
Less: Income Taxes	25%	$0.00	$2,480,195,590.75	$8,741,941,015.75	$11,222,136,606.50
Net Income		-$85,335,250.45	$826,731,863.58	$2,913,980,338.58	$3,655,376,951.72
Add: Depreciation/Amortization (equip.) @	3 Year Life	$148,566,445.67	$148,566,445.67	$148,566,445.67	$445,699,337.00
Add: Depreciation/Amortization on Land		$231,900,000.00	$231,900,000.00	$231,900,000.00	
Cash Inflow (From P&L)		$295,131,195.22	$1,207,198,309.25	$3,294,446,784.25	$4,796,776,288.72

	1	2	3	Total
Cash Flow Statement				
Capital Expenditures Other than Land	$445,699,337.00	$0.00	$0.00	$445,699,337.00
Capital Expenditures on Land, Building, M&E Dedocated Web Hos Equipment	$2,725,000,000.00	$30,000,000.00	$30,000,000.00	
Other Spending	$165,834,350.00	$995,006,100.00	$1,990,012,200.00	$3,150,852,650.00
Cash Outflow	$3,170,699,337.00	$30,000,000.00	$30,000,000.00	$3,230,699,337.00
Cash Flow Summary				
From Income Statement	$295,131,195.22	$1,207,198,309.25	$3,294,446,784.25	$4,796,776,288.72
From Cash Flow Statement	-$3,170,699,337.00	-$30,000,000.00	-$30,000,000.00	-$3,230,699,337.00
Net Cash Flow	$-$2,875,568,141.78	$1,177,198,309.25	$3,264,446,784.25	$1,566,076,951.72

		1	2	3	NPV
Cumulative Cash Flow		-$2,875,568,141.78	-$1,698,369,832.53	$1,566,076,951.72	
Discounted Cash Flow @ Various Discount Rates					
Company Hurdle Rate 5	30.0%				-*$29,542,319.0
Automatic IRR	28.96%				$0.00

Spreadsheet F-1 (continued)

(d)

Services Summary		
	Revenue ($ Million)	**NPV @**** 29%
Collocation	$6,471,600,054.60	
Dedicated Hosting	$15,413,474,428.60	
Total Services	$21,885,074,483.20	
* Capital Investment =		$445,699,337.00
** Company's Investment Hurdle Rate =		30%

Spreadsheet F-1 (continued)

APPENDIX G

Sample Customer Questionnaire

The following represents a sample questionnaire used to test market reaction to service descriptions and pricing. It is included to give an idea of the type of information required to test ideas in the market. The questionnaire should not just be given to the customer to be filled out and returned, it should be used as a guideline for the service provider to elicit information about proposed services and pricing. It can also be used as a guideline during business development.

G.1 Understanding the Current Environment and Customer Requirements

G.1.1 Background

- What does your business do?
- How do you operate?
- Where do you make your profit?
- How does IT affect your ability to make a profit?
- Has IT been viewed as a business facilitator or inhibitor until now, in your business?

G.1.2 Context

- What applications and services would you consider hosting outside your company?
- Is this in line with current organizational and/or business strategy?
- Is this part of a program of projects?
- Would this hosting form part of a chain of linked projects or program?
- What do the current applications do?

- If you are considering hosting outside your company, is there a business-critical date to have this achieved and operational? When would you consider moving these platforms? (in a month, 6 months, a year?)
- Why is a change necessary in this time frame?
- Will the results be of value to another customer, or part of your organization?
- What is the overall problem or opportunity being addressed?
- What are the difficulties or opportunities now that prompted the need to change?
- Have they been explored and understood?
- Have you made a requirements list of your needs?
- Is this an old problem or opportunity?
- How long has it existed?
- Who wants to change things?
- Have previous attempts been made to address this problem?
- What information exists about past attempts to fix things?
- What assumptions have been made?
- What are the benefits to the change?
- What are the negative aspects to the change?
- Where and how do the applications currently run?
- What operating system (OS) do the majority run on?
- Are there processes or operational procedures around these applications? If so, can you give a high-level description?
- Are the processes or procedures written down anywhere?
- Who owns these processes?

G.2 Service Provider Service Feedback

- Would you consider having SERVICE PROVIDER host your services/applications? If so, why do you want to have your services hosted by SERVICE PROVIDER? What would you consider SERVICE PROVIDER's value to you? (trusted brand, best technology, and so on.)

Service descriptions can be inserted here.

- What is your reaction to these service descriptions?
- Do they fill your needs?
- If not, what services would you add? Take out?
- Which would you use?
- What time to response do you require?
- Have you looked at any other non-SERVICE PROVIDER provided solutions?
- What do you like and dislike about SERVICE PROVIDER's solution compared to SERVICE PROVIDER's competition?
- What would you like to see SERVICE PROVIDER provide to make the solution better over what you receive now?

- Who are the end-users of the services to be provided by SERVICE PROVIDER?
- What departments/end-user groups will access the services?
- Where are the end-users located?
- How do these applications interrelate to each other?
- Do any of these applications have dependencies on any external factors? For example, weekly input from a third-party, data provided by overseas partners and so forth.
- Are there any other dependencies (application and operational) that are critical to keeping your business up and running?
- Are there any issues with the service, as currently defined, that will affect our ability to help you reduce costs and mitigate risk?
- Where does current application tailoring take place and who does it?
- Who does your Web design?
- What IT integration might be required between the SERVICE PROVIDER provided solution and solutions provided in-house, or external to your organization?
- Who will perform these integration activities?
- Do you view any other third-party as being critical to the successful delivery of services from SERVICE PROVIDER?
- Who will have responsibility for managing that third-party: your company or SERVICE PROVIDER?
- How fast would you need to be online if you switch their services to SERVICE PROVIDER?

G.2.1 Decision Making

- What budget has been agreed on for the service?
- Who is the executive sponsor of this project?
- Who will make the final go, no-go decision?
- Who will the key stakeholders and influencers on that decision?
- What is their interest?
- Why are they interested?
- What are they expecting to gain?
- How will the SERVICE PROVIDER solution affect them?
- Are they in favor of the SERVICE PROVIDER solution?
- Will the SERVICE PROVIDER solution interfere with their operations?
- Could they seriously hinder the progress of the solution if they have some issue with the solution?
- Is there any history of behavior from previous initiatives like this?
- What do they consider the major business risks to be?
- How can these risks be shared, avoided, mitigated, or absorbed?

G.3 Service Level Requirements

- What service levels agreements do you currently have with your existing provider?
- SLAs for SERVICE PROVIDER provided services are based on three different cost/benefit models for throughput, availability, and integrity. (See Table G-1.) Do these meet your requirements?

Table G-1 Cost/benefit models for SLAs.

Service	SLA	Metric	Bronze	Silver	Gold
	Infrastructure Availability	Infrastructure Uptime	99.5%	99.9%	99.99%
	Issue Response Time	Response	4 hrs/next business day	2 hrs/next business day	1 hour/next business day
	Customer Satisfaction	Quarterly Survey	Satisfied	Satisfied	Satisfied
Network Mgmt.	Network Availability	Packet Loss Latency	<1% <75 msec	<1% <75 msec	<1% <75 msec
	Disaster Recovery	RTO	1 week	4 days	1 day
		Recovery Point	1 week	3-4 days	1 day
Security Mgmt.	Breach Isolation	Time to Isolate	<60 mins	<45 mins	<30 mins

- For each service level, what are your additional service level expectations?
  - Infrastructure availability
  - Network bandwidth guarantees
  - Data backup—when, where, how often, how many levels, security arrangements
  - Data recovery—volume, file, forward-recovery capability, testing procedures
  - Disaster recovery—hot, warm, cold, offsite, onsite, testing procedures
  - Availability of support teams (Server/LAN/network administration, Help desk, and so on)—business hours, out-of-hours support
  - Issue resolution response time
  - Escalation procedures
- How often do you want reports and what level of detail do you want them to contain?
- When you expect these SERVICE PROVIDER provided services to be available based on these SLAs?
- What requirements do you have for end-user based application administration/management interaction at each service level?

G.4 Pricing

- Would you agree the following prices are fair and reasonable for each of the services?
  - Bronze Set up: $xx, Ongoing monthly fee of $xx
  - Silver Set up: $xx, Ongoing monthly fee of $xx
  - Gold Set up: $xx, Ongoing monthly fee of $xx

This is a good place to insert your prices.

APPENDIX H

Helpful Associations, Organizations, and Publications

H.1 Associations

Association for IT Companies in Mexico (AMITI): ***www.amiti.org.mx*** An association of approximately 200 IT companies in Mexico promoting business in Latin America.

ASP Industry Consortium: ***www.aspindustry.org*** A global advocacy group promoting the ASP industry. It sponsors research and promotes the advantages of this business model.

DSL Forum: ***www.adsl.com*** Established in 1994 as a consortium of more than 400 leading industry players covering telecommunications, equipment, computing, networking, and service provider companies. Its purpose is to communicate DSL benefits to the world at large.

The European Forum for Electronic Business: ***www.eema.org*** Organized to improve communications between businesses in Europe who wish to trade and communicate electronically.

Internet Business Services Initiative (IBSI): ***www.ibusinessservices.org*** A nonprofit trade association of companies supporting B2B applications over the Web. This association supports fostering the growth, development, and market acceptance of applications based on the Internet Business Services Model.

International Telecommunications Union: ***www.itu.ch*** An international organization where government and the private sector can coordinate issues relating to global telecommunications networks and services.

ISP Business Forum (ISPBF): ***www.ispbf.org*** The ISPBF is an association of ISPs that promotes ISP business success through networking, tools, and information.

Organization for Economic Coordination and Development (OECD): ***www.oecd.org*** The OECD is a group of 30 member countries providing governments a setting in which to discuss, develop, and perfect economic and social policy.

Management Service Provider Association: ***www.mspassociation.org*** This nonprofit consortium promotes standards and best practices for application management.

Telemanagement Forum: ***www.tmforum.org*** This organization is dedicated to overall excellence in communications management and to solving pressing OSS integration issues.

H.2 Periodicals and URLs

Boardwatch **Magazine:** ***www.boardwatch.com*** Information about the ISP industry. It includes things like an ISP business tool page, ISP Planet (*www.boardwatch.internet.com*) "the intelligence center for the ISP community."

www.cnet.com Sends email daily that gives information about the technology and Internet Industries.

CFO Magazine**:** ***www.cfo.com*** Case studies and helpful financial articles for service providers.

CIO Magazine**:** ***www.cio.com*** Articles about technology that relate to the service provider industry.

Network Magazine**:** ***www.networkmagazine.com*** Follows industry trends in the service provider area.

thedirectory: ***www.thedirectory.org*** Listings and mailing lists for and of service providers.

www.sec.gov/edgarhp.htm Contains information on U.S. publicly traded corporations, including service providers.

ElectronicNews**:** ***www.electronicnews.com*** Includes information on trends in the xSP markets.

Electronic Mail and Messaging Systems**:** ***www.biz-lib.com/ZBREMM.html*** A biweekly newsletter that contains articles about electronic messaging, and other technology issues.

eWeek**:** ***www.zdnet.com/eweek*** General information about technology and the industry at large.

Financial Times**:** ***www.ft.com*** News, financial, and Internet business articles with major focus on the European market.

FORTUNE **Magazine:** ***www.fortune.com*** Business information that pertains to the xSP Industry.

Industry Groups: ***www.sonic.net/~breakrec/links/industrygroups.html*** Lists of links that include many about Internet topics.

The Industry Standard**:** ***www.thestandard.com*** Bills itself as The News magazine of the Internet Economy.

Interactive Week**:** ***www.zdnet.com/intweek*** Has articles relating to ASPs, communications, CRM, e-commerce and related topics of interest.

The List: ***www.thelist.internet.com*** Links to service provider sites that include service details.

www.pcwebopaedia.com Contains terms and definitions used in the industry.

www.ripe.net/ripencc/index.html Statistical site providing data on Internet growth.

Sm@rtPartner*: *www.zd.com/sp This magazine focuses on partner issues related to the Internet and service providers.

Telecom Virtual Library: *www.analysys.com/vlib* Links to telecommunications sites worldwide.

Total Telecom: *www.totaltele.com* Articles and links relating to the Internet Industry.

www.teledotcom.com Has information about service provider industry developments and related equipment industries.

Internet World: *www.webweek.com* Has information about service provider industry developments and related equipment industries.

H.3 Industry Analysts/Consultants

Gartner Group: *www3.gartner.com/Init* Industry analysis and consulting.

HPC: *www.hp.com/go/consulting* HP consulting offers solutions and consulting services for the xSP market.

IDC: *www.idc.com* Offers analysis on e-commerce, the Internet, and information technology.

META Group: *www.metagroup.com* Offers research and consulting services focusing on information technology and business transformation strategies.

Partners in Ecom: *www.partnersine.com* Offers training and strategic consulting services in leading edge technologies for the service provider market.

APPENDIX I

CRM Process Inputs and Outputs

This appendix discusses the process inputs and outputs between functions that are included in the sample implementation discussed in Chapter 13, "Perception is Reality."

I.1 Billing System

Transfer FROM the billing system:

- Account status (unpaid, in collection, and so on)
- Bill recalculation
- Account balance (payments and charges)

Transfer TO billing system:

- Assigned customer ID
- Billing currency
- Credits and adjustments
- Payments (and prepayments)
- Request for bill reprint

I.2 Order Management

Transfer FROM the order management system:

- Order status

Transfer TO the order management system:

- Assigned customer ID
- Customer details/update
- Names
- Addresses
- Payment terms and details
- Billing details (such as bill format, frequency)
- Credit limit
- VIP status
- Service required
- Request to provision (including time delay if required)
- Service reinitialization
- Service termination

I.3 Network Trouble Ticket System

Transfer FROM trouble ticket system:

- Details of network outages, future or current
- Fault resolution and test notification
- Status of trouble ticket

Transfer TO trouble ticket system:

- Details of trouble ticket—customer ID and problem

I.4 Computer Telephony Integration (CTI)

Transfer FROM CTI:

- Caller ID
- Automatic call distribution (ACD) and interactive voice recognition (IVR) status and commands

Transfer TO CTI:

- ACD and CTI server status commands

I.5 Document Management

Transfer FROM the document management system:

- Contract details
- Correspondence (inbound fax, letter)

Transfer TO the document management system:

- Document access information (time, who)
- Status of order

I.6 Geographical Information System (GIS)

Transfer FROM GIS:

- Geographical coordinates

Transfer TO GIS:

- Address of caller/subscriber

I.7 Data Warehouse

Transfer FROM data warehouse:

- Campaign information

Transfer TO Data warehouse:

- Customer information
- CSR statistics

I.8 Credit Checking Agency

Request TO credit checking agency:

- Request immediate online credit checking where appropriate. (This function is performed by the billing system and the result returned to CRM.)

Information FROM agency:

- Results of credit check

I.9 Foreign Exchange System

Transfer FROM the foreign exchange system:

- Current exchange rate
- Historical exchange rate

(The billing system performs this function and the result returned to CRM.)

I.10 Example of Functional Specification with Implementation Timing

Tables I-1 through I-17 show examples of a functionality specification and phased implementation for the CRM example.

Table I-1 Customer service representative (CSR) capabilities.

Description/Requirement	Phase
The CSR (outbound and inbound) is empowered to perform the following actions according to access rights: Initialize service Reinitialize service Amend/Modify service package Request bills (e.g., monthly, quarterly) Cease service package Manage prepayment where appropriate Manage cessation request Rebate/Amend customer accounts through the billing system Access updated customer status (sales, faults, request for information, and so on)	1

Table I-2 Call center inbound call flows.

Description/Requirement	Phase
To support the business there are different call streams: Sales inquiries Sales order General service Billing Fault VIP sales VIP faults	1
Intelligently balanced distribution of calls between call centers. Real-time and historical information is used to enable accurate distribution.	1

Table I-2 Call center inbound call flows. (continued)

Description/Requirement	Phase
Calls arriving in Call Center 1 overflow to other call centers. The conditions under which overflow occurs are dynamic and determined by factors such as the volume of inbound calls, average wait time, number of agents available, and number of calls in queue. Calls being overflowed retain all original call details.	1
Retention/Winback CSRs. When a customer dials either the customer service or sales inquiry numbers and requests disconnection of the service, the call is transferred to the retention/winback CSR. If the screen has been populated with customer data, the CSR can transfer the caller and their associated data to a retention/winback CSR.	1
Calls may be routed based on stored customer profiles. Through integration with the CTI, system routing may be provided: Preferred language Services used Customer type (e.g., VIP) Credit history If there is no information stored for a customer, they should be sent to an IVR system to capture information such as the reason for the call, whether they are an existing customer, and their customer or telephone number.	2
Proactively identify and inform customers in case of fault by having access to details of network outages and use of scripting to guide the CSR. Information broadcast about known network outages—some form of notice board, which is shown automatically on login, and is available online, with an indication of a new message. Automated call routing at origin to recorded messages (e.g., if call from city and outage is there, direct to recorded message).	2 1 2
Support CSRs with context-sensitive scripting to provide onscreen prompting for sales conversations.	1
Script versioning	3
Scripts support a simple order pricing dialog to be able to price an order after initial order design.	1

Table I-3 CSR skill sets.

Description/Requirement	Phase
VIP Customers: Agents assigned this skill-set will only receive calls from the VIP inbound call flow. These will either be direct from the Intelligent Network (IN) or transferred from other CSR where the customer has dialed the incorrect number. Assumption: Different numbers will be dialed for different agent inquiries.	1
Sales Inquiries/Order: Agents assigned this skill-set will only receive calls from the sales inquiry call stream. These will either be direct from the IN or transferred from other CSR where the incorrect number has been dialed by the customer. Assumption: Different numbers will be dialed for different agent inquiries.	1

Table I-3 CSR skill sets. (continued)

Description/Requirement	Phase
Customer Service: Agents assigned this skill-set will only receive calls from the customer service call stream. These will either be direct from the IN or transferred from other CSRs where the customer has dialed the incorrect number. Noncomplex billing inquiries will be handled by CSRs with this skill-set. Assumption: Different numbers will be dialed for different Agent inquiries.	1
Multiskilled agents. It is expected that the majority of agents will be multiskilled and therefore able to take calls from both the customer service and sales inquiries call streams.	1
Billing Inquiries: Agents assigned this skill-set will only receive calls transferred from another CSR. These agents will be required to log into the billing system to answer billing inquiries for Phase 1. There will be no interface to billing from CRM for phase 1. Agents with this skill-set may also be allocated other skill-sets to enable them to answer customer service or sales inquiries.	1
Welcome Call: Once a customer has been successfully provisioned, CRM will be updated. An entry will be placed in the welcome call groups Inbox. CSR with access to the Inbox will be able to make a call to the customer.	1

Table I-4 Order entry.

Description/Requirement	Phase
CSR captures customer information such as name, address, billing options, payment method, and preferred date of service activation.	1
Hold provisioning until credit check is complete or customer preferred start date.	1
Customer service verification (i.e., is it possible to provide the service to the customer address?)	1
CSR captures information regarding services: Voice Data E-services	1
Workforce availability Customer appointment for installation	1
Welcome package and contract generation	1
Order validation	1
Activation	1
Update CRM on successful activation	1

Table I-5 Computer telephony integration (CTI).

Description/Requirement	Phase
The CTI server automatically displays screens to the CSR based on the customer number.	1
The CTI server populates screens automatically should the customer calling line identity be available.	1
The CTI server displays screens and populates them with data collected through customer interaction with the IVR system.	1
The CTI server supports call transfers and consultation:	
Within the same agent group (intraswitch)	1
Between different agent groups (intraswitch)	1
Between agents located in different call centers (interswitch)	1
Between call centers not using the same switch technology (disparate)—allows for outsourcing	2
The CTI server provides synchronized call and data transfer between agents:	
Agent-to-Agent blind transfer The agent passes the call (and associated call data) to another agent, but no consultation takes place. Once the call has been passed in this way, the agent must be immediately available to receive another call, or perform wrap-up activities.	1
Agent-to-Agent consultation transfer This occurs when an agent speaks with a second agent while the call is in progress. Any call-associated data must be sent with the call to the second agent so that each can review the same screen information. It must be possible for the customer to be on hold, or included in a conference call at any time. Once the consultation is over, the original agent must be able to complete the transfer of the call to the second agent, or continue with the call himself.	1
Agent-to-Queue transfer An agent must be able to transfer a call to another agent queue even if no other agents are immediately available. When an agent is available, the call and its associated call data must be transferred to the receiving agent.	1
The CTI server provides detailed on-screen call history information like talk-time, hold-time, transfers history.	1

Table I-6 Interactive voice recognition (IVR).

Description/Requirement	Phase
The IVR system supplies multilingual support	1
IVR integrates with CTI to provide screen population and screen display	1

Note: The IVR system provides DTMF features and the ability to play multilingual messages.

Table I-7 Automated outbound calling.

Description/Requirement	Phase
Information is exported to the outbound calling system and categorized according to the type of callback required.	1
Screen is displayed with the customer details and purpose of call.	1
The CSR has the ability to reschedule calls.	1

Table I-8 Internet.

Description/Requirement	Phase
All prospect or customer-activities are available on a secure Web site for requests related to:	1
Customer details	1
Information requests	1
Placing an order	1
Complaints	2
Fulfillment	2
Provisioning	2
Feeding customer data from Web page automatically into the system All Web site contacts and incoming emails, where visitors entered the minimal mandatory information (i.e., full name, address, and telephone number), must result in a new case number and have to be included in the contact history.	1
All Web site contact contents and emails of prospects or clients are stored for further reference.	1
Customer can look up personal data in read-only mode by: Account Credit limit	2
Customer can look up personal data in update mode: Change of address	2
Callback request will result in an entry being generated in automated outbound calling.	1
Customer can be identified via email in the screen display.	1

Table I-9 Data exchange.

Description/Requirement	Phase
Creation or amendment of customer details including payment method and credit limit are passed to the billing system using the process tool. This prevents the rekeying of customer details.	1

Table I-10 Credit checking.

Description/Requirement	Phase
All credit checks, including blacklists, will be covered in the billing system and will be accessed by CRM via the process bus.	1

Table I-11 Event handling.

Description/Requirement	Phase
Trouble ticket creation, management, and escalation	1
Customer creation of event via online access	2
Automatic system creation of event upon detection of a problem affecting the customer's service	2
Online information available to the customer regarding the status of event management (trouble tickets)	1 (Standard) 2 (Extended)
System notification to the customer of event status	1
System supports technical workforce management	1 (Standard) 2 (Extended)
Workforce management scheduling	1
Jeopardy case escalation to management personnel	1
Metrics and statistics	2 (Standard) 4 (Extended)
Event management interface to mail and fax	1
Event management interface to the process tool	2
Event management to GIS/Doc management	2 and 3

Table I-12 Geographical Information System (GIS).

Description/Requirement	Phase
Fixed network problems from affected areas are highlighted.	3

Table I-13 Document management.

Description/Requirement	Phase
All written inbound and outbound customer contacts for an existing customer (letter, fax, email, Web form) can be accessed and viewed from the CSR's desktop.	1
An agent for a certain customer on his desktop can create different outgoing documents (letter, fax, email).	2
Storage of outgoing documents according to a storage policy.	2
Incoming letters/fax/email from existing customers or prospects with existing individual data records are stored with a reference to the document within the individual data record.	1
If a new letter, fax or email comes in from a prospect with no existing customer information, a new customer and lead is created. The incoming correspondence is referenced.	2
The creation of a new customer or contact results in the storage of the documentation. The update of details results in the storage of the new document related to the documents already stored for the customer.	2

Table I-14 Product and pricing information.

Description/Requirement	Phase
View online general information about products, prices and services:	1
Specific product details	1
Product bundling	1
Product history	2
Multicurrencies supported	1
Simple order pricing dialogues are available to price an order after initial order design	2
View online information on competitor related price/service queries raised during the sale	4

Table I-15 Workflow.

Description/Requirement	Phase
The workload management system in the call center must manage the workload: Between agents within the same group Between different groups at the same location Between different groups at different locations	1
The agents can manage their own inbox and can reroute cases to another group's/agent's inbox or to the general queue.	1
A group supervisor can manage the load of a group of agents by accessing their Inboxes and the group's inbox and can reroute cases to Inboxes of other groups.	1

Table I-15 Workflow.

Description/Requirement	Phase
Follow-up calls by the call center after a predefined time are scheduled automatically under certain conditions.	1
Task management. Change CSR from inbound to outbound and notify CSR for noncall work items (i.e., inbox, faxes, and so on)	1

Table I-16 Billing interface.

Description/Requirement	Phase
Interface to the billing system for: Ad hoc bill creation Ad hoc bill calculation Payment inquiry Billing inquiry Change customer billing data Bill order Termination (including upsell) Change of service Information request	2

Table I-17 Miscellaneous.

Description/Requirement	Phase
Customizable screen layout on screens	1
Audit log of customer-related activities	1
Documentation of customer interaction in free text format	1
Reports—out of the box	1
Customized reporting	3
Broadcast messages to distribution lists	1
Workflow management	1
Multicustomer site support geographically distributed	1
CSR shift change without logging off	1

Table I-17 Miscellaneous. (continued)

Description/Requirement	Phase
Information security (standard)	1
Information security (extended)	3
User authorization and privileges (standard)	1
User authorization and privileges (extended)	3
Customer authorization	1

Bibliography

1. Adams, Elizabeth K. and Willets, Keith J. *The Lean Communications Provider,* McGraw Hill Book Company, New York, 1996.
2. *Application Delivery Strategies,* March 16, 1999, METAGroup, Stamford, CT, File 724.
3. Comer, Douglas E. *The Internet Book,* Prentice Hall, Inc., New Jersey, 1995.
4. Downes, Larry and Mui, Chunka, *Unleashing the Killer App,* Harvard Business School Press, Massachusetts, 1998 and 2000.
5. Harbison, John R. and Pekar, Peter Jr. *Smart Alliances*, Booz-Allen & Hamilton, Inc., Jossey-Bass Publishers, California, 1998.
6. Knight, Christopher M. *ISP Marketing Survival Guide,* John Wiley & Sons, Inc. New York, 2000.
7. McNight, Lee W. and Bailey, Joseph P. *Internet Economics,* The MIT Press, Massachusetts, 1997.
8. Newton, Harry. *Newton's Telecom Dictionary,* Flatiron Publishing, Inc., New York, 1997.
9. Parker, Marilyn M. and Benson, Robert J. *Information Economics,* Prentice Hall Inc., 1998.
10. Reichheld, Frederick F. *The Loyalty Effect,* Harvard Business School Press, Massachusetts, 1996.
11. Shahnam, Liz, *Application Delivery Strategies*, 7 Feb 2000, METAGroup, Stamford, CT, File 826.
12. Seybold, Patricia B. *customers.com,* Random House, New York, 1998.
13. Tiller, Andrew, *Billing for Mobile Data and Content Services,* Geneva Technology Ltd., Cambridge, UK, 2000.
14. Wald, Liz, *HP Service Delivery, Service Delivery in the Communications Industry,* A Hewlett-Packard white paper, Version 1.0, March 22, 2000, *www.ice.hp.com/cyc/af/00/showfile.cgi?101-0392.*

Index

C

D

H

I

J

K

L

M

N

O

P

S

T

U

V

W